# EXCHANGE BEHAVIOR IN SELLING AND SALES MANAGEMENT

# EXCHANGE BEHAVIOR IN SELLING AND SALES MANAGEMENT

**Peng Sheng**
**Aziz Guergachi**

LONDON AND NEW YORK

First published by Butterworth-Heinemann

First edition 2008

This edition published 2011 by Routledge
2 Park Square, Milton Park, Abingdon, Oxon OX14 4RN
711 Third Avenue, New York, NY 10017, USA

*Routledge is an imprint of the Taylor & Francis Group, an informa business*

**British Library Cataloguing in Publication Data**
A catalogue record for this book is available from the British Library

**Library of Congress Cataloging-in-Publication Data**
A catalog record for this book is available from the Library of Congress

ISBN: 978-0-7506-8590-0

# CONTENTS

**Part One: Exchange Behavior in Selling and Sales Management (X-Be)**

**Part Two: Theoretical Foundations and Advanced Topics**

# FOREWORD

Buying and selling have become an integral part of our daily life. It traces its origin to the ancient barter system. Barter was possible only when each party was able to supply something the other party desired. Mutual satisfaction was the key to successful barter trade.

Buying and selling today are not much different as long as the essence of exchange is concerned. Both buyer and seller seek satisfaction through the social interaction to sense and make sense of the exchange value. For a seller to effectively integrate the customer value into a sales offer, a sound methodology to cope with the buyer's value-pursuing behaviors will be among the most key success factors for any *successful* sale – a mutually satisfied-exchange.

One of the authors of this book, Mr Peng Sheng, has trained and motivated our Chinese sales team with such a sales knowledge and achieved a very big success. I see the reason for this success in taking out the complexity of a sales process with a "Simple Algebraic Language to Engineer Satisfaction" – SALES. By developing a straightforward methodology, which can be easily implemented by most of the sales persons into their daily working behaviors, they have made a big step forward to increase positive results from sales activities and make them also more predictive.

Peng Sheng and Aziz Guergachi have cleverly defined SALES with the conception of fundamental dynamics of customer's value-pursuing behavior. Keeping this in mind, the authors have excellently integrated various sales concepts into one practical and easy-to-use "Exchange Behavior Framework", which emphasizes on value-integrated selling.

The book explicitly describes $1 + 7$ building blocks that constitute the Exchange Behavior framework and explains the purchase process and the essential facts pertaining to buyer, to seller, as well as to the environment in which the buyer and seller interact. The authors have used practical examples to underline the concepts of the $1 + 7$ building blocks, starting with the stages of purchase and the seven concepts including key persons and core opinion leaders, views on criteria, buying points and selling points, deliverability and integrated product, appropriate communicator and networked resources, as well as selling status indices.

The book serves as a guide to help sales professional to understand the importance of value-integrated selling and to integrate this into their professions. Using this, the sales professional will be able to identify the key factors and use their efforts and time successfully for a successful sale.

I have met Mr Peng Sheng personally during one of my visits to China. I had a very good time reading this book, because it reflects also a lot of my own experiences in managing sales of high-tech products and leading a worldwide sales organization. By implementing this **SALES** knowledge, you make the need of changes in the sales behavior measurable. As a manager and an engineer I found that measuring a process is always the first step to improve it.

Congratulations and thanks for the very useful ideas in this book! I want to recommend this book to every salesman as a way to bring predictive results into his sales efforts.

The "Art of Selling" is what you may know, but the "Art of Re-Selling" is what we all need to master. . . .

Peter Gucher, General Manager B&R International

# PREFACE

As implied in its title, this book focuses on the value-exchange behavior of sellers and buyers. It presents a principled framework that is pragmatic and easy to implement in the field of selling and sales management. Within this framework, SALES becomes an acronym that refers to a **S**imple **A**lgebraic **L**anguage to **E**ngineer **S**atisfaction of both parties involved in the exchange – such a language constitutes indeed one of the main contributions of this book. The basic ideas of the presented framework have first appeared in the book "What is this thing called selling?" published in China by the China Social Sciences Press in 2002. These ideas have been significantly expanded upon, consolidated, and enriched in this book for the benefit of sales people, managers, and researchers. Also, and as is shown in the last two chapters, we believe that this research work may spark even more ideas that could help in advancing the topic of selling and sales management to a higher level.

We hope that this book will provide you with a valuable resource, and we welcome any feedback or comments from you.

Best wishes,
Peng Sheng
Aziz Guergachi

# ACKNOWLEDGEMENTS

We are heavily indebted to the following people who helped and supported us, in various ways, in writing this book and we would like to express our sincere gratitude to them:

Bruce Beck (University of Georgia); John Birks (NPD Hardlines Canada); John Casti (IIASA); Chuck Chakrapani (Ryerson University); Hika Chan (Mercedes-Benz China Limited); Waiyin Chan (Silicon Application Pte Ltd.); Marcus Chao (Delphi Automotive Systems (China); Holding Co., Ltd.); Bocheng Chen (Tsinghua University); Jindong Chen (Xi'an University of Technology); Kwok Leong Choo (Shell China Ltd.); Wendy Cukier (Ryerson University); Youcef Derbal (Ryerson University); Yunlong Ding (Harbin Institute of Technology); Wei Fan (Mercedes-Benz China Limited); Guoqun Fu (Peking University); Jack Gao (Autodesk Software (China) Co., Ltd.); Jin Guo (China Hewlett-Packard Co., Ltd.); Qinghua Guo (Toronto); Mahmoud Hashim (Ryerson University); Aaron Heisler (Ryerson University); Wei Hu (China FAW Group Corporation); Zuohao Hu (Tsinghua University); Pei Huang (Fudan University); Shan Huang (Chongqing Zhi En Medicine Corporation); David Jin (Sapa Heat Transfer (Shanghai) Ltd.); Xiaotong Jin (Jilin University); Ken Jones (Ryerson University); Eric Ker (Delphi Automotive Systems (China) Holding Co., Ltd.); Arkady Kryazhimskiy (IIASA); Charing Lai (Ryerson University); Ming Lei (South China University of Technology); Yingbo Li (Beijing Time Sonic Technology Co., Ltd); Chenglin Liao (Chongqing University); Linda Liu (TüV Rheinland (Shanghai) Co., Ltd); Ruixian Liu (North University of China); Wei Lu (Shanghai Jiaotong University);

Wenjin Lu (Tsingtao Brewery Group); Wei Luo (Siemens Ltd., China); Sufian Mazhar (VirisTek, Inc.); Jianing Mi (Harbin Institute of Technology); Roy Morley (Ryerson University); Alex Nazarie (Ryerson University); Eva Nesselroth (Ryerson University); Ojelanki Ngyenyama (Ryerson University); James Norrie (Ryerson University); Runtao Peng (Chongqing Zhi En Medicine Corporation); Andrew Sage (George Mason University); Shayantheca Sathiyabaskaran (Ryerson University); Bharat Shah (Ryerson University); Muhammad Shahbaz (Ryerson University); Biman Shrestha (Ryerson University); Xuebao Song (Tsinghua University); Kamal M. Syed (VirisTek, Inc.); Zhong Tang (Chongqing Datang Scale Co., Ltd); James M. Tien (Rensselaer Polytechnic Institute); Yongshi Tu (Shenzhen University); J-P Udo (Ryerson University); Tianchun Wang (Dongbei University Of Finance & Economics); Jian Xiang (Zhejiang University); Weirong Xiao (B&R Industrial Automation (Shanghai) Co., Ltd); Jenny Yan (Motorola China Inc.); Weihua Yang (Visteon Asia Pacific Inc.); Xiaodong Yang (Jilin University); Wenzhong Zhao (Siemens Ltd., China); Guijun Zhuang (Xi'an Jiaotong University).

Finally, we would like to thank very sincerely Tim Goodfellow, Jane McDonald and all the staff members at Elsevier for helping us with the publication process, the anonymous reviewers who evaluated the content of this book, and our wives, Yaping Zhang and Leila Tijini, for their patience and constant support.

# INTRODUCTION

This book is intended for those readers who are looking for thought-provoking ideas and intellectual challenges in the field of selling and sales management. It consists of 12 chapters; the first 10 chapters will benefit all readers including the sales practitioners, while the last 2 are written mainly for researchers in the areas of sales, systems modeling, and management.

Throughout these chapters, we present the sales knowledge that we have developed through our research. This knowledge is encapsulated in a framework (the *Exchange Behavior framework, or simply X-Be*) that is practical and easy to implement. A unique feature of this framework is its consistency with the scientific principle of parsimony and its logical development of selling and sales management knowledge from the ground up – the framework is made up of only a few building blocks (1 + 7 building blocks), yet is able to account for various selling and sales management situations logically and effectively. It has applications in many key activities that take place in a sales department and beyond; this includes, but not limited to, managing sales opportunities, generating sales forecasts, constructing sound judgments about customers, planning sales calls, managing customer objections, guiding the communication and interaction with the customers, designing adequate sales offers, developing a team-oriented environment for selling and sales management, constructively evaluating sales performance, effective handling of competition, activity-based costing, practicing management by objectives, and ultimately transforming the corporation into an integrated sales organization – all of this can be done by performing the appropriate operations on the (1 + 7) building blocks of the X-Be framework. These building blocks and the various concepts associated with them form the *alphabet* of a *language* that can be used to conceptualize and analyze the selling and sales management activities. As will be demonstrated throughout the book, this language is easy to use, and the various operations that can be performed on its alphabet help infer useful and actionable information. Thus, one of the main contributions of the X-Be framework is a **Simple Algebraic Language to Engineer Satisfaction** (SALES) of both parties involved in the exchange.

We want to highlight the expression "Satisfaction of both parties." The X-Be framework is not about teaching sellers how to "sell ice to Eskimos." If that is what you are looking for, then this book is not for you. It is our belief that those salespeople who boast that they are able to sell anything to anyone damage their own image and the image of the sales profession more than anything else. The X-Be framework is about the creation and exchange of real value. Its purpose is to reveal the fundamental factors that affect the behaviors of the buyer and the seller and, based on them, provide businesses with effective and efficient tools to carry out successful selling and sales management tasks, innovate and strengthen their internal production systems, build long-term relationships with their customers and other partners, and thus contribute to the creation of the overall wealth and growth of the society. This is why the X-Be framework as well as SALES emphasize the satisfaction of both the seller and the buyer in the exchange relationship. In this line of reasoning, we define selling in this book as follows:

> *Selling is the process in which a party (the seller) searches for, communicates, and interacts with another party (the buyer) for a certain exchange to take place to the satisfaction of both parties.*

The $(1 + 7)$ building blocks of the X-Be framework include a model for the purchase process, plus seven concepts to capture the dynamics of the value-exchange behavior of the seller and buyer. Here is a brief description of these concepts:

1. *Phases of Purchase Process* (PPP): a model that describes the process of value formation and exchange on the part of customers;

and the seven concepts:

1. *Key Persons* (KP) and *Core Opinion Leaders* (COL): the roles in value formation and exchange on the part of customers;
2. *Views on Criteria* (VOC): the base for judging value;

3. *Buying Points and Selling Points*[1] (BP/SP): the expression of customer value;
4. *Deliverability and Integrated Product* (D/IP): the totality of a purchase in terms of value;
5. *Appropriate Communicators and Networked Resources* (AC/NR): the facilitators of value formation and exchange;
6. *Selling status Indices* (SI): measures for monitoring the value integration process;
7. *Dealing with Competition*: an approach from the perspective of customer value.

The first three of the seven concepts (KP/COL, VOC, BP/SP) pertain to the buyer, while the second three (D/IP, AC/NR, SI) pertain to the job of the seller, and the last one concerns the environment where the buyer and seller interact for the purpose of an exchange.

An important issue that we would like to point out before we move on to the detailed description of the (1 + 7) building blocks concerns the ethics of selling and buying. The X-Be framework aims at accounting for all the relevant aspects of human interactions in an exchange relationship. As a consequence, it does reveal the impacts of possibly unethical exchange behaviors in seller–buyer interactions, which is nothing but a reflection of the realities that both buyers and sellers might have to face in certain situations. But we obviously do not recommend any party, seller or buyer to engage in ethically unacceptable transactions.

---

[1] It should be noted that the meaning of the expression "Selling Points" in X-Be is different than its traditional meaning in the sales literature.

# ABOUT THE AUTHORS

 **Peng Sheng** has over 20 years of experience in selling, marketing and sales management. He has worked for Shell and Delphi for 10 years, and provides sales and sales management consulting services and training for many companies including Fortune 500's such as Delphi, Mercedes-Benz, Motorola, and Siemens. He is often invited as a guest speaker or visiting professor addressing MBA, EMBA, and Executives Programs at renowned Chinese universities such as Tsinghua University, Peking University, Shanghai Jiao Tong University, and Xi'an Jiao Tong University. He is the author and coauthor of other two Chinese sales books: "What is this thing called selling?" (2002, awarded as the "Nation's Excellent & Best-selling Work in Social Sciences for 2003" by the BPDAC) and the "Selling Behavior" (2005, the first author, recently approved as a "Nationally-Planned University Textbook" by the Ministry of Education of P.R. China). Peng holds a B.Eng. degree from Hefei University of Technology (China) and an MBA degree from Cardiff Business School of Cardiff University (UK), and his persistent research efforts focus on selling, sales management, and other reward-oriented behaviors in different socio-cultural settings. He is also the CEO of BTS-T, the Board Director of LEC, and can be reached at sp@5sbts.com.

**Aziz Guergachi** specializes in advanced and interdisciplinary problem-solving techniques for business professionals. He is the author or coauthor of over 30 articles and industry reports spanning the fields of business management, engineering, information technology, environment, and sustainable development. He was involved in several industry projects including the development of a large software system for trade promotion management and collaborative sales forecasting in the retail/manufacturing sectors. He is the recipient of the New Opportunities Award from Canada Foundation for Innovation and the principal investigator of a research project on the applications of machine learning and knowledge management funded by Canada's Natural Sciences and Engineering Research Council. He is a visiting scholar at the International Institute for Applied Systems Analysis (Vienna/Laxenburg, Austria), and a member of the Institute of Electrical and Electronics Engineers. A graduate of the École Supérieure d'Ingénieurs de Marseille, France, he also holds a B.Sc. in Mathematics (Mention *Très Bien*) from Université de Provence, Marseille, France and a Ph.D. in Engineering from the University of Ottawa, Canada. He is currently an associate professor at the Ted Rogers School of Management in Ryerson University, Toronto, Canada, and is the director of the Research Lab for Advanced System Modelling. He can be reached at Dr.Aziz@ieee.org.

# PART ONE
## EXCHANGE BEHAVIOR IN SELLING AND SALES MANAGEMENT (X-Be)

# 1

# OVERVIEW OF THE (1 + 7) ELEMENTS OF X-Be

Exchange behavior in Selling and Sales Management, or X-Be in short, is a comprehensive conceptual framework that deconstructs, systematizes and elucidates selling, sales management and the various actions that are related to them. Composed of (1 + 7) fundamental building blocks or elements (a model for the purchase process, plus 7 concepts), X-Be has its theoretical foundations in psychology and sociology. Its central precepts reflect extensive experience within the field and are based upon various kinds of selling and sales management practices that the authors have been exposed to. As will be demonstrated later in this book, the (1 + 7) building blocks of X-Be are logically integrated by a series of bonds that make use of relevant theoretical knowledge about buyers' cognitions, psychographics, and behaviors. While X-Be and its building blocks are easy to comprehend and implement, the framework also allows the sales staff (salespeople and sales managers) to define a complete roadmap for selling and sales management that accounts for various complex issues related to the latter activities.

The goal of this chapter is to provide an overview of the (1 + 7) building blocks of X-Be, while the next eight chapters of the book will focus on presenting a detailed discussion of each building block.

## THE PHASES OF THE PURCHASE PROCESS

The first building block of X-Be is a universal model that describes consumer and organizational buying decision-making processes. We shall refer to this model as the Phases of the Purchase Process, or PPP. The basic idea that underlies the PPP is that consumers and organizations are value-pursuing engines and that buying decisions are at the root of value formation and exchange. Above all, X-Be does not consider the buyers' underlying motives to be a black-box that cannot be understood, described, or explained.

The PPP model has five phases which we will refer to as follows:

1. Need Emerging (NE)
2. Need Defining (ND)
3. Selective Qualifying (SQ)
4. SeLecting (SL)
5. Follow-up and Control (FC)

This model provides an effective tool to analyze the purchase decision-making processes of almost any organization. While the nature, content, and effectiveness of buying activities may vary by organization or products, the basic flow of the purchase decision-making processes remains consistent with the PPP model regardless of context. The following Figure 1.1 describes this flow in a graphical form.

As a purchasing organization goes through these five phases, not necessarily in a linear manner though, its structural focus, behavior, and rhetoric will change. When X-Be is implemented, it allows the seller to establish which one of the five stages the buyer currently occupies and thus devise an appropriate strategy of approach and communication to get involved most effectively in the process of value formation and exchange on the part of customer.

The PPP model not only applies to organizational purchases, but to consumer purchases as well. However, consumers tend not to follow

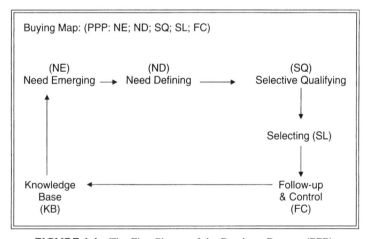

**FIGURE 1.1**    The Five Phases of the Purchase Process (PPP).

quite so formal a process as organizations may be inclined to. Consider a simplified example: Imagine that you want to buy a house, here representing any product or service that is particularly significant. To carry out the purchase, you would normally go through the following phases:

- NE: Before buying a house (regardless of what or who caused you to think about it), you would ponder whether or not one was needed.
- ND: If you thought that a house was needed, you would then look at its criteria – for example, the location, the price, and the type of house. At the end of this stage, you would define your views on the relevant criteria, which you would use to carry out your search in the real-estate market.
- SQ: Based on your own views on criteria (VOC), you would select a specific set of real estate agencies and/or builders who could provide you with your dream home.
- SL: Once you have selected the agencies and builders, you might weigh-out the pros and cons of each house based on your VOC. At the end of this stage, you would select a house that best satisfies your VOC.
- FC: After living in a house for a year or so, you would probably be able to gauge your satisfaction with the house and its features. In the end, you would realize whether the choices you made corresponded to what you had originally thought of the house (before actually living in it). Through this process of post-purchase evaluation, you would enhance your existing knowledge about house purchasing and/or develop new knowledge that would contribute to your own internal knowledge base (KB). This KB would in turn influence future behaviors in situations that are similar to that of buying a house.

Although the above example is necessarily abstract and simplified, it provides an illustration of the PPP model and shows the processes by which value formation and exchange occur for customers when dealing with important purchases.

The question that arises now is that how does the PPP model account for consumer behaviors that underlie the purchase of more everyday items? For example, if a person feels thirsty while walking, she may visit a nearby shop and buy a drink. This kind of spontaneous purchasing behavior is very common and occurs in most economies. Because of its seemingly impulsive nature, it has led many researchers and academes to doubt whether it is possible to develop a model to account for it. Purchasers do not seem to take much time to go through all the PPP when dealing with less important products or services. Once they realize that something is needed, they go ahead and buy it. They seem to go from the phase of NE straight to the SL phase. But this behavioral shortcut does not mean that buyers have never gone through the five phases outlined in our model; it is an indication that buyers tend to rely on their prior knowledge to deal with these "inessential" purchases. Thus, they do not require a formal decision-making process in which they may have to repeat all the five steps of the above PPP model. It is similar in nature to the shortcut one usually uses to carry out the multiplication of a whole number by 100, for example. There is no need to apply a complex algorithm to reach the product; two zeroes appended to the initial number shall suffice. However, this algorithmic shortcut is not the result of impulsive thinking, but is rather a consequence of knowledge previously acquired through experimentation, examples, formal education, and/or learning in general.

Consumer behavioral shortcuts develop in a similar manner, but with one difference. Algorithmic shortcuts in computer science and mathematics can be accounted for in terms of logic, while consumer behavioral "shortcuts" are accounted for by means of the introduction of a new concept *default-value behavior* (DVB). The "default-values" in a person's behavioral makeup can be compared to defaults found in a computer's operating system. For a computer to begin working properly after it is powered up, its operating system needs to internalize (which is to say, commit to memory) those defaults in advance. These defaults are also required for the computer to respond adequately to the user's requests. Similarly, it is the internalized behavioral default values that guide a purchaser through less multifaceted purchasing contexts, especially those involving inessential purchases. For our purpose, we consider default values as the result of direct or indirect experiences of similar events and/or similar situations assimilated into one's system of actionable values.

In Figure 1.2, we have updated the PPP's Buying Map and added the concept of DVB to it.

The DVB and the corresponding behavioral "shortcuts" can be illustrated by various examples in everyday life. For instance, it is not very likely that a person will wander into a shoe store and ask for a plate of spaghetti. Cases like this are not considered in X-Be, because they are fundamentally irrational. Our discussions will focus on people who act with reason (no matter what this reason is) and are responsible for their own behaviors. PPP can provide a universal model that accounts for the purchasing behaviors of any rational person ("rational" refers here to a behavior that is agreeable to some set of reasons, no matter what these

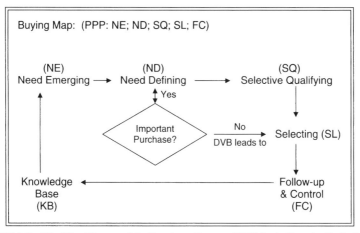

**FIGURE 1.2**    The Five Phases of the Purchase Process (PPP) Including the Default-Value Behavior (DVB).

reasons are or how they have been defined by the individual under observation). "A shoe store is a place that sells shoes" – this is a default value engrained from youth, deep into the minds of anyone living in the context of a market economy (in Chapter 5, you will read the case of a nightclub owner who takes advantage of these default values in naming his establishment to attract a younger customers base). Education, experience, or learning in general endow us with many default values which precipitate and facilitate seemingly thoughtless and "natural" behaviors – these are referred to as DVBs. Children, for example, who have been taught that electrical sockets are dangerous to the touch will fear them, even if they have never touched one. Adept cyclists can ride on the road gracefully; the peculiar rhythms and precarious balance of bicycle riding is second nature to them.

Default values shall be discussed at length in the next several chapters of this book. For now a précis:

- Buyers may go through the entire cycle of the PPP model, even when facing routine purchasing situations in their daily lives. The distinction lies in the fact that the less essential and more frequent purchases would rely more heavily on the customer's DVB.
- DVBs exist even in corporate purchasing processes. The experience and belief systems of organizational buyers working within a company influence the company's buying decision-making processes.

• One can view the DVBs of the customers as a consequence of the deployment of their KB (as per Figure 1.2), the content of which has accumulated in the past in many different forms. Various activities such as advertisements and promotions, personal experience, "word of mouth," and other sources all have something to do with the formation and development of our default values, which often influence our purchasing activities.

## KEY PERSONS AND CORE OPINION LEADERS

The second building block of X-Be is concerned with people who play key roles in the purchasing decision-making process. We usually refer to those people as "customers," "purchasers," or "buyers". In complex selling situations, however, this term is too general to provide an effective description of "who really does the buying." For instance, when one sells goods or services to organizations, several or even more people – with widely varying interest in the purchase – can exert their influence over purchasing decisions. Thus, various labels are applied to these figures: decision makers, advisers, influencers, gatekeepers, coaches, mentors, anti-sponsors, sponsors, and users. These terms are rather inexact, though, and indiscriminate in responding to the question of "who really does the buying." In X-Be, we adopt a simpler approach. In addition to those people who are often highly visible during the purchase process (e.g., buyers, purchasing managers, purchasing engineers, etc.), we also propose a straightforward model – the **MAP** (see Figure 1.3) which allows a seller to identify other people who may not be so visible at purchase, but can also play key roles in the purchasing decision-making process. All these people, visible or

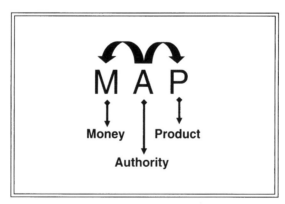

**FIGURE 1.3**   The Key Persons are Those Who have Authority Over Money Spending and Product Selection.

not, could each have an impact at different phases of this process; we shall refer all of them as *key persons*. Among them, there are those whose influence is most acute, who exert the strongest influence (be it positive or negative) upon the purchasing process and its result, and consequently upon the selling activities – these people are the *core opinion leaders* (COLs).

In some simple selling situations, sellers may deal with a purchasing process that involves one key person – the customer. In a hypothetical situation in which the customer is not influenced by anyone else, the key person may also necessarily be termed the COL [in the sense of "communication with self" – Mead (1934)]. In this case, the sales task of identifying key persons is easiest to parse and evaluate. But these sales situations – even in a retail setting – are fairly rare. Most of the time, the customer is under the influence of others who also function as key persons and even COLs in the various PPP. Although these people may be absent from the actual site at which the product is bought, they contribute to the synthesis of the customer's decision. These people could be the buyer's peers, acquaintances, relatives – or, they could be the seller's competitors, who may have succeeded in inculcating certain default values to the customer through previous interaction or communication. These variables present difficulty to the act of selling, particularly when a customer's or key person's default values run contrary to the seller's value proposition.

By nature, organizational sales tend to be this complex. For, in sales involving companies, or governmental departments or offices, the personnel concerned with and interested in the sale can be myriad, and differences of opinion are to be expected. Sales of OEM products, industrial products, or large quantities of wholesale products are examples. In these cases, the sales process will most likely involve several and even more key persons – perhaps even several COLs. Well-organized purchasing entities are likely to ensure that each key person or specialized group of key persons is concerned with a different aspect of the purchase in question. Each key person and COL involved in a purchase develops his or her own self-defined views on how the customer's needs can best be addressed.

## VIEWS ON CRITERIA

Many companies currently rely upon the express "voice of customer" – *vox populi* – to describe the customers' expectations from a sales transaction. But the term's definition is vague, and, worse yet, the "voice of customer" is inexact and can be unreliable in practice.

In X-Be, the customer is not simply taken at face value. Steps are enacted to meaningfully and usefully interpret a purchaser's behavior, in the context of his or her phase of the purchasing process. To do that, we propose rethinking this old concept in terms of views on criteria (VOC), which, applied to a customer's expressed and implied attitudes and beliefs, can be a reliable measure of this customer's values, wants, and expectations before, during, and after a transaction.

VOC are characterized by two elements: one is a key person's perception about the specific factors, aspects, or dimensions relevant to his purchase decision situation, termed *selecting points*. Each selecting point has the rationale behind it – the feeling, belief, or logic accounting for a key person's or COL's valuing the corresponding selecting point in terms of importance. This rationale, whether it is explicit or implicit, clear or not, felt or emotional, may be termed *selecting rationale*.

It should be noted that the VOC might not be directly related to any specific sales offer on table at all, although in many cases, the previously experienced sales offers often do contribute to its formation and contents.

In the real estate industry, there is an old motto that runs, "Location, Location, Location!" While location is certainly a selecting point (relevant aspect) for many home buyers, the rationale that account for why location is so important differs considerably from buyer to buyer. Deploying the nomenclature of X-Be, one may note that each buyer boasts a different selecting rationale for the selecting point of location. For a seller (salesperson or sales organization) to succeed in correctly interpreting the voice of a customer, and understanding his needs and wants, she must take heed that rationale is as important, if not more so, than the selecting point it entails – as per the following critical formula of X-Be:

$$\text{Views on Criteria} = \text{Selecting Points} + \text{Selecting Rationales}$$

Consider the following case. A young, middle-class sports reporter is looking to buy a house and her real-estate agent quickly recognizes the purchaser's concerns regarding the potential home's location – contiguous, she has suggested, to public transportation. But the salesperson's approach is much different, and he largely discards this nugget of information. And, all this is the product of the agent having paid scrupulous attention during the cul-de-sac of small-talk that presaged the sales discussion in earnest: the woman made passing reference to a fondness for leisure sport – golf, tennis, equestrian. Ah! – thinks the real estate agent – this customer must belong to the upper crust. So he thinks and congratulates himself for so astutely isolating the basis of his customer's interest in location. Based on his perception of his client's economic strata, he shows her an assortment of homes in ritzy suburbs, promoting at all times the adjacent natural environment, golf courses, exclusive tennis clubs, and other local frills congruent to what he perceives to be her social class. He spends two hours on this tack – trying to "sell" her on these features, only to realize that this very patient client still seems to have no particular intention to buy. Why? Because the agent built his selling strategy on the wrong buying rationale. This "wealthy" customer had, in fact, limited means, and while she desired the best possible home in the safest possible place for her money, she was entirely uninterested in living in some far-flung suburb with no access to the public transportation that would link her to work downtown. The agent was not skillful enough to understand that, zealously pursuing his own interests and his presumptions about her, and the client was too reticent (feeling that the agent has ignored her insinuations) to surrender any further information.

## BUYING POINTS AND SELLING POINTS

The fourth building block of X-Be is concerned with factors that help bring about a motion to purchase (a state of readiness to buy) in the customer – they are related, very specifically pertinent to the sales offer at hand, and of paramount importance. These "purchase catalysts" may be categorized into two types: *buying points* and *selling points*. As far as their content or denotation is concerned, buying points and selling points can either be identical, completely distinct, or overlap. They relate to those aspects of the sales offer that are attractive to the individual purchaser as a solitary entity and to this same individual purchaser as a social entity, respectively. They are accordingly related to this individual purchaser, even if they reflect tangible aspects of a sales offer.

The purchase behavior of a key person is influenced by two discrete spheres: namely, the personal and the socio-cultural. buying points originate from the former sphere; they refer to those factors that may motivate the key person, as an individual agent beholden to no-one, to make a purchase. They thus reflect personal benefits – the immediate dividends the sales offer may pay to the purchaser's private life. Selling points originate from the latter sphere and refer to those factors that enable the key person to socially justify – in effect, "sell" – his buying behavior to those whose opinions he values or whose approval he requires. Since these people can influence the key person's buying decision, they act as *de facto* key persons during the purchaser's decision-making process. Selling points, thus, reflect collective benefits and dividends rather than individual ones. So, customer value is like a coin – one side of it involves a key person's buying points, and the other his selling points. Below is an example that illustrates the concept.

A young man enters a fashionable boutique and is struck by a particularly ostentatious suit, pastel-colored and with a sexy, tapered cut. Impressed with his choice, a salesperson compliments his daring nature, as the suit is also form-fitting and iridescent. The man thought the suit was innovative and would make for a memorable entrance at an important party he is organizing with a friend of his. As he removes the jacket, however, he recalls that his friend's parents will be joining them for dinner and fears the suit would be inappropriate for such an occasion. He, therefore, abandons the idea of buying the suit on the basis of its contextual inappropriateness in the eyes of his friend's parents, whom he wishes to impress, and opts for a more conservative suit instead.

In this example, the customer's buying point was the striking design of the suit. The customer, in a social vacuum, would have, in an instant, been willing to purchase the suit for this reason (assuming the presence of another buying point – a reasonable price). However, he could find no attached selling point which would permit him to justify wearing this suit in front of people with whom he was to interact – (in fact, in this case, the buying point was clearly in conflict with the customer's ability to "sell" his buying behavior). Because of this, the sales transaction could not be consummated.

## THE INTEGRATED PRODUCT – DELIVERING UPON BUYING POINTS AND SELLING POINTS

The fifth building block is concerned with the customer's perception of the deliverability of the buying points and selling points in a sales offer. Sellers are relied upon to deliver what we term the *integrated product* – not merely the items (or services) changing hands, but those items with all the accrued and encrusted add-ons and incentives which constitute the customer's buying points and selling points. The integrated product's importance stems from the fact that purchasing, like any action or decision taken in the course of life, has risks associated with it. The customer's aim is to minimize this risk. In the case of purchasing, the risk is as follows: when the buyer makes the final decision to consummate a purchase, he also makes a decisive assumption that the sales offer provided by the seller will satisfy his buying and selling points. But this assumption could very well be faulty. The risk is even higher when the purchased product is one which, for example, is new or has been newly introduced or considered, and thus there is no or little "KB" in place to guide a potential purchaser, who must necessarily also have no personal experience with the product. And, thus, the sales offer's and/or seller's ability to convince the customer and actually deliver upon his buying points and selling points (before, during and after sales) is paramount. Below is an example that illustrates the interrelation of buying points, selling points, and the integrated product.

A woman looking to buy a lap dog is told (by the pet store owner) that the breed in which she is interested is one which displays particular devotion in catering to the whims of its master. As the customer examines the dog, she is enamored; its beautiful coat and slightly melancholy mien wins her heart, and she is also reassured as to the dog's docility and intelligence by observing it carrying out various complex commands with grace. She then bargains with the store owner and accepts the price; the woman's buying points (the promise of the dog's affection and obedience, and the good price) are addressed. But the expenditure, however reasonable, is still substantial, and the customer has yet to consult her husband, with whom she shares control of the family's finances. She hesitantly closes her purse. Now, the store owner has to address the potential purchaser's selling points. He appeals to her, suggesting that her children could stand to gain enjoyment and edification from the company of a pet; he is certain that her husband would agree and invites her to call and check with him.

The store owner developed this argument on the basis of the following precepts: (1) if the woman is to "sell" the purchase to her husband, she shall have to deploy a line of reasoning congruent with his own values; (2) the husband's values include a desire to keep his children happy and educated.

The woman then phones her husband and convinces him to buy the dog after explaining how happy the children will be. And despite his passing misgivings about the investment, he acquiesces. The customer's selling points were addressed: this lap dog may bring happiness to the children and teach them about responsibility – it is also a cost-effective means of doing so and has been approved by her financial partner (another key person). Her purse reopens.

Just as the store owner begins the maneuvers by which he may close the deal, the telephone rings – it is the husband, in a panic, inquiring as to who will bathe the dog – an arduous task particularly for a family who already have children to whom to attend. The store owner thinks quickly and offers her an incentive to buy the dog: he will provide a dog bathing service, under certain conditions. (He also realizes that this could serve as a way of bringing in new business and internally revises his establishment's promotions strategy.) This promise does indeed soothe the couple's concerns and leads to the store owner's success in delivering upon the buying and selling points associated with the sale transaction. Coupled with the dog-bathing service, what changed hands was not a mere lap dog, but an integrated product – personalized to the individual customer.

It may also be useful to define selling by means of a functional formula:

Selling = f(VOC, buying points and selling points, Deliverability)

In other words, selling is a function (f in the above formula) of (1) the VOC of the key persons and COLs; (2) the combination of buying point and selling point aligned with these same people; and (3) the deliverability of these points by the seller or the sales offer. Thus, according to the above formula, if a seller has a good handle on the purchaser's VOC, and specific buying points and selling points expected of a sales offer, as well as on the proofs of the deliverability upon the latter two, the sale itself should be within the seller's effective control.

## APPROPRIATE COMMUNICATORS AND NETWORKED RESOURCES

Not merely does a salesperson orchestrate sales "dialogue" – direct seller-to-customer interaction – but salespeople also play an active role in facilitating communication among any other parties that may be involved or interested; for the seller may not necessarily be the most appropriate communicator of ideas and values at all stages of the selling process. Depending on the complexity and nature of the sale in question, the salesperson may have to involve different people, at different PPP, to best position the sales efforts and the offer to the key persons. Hence, the concept of the *appropriate communicator* – the sixth building block of X-Be.

The appropriate communicator can be anyone who helps a seller with the sales process (address the customer's concerns, and advocate – at any given time – for the seller's cause to bring the sale to consummation). The concerns and attentive focus of the purchaser or purchasing organization may change with the phase of this process currently occupied. Indeed, different key persons become involved at different phases to emphasize different selecting points – and each possesses its own corresponding selecting rationale. As a consequence, besides the salesperson herself, she may need to consider finding and mobilizing other communicators to effectively facilitate communications with specific key persons. For instance, the appropriate communicator for a key person concerned with quality will probably be a quality-control engineer or manager, while the appropriate communicator for a key person concerned more with storage and stock management will be a logistics manager.

Nowadays, selling is becoming increasingly teamwork-oriented and often involves and deploys different people from various departments within a sales organization. Companies that limit sales functions to only their sales and marketing departments often needlessly jeopardize their own true selling capacities.

Most successful salespeople have built a network of professional relationships, which are termed *networked resources* within X-Be. The networked resources a salesperson has, whether they are from the relevant industries, her own company, or are simply satisfied customers, are indeed a priceless asset in getting needed customer information, in convincing new customers as to an offer's value, and in putting them at ease during the transaction. And a truly skilled salesperson should be aware of the benefits of linking an appropriate communicator to a similarly concerned key person; knowing whom is just as important as knowing how.

Later on in the book, we will further explore why and how various relationships can help salespeople hone their selling techniques. The question will be considered sociologically and explore why some key people are willing to provide valuable information, while others are not.

## SELLING STATUS INDICES

Selling, in a sense, amounts to a process of communication – the exchange of information among individuals with disparate interests and levels of interest in completing a transaction. But the trouble with processes of communication is that they are, to each participant, a necessarily subjective experience; the underlying thoughts and motivations of the involved key persons may be elusive or deliberately clandestine. It is a difficult proposition, then, to systematize, monitor, and evaluate communicative relationships.

And yet salespeople are often called upon to "think on their feet," to effect rapid changes in sales strategy or positioning in accordance with level and quality of communication with the purchasing party. They must be able to assess the direction in which the sale is moving, but, to do so, they have no agreed methodologies by which to abide and can rely only upon their own erratic "gut feeling" or "instinct." Such uncertainty should be unacceptable in a sales environment demanding maximum efficiency.

While subjective feelings do represent an important barometer for the progress of a sale, they are by no means sound enough to be the sole one. More objective, rational measures are needful, with built-in contingencies to guide sales behavior through crises and past bulwarks. Any process must have some monitoring indices established for it; otherwise, the process would not be manageable.

To this end, X-Be introduces three easy-to-implement selling status indices – spectra based upon consideration of which the seller may form judgments on how the sale is progressing, and to what extent one can be confident about its success. These indices are defined in a way that reflects the value-pursuing behavior of customers.

### Relating Status Index

Can you assess relationship in an objective manner? And how? The *relating status index* is concerned with the personal relationships that the seller shares with those key persons to whom the sale is being targeted. In simple terms, it evaluates a key person's "comfort level" with the seller. It is measured by the following four incremental stages:

1. Critical Stage: the key person is silent – or obviously unwilling to discuss any issues pertinent to the sale.
2. Public Relations (PR) Stage: the key person speaks only officially, divulging information that can be easily obtained through public channels.
3. Acquaintance Stage: the key person speaks relatively freely on business matters. The information offered is probably not secret, but perhaps difficult to glean through public channels.
4. Partner Stage: the key person is willing to share any relevant information with the seller, including but not limited to information that may or may not be considered privileged.

The relating status index evaluates a seller's progress by measuring the amount of information (conducive to the sales process) that a key person has volunteered. It is ultimately objective, as the rate of information exchange (and the nature of its content) is outward and tangible; furthermore, the seller is rationally aware of the extent to which the information in question is pertinent to the sale itself. The resulting assessment of status is therefore unambiguous.

## The Attitude Index – the Purchaser's Attraction to buying points

Can you assess a key person's motion to purchase? And how? The concept of "attitude" has been widely discussed in psychology and in studies of organizational behavior; generally, the term itself is defined as an individual's disposition toward a particular event or person. Within X-Be, the attitude index refers specifically to a measure of how a key person ranks the importance of the various buying points in the sales offer, and how important this key person deems these buying points in the grand scheme of things; in other words, it measures a customer's interpretation or feeling of how effective the sales offer will be in bringing him closer to happiness.

Of course, nothing in the world is ideal; no key person expects any offer to fulfill at once all his various and varicolored needs. However, as regards any given offer, there are some things (buying points) that are utterly essential to piquing a purchaser's interest and convincing him that an action to obtain them will be worthwhile; the very idea of a purchase cannot be entertained unless these buying points are included. Other buying points would be just nice to have or otherwise minor. So the attitude index assigns a rating to each buying point describing the purchaser's relationship to it: some buying points are essential; some are desirable; the rest are minor. The seller's goal is to ensure that the customer views as many of the sales offer's features as possible as essential.

Chapter 8 will outline how the seller can make use of this ranking system to evaluate her own success in highlighting the virtues of the sales offer – and also in reconciling the customer's expectations with the offer's limitations.

## Confidence Index – Attitude Toward selling points

"How confident are you about sales targets?" This question has obsessed companies and salespeople since the dawn of organized sales. In many Enterprise Resource Planning (ERP) and Customer Relationship Management (CRM) software packages, for example, salespeople are required to input their confidence levels for each sales task. Such an input amounts, though, to an educated guess at best.

Because of the way it is generated, this input will vary with the individual salesperson who formulates the judgment about her confidence. And close to the end of the year, concerned managers invariably become highly apprehensive about achieved target for the year and sales forecasts for the following year, lacking as they do a comprehensive assessment of sales performance for the preceding year. This apprehensiveness stems from not having an objective, rational means measuring the company's success or failure before the finished figures of an annual report are in; in many cases, managers find themselves mere spectators to their own businesses, as a litany of unpredictable factors make themselves felt upon sales levels and rates. It is, therefore, critically important to develop a method that allows salespeople to evaluate their confidence in an objective way, while acknowledging the various risks that surround the selling process.

This is why we introduce, within X-Be, a third selling status index – the *confidence index* (CI). The CI is defined as the extent to which a key person has publicly acknowledged the selling points of a sales offer. "Extent," here, is understood to refer both to (1) the *amount* and *prominence* of acknowledgment and to (2) the *type* of forum.

Indeed, forum is of particular importance during occasions for attitude declaration – those times when a purchaser (or purchasing organization) articulates his attraction to the selling points in the sales offer. A casual mention to low-level workers should give rise to a low CI; acknowledgment only to the salesperson is even lower, but certainly not unfavorable. But if a key person's attitude is expressed in public, in the media, or at a meeting of executives or shareholders or any significant others, the CI rises sharply.

The rationale behind the CI is pretty simple; when a specific attitude and/or behavior are publicized, people who have done so will find it difficult to reverse this attitude – because to do so would be to contradict what has already become a matter of corporate or social record or policy; it may damage his image, and he may not be worthy of trust by others any more. This might explain the phenomenon of so-called escalating commitment (Staw, 1981) among decision makers: the tendency to continue in a previously chosen course of action even when feedback suggests that it was a failure.


## COMPETITION

Unless business is transacted in a no-competition or weak-competition environment, or a product is essential and available nowhere else, a seller's position relative to that of (his or) her competitors within the marketplace is a key factor in any sales activity.

Within X-Be, competition is viewed in its broadest sense, encompassing all – and any – factors that might impede a seller's success. General market information about the seller's industry competitors is to be solely used as a reference point. X-Be's concept of competition is not represented by, for example, an opposing sales organization offering the same item or service, but rather by how those factors in the key person's VOC tend to hinder the seller from winning the sale.

To develop a working concept for salespeople, X-Be introduces the concept of impeding factors – impedance to sales progress in the form of buying points and selling points about which key persons may feel the seller and/or her sales offer will have trouble delivering. It should be obvious that a seller needs to parse and develop an understanding of all those factors which may prevent a key person from commencing their motion to purchase – and fundamental to this process is to establish why deliverability is in question. X-Be allows a seller to reach conclusions on these questions and to establish or ameliorate a competitive position.

X-Be provides sellers with a conceptual framework for virtually all sales activity – personal selling or non-personal selling – organized in a systematic and easy-to-follow fashion. Because of the clear logical relationships that X-Be establishes among its internally defined elements, this conceptual framework will help salespeople or sales manager to evaluate and direct sales activity with a degree of effectiveness much greater than that of a sales framework based upon subjectivity, mere experience, or trial and error. X-Be's building blocks reflect the highly dynamic nature of the cognitive, psychological, and behavioral characteristics of the customer, a value-chasing engine. The logic and internal consistency among these building blocks represent the key features that make X-Be universally applicable and effective in day-to-day selling work and its management.

The following chapters will provide a thorough discussion of the building blocks of X-Be and their applications in various selling and sales management cases.

# 2

## PHASES OF THE PURCHASE PROCESS MODEL: VALUE FORMATION AND EXCHANGE ON THE PART OF CUSTOMER

Most sales textbooks and companies' sales manuals tend to describe the sales process in a similar way by including various steps, such as (1) prospecting – finding the leads and qualifying some of them as good potential customers who have Money, Authority and Desire to buy (MAD); (2) approaching – obtaining meeting opportunity and establishing rapport; (3) presenting with trial closing – relating product to customer needs and checking the attitude of the potential customer toward the sales presentation; (4) overcoming customer objections; (5) closing – getting orders; and (6) follow-up.

Such a description of the selling process makes sense, but only from the seller's perspective. It does not say much about the buying decision-making processes of the customer who, obviously, has no reason to dance with this kind of "imposed" logic of the selling process. The steps that customers take to make a purchase may have little or nothing to do with the way the seller decides to run his or her selling processes. Even worse, the above selling logic often misaligns with the customer's buying logic, and thus tends to generate numerous insurmountable objections from the customer's side, leading to failures of the sales process.

Yet, the typical management adage is that sellers' activities should be customer-oriented. Therefore, it only makes sense to attempt to first understand and describe the buying decision-making processes from the customer's side. But, the customers can be awfully diverse: they come from differing cultures and have different processes and behaviors, even within a selected segment or target market that is believed to share similar needs and desires. This fact makes the difficulties in attaining a truly customer-oriented framework seem insurmountable, for no company has the limitless resources by which it may attune itself to every imaginable customer idiosyncrasy.

The result of the above difficulties is of management and sales staff taking two different approaches: one is a managerial, gregarious approach to customer interaction, relying primarily on a sales process like the abovementioned one; the other one is a *laissez-faire*, individualistic approach to customer interaction, relying primarily on experience and acquired human skills to broker deals. The former approach is process based and tends to reflect the belief that "well managed behaviors produce good results"; but, because the sales process it uses is designed from the seller's perspective and, thus, is not customer focused, this approach often fails to generate satisfactory results. The latter approach champions the opposite stance: "everything goes depending on the sales situation – only the results count"; this results-driven approach centers upon the sole salesperson's charisma and performance; achievements are personalized, and the individualistic climate this approach creates becomes difficult to manage effectively. But things need not be this way if there is an integrated framework for both selling and sales management developed along the process of value formation and exchange on the part of customer.

Through in-depth understanding of selling and sales management practices, this chapter will attempt to show that in all customer interactions, no matter how intricate, with all clients, no matter how many or how few, and in any context, X-Be's Phases of Purchase Process, or the PPP model (which involves the intrinsic logic underlying the way a customer pursues value to satisfy a purchase need), should always be the first and foremost element that sellers need to consider when entering the interactions with a customer. Intimacy on the part of the salesperson or sales manager with the PPP model, as briefly illustrated in Chapter 1, will allow the process of selling and sales management to become, at last, a truly *manageable* customer-oriented operation. The PPP model, indeed, not only does it enable sellers to center their interactions with customers on customer needs (which vary and change by situation), but, more importantly, on the entrenched buying logic that underlies the process of value formation and exchange on the part of customer. The idea we are championing here for customer-oriented interactions is built upon the very understanding of how individual customers perceive and act for customer value in their purchase process, as opposed to assuming that *standardized* sales offers developed by marketing efforts already have their ready customers to buy in and, thus, all that selling needs to do is to simply communicate the *intrinsic* merits of these sales offers to the target customers. The fact of the matter is that different customers, in different situations, coming from different background, with different interests, will have different perceptions of customer value in the very same sales offer.

## ISSUES CONCERNING THE CONCEPT OF NEED

In order to survive and develop, individuals always act to satisfy their various needs. In our modern society, most of these needs can be satisfied through various types of exchange with others, one of which is the buying activity.

Similarly, organizations have their needs too; they indeed require various goods and services to operate and expand their businesses. However, any organization is staffed and run by people. It is these people who perceive the needs for their organization, and all of these so-called organizational needs can ultimately be reduced to the individual needs of the people who perceive them, though all is done in the name of organization. Therefore, it is legitimate to study organizational needs in relation to those of the people involved.

As for individuals, the concept of need can be understood and analyzed within different theoretical frameworks. Among these frameworks, there are some that are often quoted in the literature such as Maslow's Hierarchy of Needs theory (see below) and McGuire's classification system of various needs. In response to the accusation that marketing often creates a lot of undue needs, some marketers often argue that needs are not created but are part of basic human motives; marketing, rather, creates wants or demands.

For our purpose here, we shall not delve into this kind of argumentation, but simply adopt the understanding that a perceived discrepancy between a desired state and the actual state in one's current situation could act as a driver for the need to do something; if the action of doing something can be related to a purchase, we refer to the need as a purchase need.

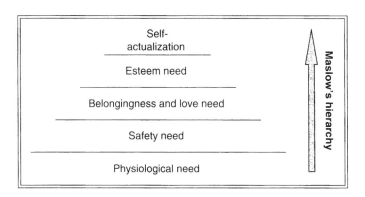

Thus, as studied in psychology, the origin of a need is in a feeling of dissatisfaction on the part of a potential customer regarding some element of his life or work, or situation in general. But though this feeling is the basis of a need, it is not necessarily the need to purchase in itself. This distinction shall be clarified later in this chapter. For now, though, let us note that this perceived deficiency can bring about the emergence of need (NE), and can be the result of either internal or external factors, and can afflict individuals or organizations. As regards individuals, Maslow's Hierarchy of Needs and many other studies on human needs illustrate a number of needs that can arise due to physiological, psychological or social catalysts. But, external factors such as social interactions, advertising, and word-of-mouth have a similar effect.

The same is true of companies, as internal operations and pressures give rise to different perceived purchasing needs. The production department may require a replenishing of raw materials or stocks in general; the personnel department may desire counseling services on the matter of human resources; research and development may demand a more advanced diagnostic apparatus. External factors may also create needs: increases in sales; changes in social trends; new competition; governmental interference. However, and as pointed out above, all these organizational needs can be related to the perceptions of needs by different people in the organization and should, therefore, be somehow connected to these people's characteristics.

Regardless of who and what may cause a need, the need itself precipitates the PPP as outlined in the previous chapter.

It should be noted that it is in the seller's benefit to accurately identify the phase of the client's purchasing process in which she finds herself at any given time (during her communication and interaction with the customer) and adjust her selling strategy accordingly. She could carry out such identification by asking appropriate questions to understand the customer's current concerns, how he perceives these concerns and how clear he is about other relevant issues related to them; getting such information will help the seller make a sensible judgment as to what the phase the customer is currently occupying. Similar actions are taken by those professional sellers mostly concerned with brokering complex sales among organizations or companies with myriad key persons on the customer side. In general, for sellers to effectively interact with their customers for successful exchanges, they need to understand how these customers pursue purchasing value in the course of their purchase processes.

The following is a brief gloss of the purchasing process (PPP model) as conceptualized within X-Be.

- The purchasing process is forward-looking and embodies a series of characteristic cognitive, psychological, and behavioral events.
- It is followed by almost all individuals and organizations, who may shortcut such stages as ND and SQ by resorting to the Default Values already internalized.
- Its phases and the actions and decisions pertinent to each phase can be plotted logically and in an orderly manner.
- Central to it are the key persons who play various value roles (resource type, product type or process type) in the course of the process of value formation and exchange. Who these key persons are and what influence they have can vary from sale to sale.
- At each stage of the purchasing process, key persons tend to behave in a specific way that will be conceptualized within X-Be to shed light for sellers on how they can get involved effectively in the customer's value formation and exchange process.

## WALKING THROUGH THE PHASES OF THE PURCHASING PROCESS

Within the framework X-Be, we emphasize the customer value questions that sellers need to address, regardless of the nature of the physical communication or interaction methods these sellers are going to use in, say, non-personal selling (advertising, direct mailing, and interactive website), personal selling or a combination of both. To make this focus on customer value questions clearly visible to the reader, we shall discuss the PPP, below, in a systematic way.

### Need Emerging – The Customer Precipitates the PPP

When we decide to sell to or happen to meet with the customer in the phase of NE, what customer value questions we need to address to be effective? The following key customer value questions ought to be considered within X-Be:

- "No gap, no need":
  What are the discrepancies in the key persons' life and work that could be associated with the sales offers? Should key persons not perceive such gaps at all, could we help them become aware of some?

- "The higher the urgency, the higher the probability of purchase":
  Have the key persons realized the significance or magnitude of the
  discrepancies that (will) affect their life and/or work? Do they
  perceive any urgency to resolve these discrepancies? If not, could
  we help them become aware of it?

Clearly, there are often many discrepancies that make people's life
and work unsatisfactory, but only those ones that are perceived by the
customers to be significant enough to them, and that can be addressed
or reduced at least for some time through exchange efforts, may lead to
purchase needs. The clearer the sellers are about the above-mentioned
customer value questions, the more effective they will be with their own
exchange behavior in selling and sales management when they communicate and interact with the customers in the phase of NE.

Also, there should be a consideration of what means for communication and interaction the sellers should select in their selling activities at this
stage, and this usually depends on the customers' preferences for the types
of communication media. It also depends on the level of involvement of
the customers when facing different buys in terms of product, industry,
situation, finance, availability of the current communication technology,
and so on.

One more point to make about selling in this phase: sellers must
be proactive and strive to comprehend fully the customers needs and
the dynamics that surround them (perhaps better than the customer him
or herself) and should, as a consequence, be able to arouse purchase
needs, which would otherwise not be considered or even realized by the
customer. The ability to arouse needs for new products, new life styles,
new processes, and consulting services of different kinds is very important
and not uncommon in selling.

### Need Defining – The Customer Looks at Establishing Criteria for Value

When we decide to get involved with or happen to meet with the customer
in the phase of ND, what customer value questions do we need to address
to be effective? The following customer value questions are recommended
for selling in the phase of ND:

- "No criteria, no decision":
  What are the specific issues, concerns, and standards of judgment
  that the individual key persons tend to focus on for making a
  decision (Selecting Points)? What are the feelings and beliefs

behind the focus on these points (Selecting Rationale)? Answers to these questions help us to understand what we called the VOC.

- "The less favorable the VOC, the harder the selling will be and vice versa":
  What, in the VOC of the individual key persons, is favorable and what else is unfavorable to your selling?
- "The more flexible and unsettled the VOC, the more uncertain the result of selling":
  Are those unfavorable criteria settled or are they changeable, and to what extent? What specific actions should be taken to effectively promote the favorable and convincingly downplay the unfavorable?

The effectiveness of selling and sales management behavior in the phase of ND can be judged by how well the sellers answer the above customer value questions.

## Selective Qualifying – The Customer Senses Value

When we decide to engage or happen to meet with the customer in the phase of SQ, what customer value questions do we need to address to be effective? The following customer value questions should be addressed in the phase of SQ:

- "Personal Gains" (something for self):
  Buying points – what are the characteristics of the considered sales offer that are of specific value for each key person as an *individual* and as per his VOC?
- "Social Justification" (good in others' views):
  Selling points – what are the characteristics of the considered sales offer that renders the needed social justification for each key person as a *social being*, so that he could "sell" his own buying behavior to his significant others (the people whom he likes, respects, or who have influence over him?). The customer's own selling points are of significance in numerous purchasing situations.

The effectiveness of exchange behavior in selling and sales management at the stage of SQ can be judged by how well the sellers address these customer value questions.

It should be noted here that the concept of "Selling points" as it has been traditionally used in selling and sales management literature has nothing to do with that used in the X-Be framework. In fact, the old-fashioned sales-side "selling points" do not warrant any reflection on customer value at all.

## Selecting – The Customer Confirms the Acquisition of Value

When we decide to interact with the customer in the phase of SL, what customer value questions do we need to address to be effective? There are at least two customer value questions that should be addressed in this phase:

- Deliverability of buying points (Personal Gains) and selling points (Social Justification):
  What are the requirements and expectations of the key persons in terms of the deliverability of the buying points and selling points for the customer to act and purchase?
- Actions to reinforce the sense of deliverability:
  What are the specific actions that may increase the customer's sense of deliverability of the buying points and selling points for the customer to buy?

The effectiveness of exchange behavior in selling and sales management at the stage of SL can be judged by how well the sellers deal with the above questions.

It should be noted here that the notion of deliverability aims to reduce the buying risks as they are perceived by the customer. Any action may be associated with risks, and so do the buying activities. The goal of reinforcing the customer' sense of the deliverability (by the seller) of the buying points and selling points is to assure the customer that the buying risks have been dealt with in the sales offer before, during, and after the purchase decision.

## Follow-Up and Control – The Customer Evaluates the Acquired Value

When buyers are in the phase of FC, they are using either the seller's product or the competitor's product. What customer value questions do we need to address in either case?

If the buyers are using the seller's product, there are at least two customer value questions that should be addressed in the FC phase:

- Promises must be kept:
  What are the specific actions that you have seriously considered taking to ensure a satisfactory deliverability of the buying points and selling points, as they are expected by the customer?
- Customer perceived results count:
  What is the customer's perception about the deliverability of the buying points and selling points after the purchase? If the customer

feels, after the purchase, that he gains more than the previously expected deliverability of his buying points and selling points, he could become a delighted customer, and this is certainly the dividend for future business; if he perceives a satisfactory deliverability, he will be a satisfied customer, and this result might help future sales; if he experiences an unsatisfactory deliverability, he will become a dissatisfied customer, and this may have a negative impact on future sales.

The FC phase is usually the stage where it is easiest to sell well and maintain a long-term customer relationships to generate more business, win even more customers through good referrals and words of mouth, and establish and sustain the strength of the brand in general. Thus, exchange behavior in selling and sales management should never end at the acquisition of purchase orders from the customer.

If the buyers are using a competitor's product, there are at least two customer value questions that should be addressed in this phase:

- How well has the competitor delivered the customer's expected buying points and selling points?
- If the competitor has not satisfied the customer's expected buying points and selling points, is it a new opportunity to win back the customer in the future? Or should you just ignore it?
  Keep in mind that there are hardly such buyers that will be your competitor's customers forever. The fundamentals that support any buyer – seller relationship always consist of the deliverability of customer value. To illustrate this, we will present a real business case later in this chapter.

The effectiveness of exchange behavior in selling and sales management at the FC stage can be judged by how well the sellers can answer the above questions.

To summarize our discussion in this section, we convert the PPP model into a buying map (see Figure 2.1 below) that illustrates the dynamics of the buying decision-making process. The map also shows the articulation between the PPP model stages and the basic concepts of the framework X-Be. It provides the logic that underlies the transitions from one step to the other and explains it using these basic concepts. At the fundamental level, as it will be explained in the later chapters of the book, the rationales behind this map are grounded in psychology and sociology and aim to analyze the value-pursuing behavior of buyers. When a feeling of dissatisfaction takes place, buyers will either have to go through a formal process to define the purchase need to address this dissatisfaction or simply make

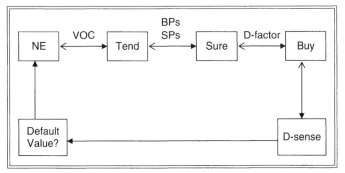

**FIGURE 2.1**    Buying Map Illustrating the Phases of the Purchase Process (PPP) Model. BPs, Buying points; SPs, Selling points; VOC, Views on Criteria.

use of the learnt default values to come up with such a definition. In both cases, the need definition is expressed in terms of the buyers' views on the criteria for value (VOC). Armed with the VOC, the buyers might decide to tend to the customer value through the acquisition of a sales offer with a certain set of buying points and selling points. If they are sure of the deliverability of the buying points and selling points (D-factor in the figure), they might take action to buy. After purchase, they will actually feel and evaluate the "real" deliverability of the customer value during the use of the product or service (D-sense in the figure), and some of these feelings and evaluations might become the new default values which may affect their future buying perception, psychology, and behavior in similar situations; they may also share such experience and knowledge with others and, thus, affect those who trust them.

It should be noted that customer's purchase involvement in each of the above purchase phases vary with the individual buyers and with the situations. For instance, the phase of NE in some purchases such as consulting services could be much longer than that of purchasing many physical products, and the phase of SL is often identified as a long negotiation process in some purchases of OEMs.

## THE PPP IN COMPANIES AND ORGANIZATIONS

Generally speaking, by the time an organization has entered the process of purchasing, it has likely already sketched out a timetable with deadlines for its needs to be satisfied. Though there may be some flexibility in these deadlines, and though this timetable may be revised during purchase, an organization tends to operate in accordance with schedules in order to ensure that its operations are efficient.

However, it should be noted that, though an organization as a whole is generally at a single stage of PPP, the various key persons involved might individually be ahead or behind the company itself in the process.

For example, even though the company may be on the cusp of the final Selecting Phase (SL), certain dissenting key person(s) may feel that the company ought to do more exploration in the interest of finding better-qualified or competing suppliers (the SQ phase), or may even dispute the existence of a need to begin with (NE phase). Similarly, certain key person(s) may already be scouting potential suppliers (SQ) by the time the company as a whole is still weighing whether or not a need exists (NE) or what its precise nature might be (ND).

So perhaps it would be useful at this point to distinguish, functionally, between the PPP of organizations as a whole and the PPP of individual key persons within those organizations. Here is how they differ:

1. Organization-as-a-whole PPP: This PPP requires the seller to complete a certain sales task in a certain time, according to deadlines installed into a schedule as set by the organization as a unified body.
2. Key person PPP: This PPP requires the seller to check, balance, and regulate the above task by means of communication, ensuring that proper decisions are made; the effectiveness and purposefulness of the sales activities are thus ensured by flexibility and research.

The distinction of the above two types of PPP has an important implication for selling. Competition presents itself primarily in the cases in which there are key persons who lag behind the organization as a whole PPP, while you are ahead of the competitors. But, conversely, there could be a competitive advantage with the key persons whose individual PPP lay behind the PPP of the organization as a whole when you are behind the competitors. The following section presents a real case study that illustrates such happenings, together with the customer value questions that need to be addressed at the FC stage.

## A SALES CASE STUDY ABOUT THE FC PHASE (SHENG, 2002)

In the second half of 1999, a multinational manufacturer of automotive parts (Supplier S) begins targeting an automobile company (Client C) located in one of the emerging Asian economies. The mission of Supplier S is to gain clients for their new engine management system (or "electro-inject system" in local parlance). The salesperson sent to Client C arrives aware that this potential customer's new minivan can make use of their electro-inject system. Indeed, Client C was one of the first manufacturers of minivans in the country and, at one point, occupied a competitive share in the domestic market, but with corporate regrouping, minivan production was halted. This time, Client C intends to re-enter the market with a minivan equipped with a new electro-inject system.

That being said, the salesperson sent to broker a deal with Client C does not represent the first supplier to have visited this potential customer. Indeed, upon her first visit, she was clearly told that Client C was already at the phase of post-purchase tracking, controlling, and assessing (FC phase).

At that time, one of the key persons who was most influential upon this purchase in Client C's organization had already enjoyed a satisfactory collaboration with a competitor, the joint venture of a European company. As one of the main overseers of this deal, he utterly refused to take on a second supplier. And though other relevant key persons were not so firm in this position of denial, the fact of the matter was that no number of visits to Client C would dislodge the extant contract with the competing supplier. All that the salesperson in question could do is maintain frequent telephone contact with Client C, and those key persons who dissented with the firm denier. This supply contract, if secured, would be too lucrative to ever surrender the hope of success.

By maintaining this casually communicative relationship with the executives at Client C's company, the salesperson keeps abreast of the sort of personnel changes characteristic of any large company with the passage of time. One day, in the course of these friendly exchanges, he discovered a few heartening developments:

- One of the key persons, whose PPP had lagged behind that of the company as a whole, has come to prominence in the organization, becoming more influential – and indeed currently oversees the project in question.
- That makes the key person a COL, because he satisfies the three criteria which characterize a COL:
  1. he is a key person regarding this purchase (indeed, he has been a key person for this project right from the beginning, though he was not as influential as he is now);
  2. he has won the eminent trust of other key persons; and
  3. he possesses comprehensive knowledge and his opinion, as a result, is influential.

- More importantly, the competing supplier has not satisfactorily helped the previous COL realize an important selling point – reliable post-sale service – that was intended to justify why this COL had bought from that supplier; it was indeed this selling point that was used to rationalize the decision of buying from this very supplier who, in the end, did not deliver. And this failure to deliver the promised selling point was the cause of that COL's removal from his previous position, as the salesperson learnt afterwards. Indeed, for a domestic auto factory that was making its first acquaintance with such a new system, reliable post-sale service was one of the cardinal "selling points" for that COL to justify his purchasing decision, particularly in the early going. And yet, this post-sale warranty has become bogged down in contract semantics and the competitor's inability to cope with unforeseen technical glitches.

In possession of this knowledge, the salesperson slightly alters her sales plan and starts the process of designing the appropriate integrated product: she appeals to the new COL on the basis of a *strong post-sale service* and offers examples from her company's history as a reliable supplier. Keenly aware as well of the disparate buying points favored by other relevant key persons, she emphasizes, for example, a logistics arrangement for the electro-inject wire harness – one deliverability factor that will make another influential key person's job much easier (as this is an important buying point for this key person).

Soon the Client C's purchase director has successfully proselytized this company to the supplier she represents, having taken advantage of the errors and omissions in client relations committed by his former competitor in the stage of FC. And, indeed, the CEO of the automobile company, Client C, greets her as soon as the deal is signed, to thank her for her impeccable understanding of his company's needs and for the quality and comprehensiveness of the service she supplied.

The above case has illustrated at least the following points we have made before:

- it is the right customer value question that really catches customer's attention;
- it is the deliverability of the customer value in terms of key persons' own buying points and selling points that really accounts;
- there could be a competitive advantage with the key persons whose PPP lay behind the PPP of the company as a whole when you are behind competition.

## ON THE THEORETICAL REVERSIBILITY OF THE PURCHASE PROCESS

Salespeople tend to be satisfied if the customer's purchasing process runs in their favor. But, if it does not, they would wish they could reverse this purchasing process and make it take a direction that is in their favor. Although the logical phases listed in this chapter for the PPP model are reversible in theory, the process of reversal in practice is asymmetrical and tortuous. There are two reasons for this:

1. Purchasing needs: As soon as the need to purchase presents itself, it directs individuals or organizations to the gratification of that need, presumably within an established, and fairly rigid, time frame. For example, if a company has scheduled a deal regarding materials for the maintenance of production to be consummated by the end of March, it results in a certain inevitability of that consummation. Otherwise, the company might not be able to meet its next production commitments.
2. Purchasing behaviors: Each phase of the purchasing process precipitates and facilitates the next one. Most individuals and companies would be unwilling to abjure an earlier decision in the process, unless presented with a radical change of situation or taking on a radical renovation in personal or institutional ideals or goals. Also from a psychological point of view, human beings tend to think and behave with as much consistency as possible (the quality of consistency is judged according to a certain set of criteria selected by the person in question him or herself); it is very hard for them to change their own decisions, especially those ones that have already been made public. Doing so would not only create cognitive and psychological dissonance, but would let them down and damage their credibility. The so-called *escalating commitment* phenomenon (Staw, 1981) in decision making is a good illustration of this fact.

## MORE ON THE PPP MODEL

The individual consumers' or organizational buyers' definition of what is essential and what is not varies by situation and is generally influenced by several internal and external factors, including quality of finances, cultural and personal values, health (in the broadest sense of the term), safety, quality of life, the opinions of others who are important to them, and so on.

A seller who convincingly associates her sales offer with these factors may be able to induce a purchase need, or more accurately, the appropriate purchase need, even in the cases where such a (purchase) need has been absent. For instance, she may be able to do that by attaching novelty to products or services already known by most potential customers. Also, it is worth making a point here that when the novelty becomes evident, customers might render more interest and time (i.e., increase the level of purchase involvement) to a seller than otherwise. It might even encourage the potential customer to walk through a complete and explicit purchase process, rather than following an otherwise default value driven and low-involvement purchasing behavior. It is this ascription of the "essential" status to common products that is one of the cardinal virtues of a well-structured sales plan in a competitive environment.

Another point we like to make is that the PPP model does not include such a stage as "Information Search," as it is usually conceptualized in many commonly known purchase process models. It is clear that customers have to search for the needed information at any of the stages of the PPP, be it an internal search, external search, or both. For this reason, therefore, we do not think it is proper to specifically isolate Information Search as an independent purchasing phase in a purchase process model. From a cognitive point of view, indeed, humans constantly search and process information (internally or externally or both) in order to take actions, to assess the result of these actions, and to react according to the assessed result at any stage of their decision-making process.

Lastly, marketers can be sellers too, and the purchasing process can also be catalyzed and overseen by pure marketing (i.e., non-personal selling methods such as advertising, direct mailing and so on), with sales made with little or no involvement of a salesperson, particularly in the case of small ticket consumer goods purchased by end users. This sort of sale can be witnessed in any large-scale supermarket and might be best termed "marketer's selling" or, as it is termed in this book, non-personal selling. Here is an example.

A large-scale supermarket is looking at whether – and how – to promote a product termed Item X. Of course, they have already themselves gone through their own purchasing process in order to reach the decision of acquiring Item X. Indeed, before the item is even allowed onto store shelves, they have already considered questions, such as, is this the right time or socioeconomic climate in which to introduce this product? And if it is, what would be a successful promotion strategy? The supermarket has employed professional marketers to conduct research, the result of which is the confirmation that a rich target customer demographic exists; the marketing firm has also designed a television campaign with the opportunity for customer feedback by means of a toll-free number and a buy-back promise. This communication strategy was codenamed Populi and persuaded the manager of the supermarket to make use of it.

The excited manager implemented the suggestions of the marketing firm and confidently stated that, with the benefit of the X/Populi plan, all that is necessary for the supermarket to reap a substantial profit is to place Item X in the store, visibly, and in abundance. The resulting creation and cultivation of customer need proceeds without the involvement of salespeople.

But in this case, the marketers have acted as salesperson surrogates, mining various data to find customers for the existing product; they have communicated and interacted with the "client" in advance and effected the sale. This is the sort of intense intimacy with the behaviors of potential buyers that characterizes familiarity with the PPP. The process is fundamentally a communicative one. And a successful sale is a triumph of communication, of "reading" the customer.

Failed sales techniques are often the result of a failure on the part of a sales organization at this exercise. A common example is that of trendy, teen-targeted clothes as displayed by many large department stores; regardless of how appealing the clothes might be to their target demographic, they are arrayed in the stultifying, rote fashion that is the nature of most department store designs, and are attended by stuffily "adult," uniformed shop assistants, who offer passionless, programmatic salesman blather. The targeted teenage demographic is unengaged, the trendiness is dissipated, and the sale is lost. This is a client that the salespeople – all of them, including floor workers, promoters, managers, and interior decorators – have failed to "read."

To conclude, while it is important to keep in mind the non-linear nature of purchasing behavior, a good conceptual model for the purchase process will provide valuable insights to the sellers. Potential buyers all experience a conceptually similar purchasing behavior flow regardless of the sort of the purchase being undertaken. By means of theoretical, practical, and interpersonal understanding of this behavior flow, sellers may enable themselves to effectively participate in the value formation and exchange process on the part of customer, and thus to address the customer value questions which are right in the customers' mind at each of the stages in which they have found themselves. And the PPP model within the context of X-Be is developed just for this purpose.

# 3

# KEY PERSONS AND CORE OPINION LEADERS: VALUE ROLES ON THE PART OF CUSTOMER

Who really does the buying? The answer to this basic question is demanded not only for the success of particular selling processes but for the continuous improvement in the seller's connectedness with the target market as well. Yet getting the right answer for it does not seem to be an easy job in many sales situations that include not only organizational selling, but consumer selling as well.

To address this question, various buying roles that people can play on the customer side have been proposed. A popular view about these roles reported by various authors [e.g., Kotler & Keller (2005)] states that there are five buying roles for consumer marketing (Initiator, Influencer, Decider, Buyer, and User) and seven for industrial marketing (Initiator, User, Influencer, Decider, Approver, Buyer, and Gatekeeper). Within X-Be, we present a more practical classification of these buying roles (key persons and COLs) that help sellers focus on the customer value questions and provide direct indications about the value preferences of those people who assume these roles in a purchase process. We also address the issue of influential power of individual key persons from the perspective of social exchange theory, which will lead to the discussion of the notion of COL.

## UNDERSTANDING, IDENTIFYING, AND TARGETING KEY PERSONS

Those who observe everyday consumer behavior tend to notice only those who end up paying for the goods; this is especially true in retail situations. But this could be an oversimplification of the way decisions are made, even in the area of consumer marketing; it is, indeed, a misrepresentation of the complex network of influences that act within the purchasing organization. Indeed, the micro-social behavior that underlies this network of influences is so intricate that sellers often feel uncertain and spend a great deal of efforts and time on their relationship marketing, relationship selling, and relationship management, in order for them to, hopefully, happen upon the "rosetta stone" which would decode that interweaving of forces that conspire to thrust a customer to buy.

But the notion of customer is itself too fuzzy and does not provide much help to the sellers regarding the way they should interact and communicate with an individual consumer or a purchasing organization. "Customer" has indeed a broad meaning and is used by many people in many different circumstances. To deal with the fuzzy and broad nature of this term, we sometimes make such a statement that a customer can be an individual or an organization. But, such a categorization does not provide much help as to who will influence the buying decision, to what extent, and for what reasons; indeed, while sales that involve organizations are known to be complex, the ones that target individuals are not simple either; individual customers evolve within their social surrounding which tends to influence their behavior to a significant extent. Thus, and as many other researchers have already realized, the term "customer" remains not so instructive for us to understand the complexity of communications and interactions with the other entity that will end up paying for the products and services we sell. It is for this reason, perhaps, that the concepts of buying center and buying roles were proposed (Bonoma, 2006; Webster & Wind, 1972). There are, of course, other sales frameworks and models that implement the idea of buying roles, mostly in practitioners' sales manuals and handbooks, but the essence of the implementation remains the same. These views have certainly enriched our understanding of the notion of "customer," but what concerns us about the existing sales frameworks is that they still have not addressed the very core question of any purchase process: what kind of roles a person could assume in order to directly procure the perceived customer value for himself or for the people and/or the organization he is part of? In what follows we would like to address this question, and describe this kind of roles, which we will call "value roles." We also would like to study the level of influence of an individual who plays certain value role(s) in the purchase process; we propose to examine this influence from the perspective of human interaction and interdependence. In this regard, the principle of least interest from social psychology might be helpful in revealing enough information about the network of influences within a social setting or in an organization; it should also assist salespeople in identifying the persons who have more influential power over the others in social interactions in general and in a purchase process in particular.

In B-to-B context, the most familiar buying roles are played by those people with formal titles such as "buyer" or "purchaser," "purchasing manager," "purchasing engineer," and so on. While these obvious key persons get involved in different purchase processes, the level of influence and the nature of activities they carry out tend to vary greatly with the nature of the buy (e.g., straight re-buy, modified re-buy, and new buy), complexity of the product (e.g. complex solutions or small-ticket items for office use), competition (low or high), management style (delegated or controlled), and so on. We will refer to these often formal roles as *process-type roles*.

The other roles we focus on within X-Be are as depicted in Figure 1.3 (MAP) in Chapter 1; they are played by those persons who have formal or informal authority over the money to spend (resource-type roles) and those who have formal or informal authority over the product to be selected (product-type roles) in a purchase process. The existence of these roles is what makes it possible for a seller (the salesperson or the sales organization) to get involved even more deeply in the process of value formation and exchange on the part of customer. It is important that all efforts of selling and sales management engage the *key persons* (i.e., the people who play one or more of the abovementioned roles) involved in the purchase process. key persons should be viewed as the sockets where the plugs of customer value are to be inserted; once the right plugs (i.e., the right customer value is selected) are properly inserted, and the electrical circuits are well set-up (i.e., the organization or the consumer's social surrounding function well), light (i.e., the expression of value) is turned on and all the associated items (i.e., the company's departments and services associated with the key persons in question, or the consumer's social associates) are illuminated. So, appealing to and connecting with key persons, especially those ones whose opinions are most influential (the COLs), is the key to any embarking upon a successful sale.

But, a major question that needs to be addressed now is how to identify these key persons and COLs in multifaceted sales involving a large cast of players. Social identities or business cards with titles can be handy, but they are sometimes misleading. As usual, good relations and observation are the key. The ultimate question remains, and it is a deceptively simple one – to whom, ultimately, does the seller really sell to?

A comprehensive, adaptable answer comes from a thorough understanding of the causal and influential interrelationships of three entities: *persons*, *money*, and *products*. Many novice salespeople tend to talk and

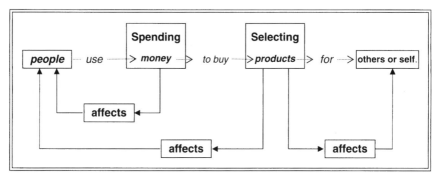

**FIGURE 3.1** Causal and Influential Interrelationships Among the Three Entities "People," "Money," and "Products."

interact mostly with acquaintances or easy-goers, and that is a mistake. Salespeople must focus on those persons whose job and life would be affected by the products to be selected and the money to be spent. And ultimately, as indicated in Figure 3.1, the following maxims become evident:

- *Maxim* 1: the purchasing behavior and its outcomes are under the influence of those people who are in some way related to the purchasing resource (money).
- *Maxim* 2: the purchasing behavior and its outcomes are also under the influence of those people who are in some way subject to the impact of the purchased object (product).

Consider the simple case of a pair of parents preparing to purchase sessions with a tutor for their son. In this case, the entity, "purchaser," consists of both parents, and the key persons are the parents and the son. The parents, being equally in possession of the purchasing resource, discuss the amount of hours and the subject areas most appropriate for their son's purposes. They are, in effect, influencing one another as key persons ultimately influence the "purchaser." This exemplifies the first maxim of the person-money-product relationship. Note too that the son shall attempt to inject his own opinions regarding who the tutor might be, what subject areas he needs, and when the best time might be to suffer his lessons; this is an illustration of the second maxim, namely that of a person who might be impacted by the specific product being purchased exerting his influence on the transaction.

A similar dynamic characterizes selling in the corporate world. Lately, many governments have offered tax incentives to corporations to upgrade to more environmentally friendly modes of production, and it is from within this climate that a germane example may be drawn. With the advent of an eco-reform tax benefit package from the government, and a bank loan, a crown corporation plans to purchase a new, ecologically sound production line from abroad. To insure the success of this purchase, the corporation obtains the services of an independent environmental technology counselor as well as a foreign law consultant. In this case, the people capable of influencing the final purchase can come from various interested parties, both internally and externally. The level of their presence and interference during various phases of the purchase process will fluctuate. How might a seller in this scenario apprehend all the relevant key persons in each successive phase comprehensively and systematically? How may she win in the influence of each of these key persons? And, perhaps more importantly, what might she be able to do to identify expeditiously the COL? What are the characteristics of a COL?

For selling and sales management in complex situations such as the one described in the above example, a more detailed structure of the three abovementioned value roles would be useful. In the X-Be framework, this detailed structure classifies the value roles as:

- Resource-type value roles: Budget Approver, Budget User, and Budget Adviser;
- Product-type value roles: Product Approver, Product User, and Product Adviser.
- Process-type value roles: Buyer or Gatekeeper to whom the monitoring, coordination, and execution of the purchasing activities are delegated on behalf of other value roles for the acquisition of customer value.

The confidence of a seller at any given point of the selling process first stems from her ability to specifically answer the following questions so that she can identify the value roles that are relevant to her job:

1. For resource-type value roles:
   a. Who approves/disapproves budget?
   b. Who controls the use of this budget?
   c. Who advises, recommends, and provides rationales for budget approval and use?
2. For product-type value roles:
   a. Who approves/disapproves the products?
   b. Who uses/manages the use of the products?
   c. Who advices, recommends, and provides rationales for products selection and purchase?

3. For process-type value roles:
    a. Who executes or coordinates the exchange activities?
    b. Who monitors the exchange activities?


To address these questions, the seller could attempt to find out what types of messages are of interest to different key persons. Here are some guidelines to help the seller do that:

*For resource-type value roles:*

- The messages on investment justification and return on investment (ROI) are of value to the budget approver;
- The messages on cash use efficiency and financial gains are of value to the budget user;
- Both types of messages are of value to the budget adviser.

When addressing these resource-type questions, one should keep in mind that all sales compete for the buyer's resources which might be used in other ways to satisfy the resource-type key persons.

*For product-type key persons:*

- The messages on solution justification and effectiveness in solving problems are of value to the product approver;
- The messages on product use and service efficiency are of value to the product user;
- Both types of message are of value to the product adviser.

When addressing these product-type value questions, one should keep in mind that the product bought will directly affect the life and work of the product-type key persons involved.

*For process-type key persons:*

- The messages that are of value to resource-type and product-type key persons are of value to the fully habilitated process-type key persons;
- The messages on the efficiency of purchasing activities are of value to all process-type key persons;
- The messages on the contractual terms concerning the purchase (e.g., legal or contractual issues) are of value to all process-type key persons.

When addressing these process-type value questions, one should keep in mind that all issues and consequences arising from purchasing activities will directly or indirectly affect the life and work of the process-type key persons involved.

We should note that the above concepts and guidelines could also be of value to sellers working in consumer marketing; they will help them to continuously improve their connectedness with the target market. Indeed, selling of many consumer goods can be improved by constant communication and interaction with not only the consumers, but also with the members of their reference groups, interest groups, and consumer watchdogs. All these people could influence the buying behavior of the target consumers simply because they have assumed some of value roles that were pointed out in the above discussion (typically, "budget and/or product advisor," but occasionally "budget and/or product approver," as in the cases of consumer incentives offered by the government for some types of consumption).

## INFLUENTIAL POWER DEFINED

In many consumer marketing practices, focusing on people who have the most influential power over the consumer's buying behavior and communicating and interacting with them is the key to successful sales. Examples of these practices are abundant in the literature: focus on and interact with professional baby-care nurses for selling baby-care products, with beauty advisers for selling beauty products and services, and with professors for selling textbooks. In complex sales situations, it is also imperative to recognize the distinct influential powers and responsibilities of the various key persons concerned. And, as noted previously, business cards and titles are not always the most effective sources of information for doing so. Many sales organizations engaged in large-scale sales attempt to isolate key persons and COLs by formulating "customer power maps," or internal hierarchies, of the purchasing organizations. But these maps, like titles, can be deceptive. Research findings regarding organizational behavior attest to the following:

- The influential power allotment in organizations can be observed along two discrete lines, namely, formal authority and informal interpersonal influences. The former powers in a well-structured organization are normally thought to be much more specialized, and best expressed by means of the hierarchies or ranks described by business cards, titles, and "customer power maps"; the latter are unspoken, casual, and sweeping, regardless the organizational structure.

- Those people, especially good managers and communicators, in possession of formal authority often do not implement their influential power through administrative commands, but rather via good and effective communication. And, it goes without saying that doing so works actually better for them and for the organization. But, of course, there is also the other extreme of big bureaucratic organizations where very slow and inefficient purchase processes prevail; although the administrative commands and formal authority are stronger in such organizations, informal interpersonal influences cannot be neglected.
- In the case where the organization is faced with great deal of uncertainty and the decisions are perceived to have significant consequences, the decision-making behavior might be characterized by the so-called Garbage can model (Cohen et al., 1972), in which decisions are a product of four independent streams of events – problems, solutions, participants, and choice opportunities.

Moreover, if the formal hierarchy is being subverted or undergoing a reorganization, which is not an exception anymore, titles and business cards would definitely be of little or no use.

In summary, then, a business card, title, or the size and furnishing of an office cannot be used as a reliable barometer for a person's influence within an organization. A different approach to apprehend the actual influential powers that are in the hands of the relevant key persons is, therefore, needed. Within the framework X-Be, we propose to make use of the following definition of influential power to design such an approach:

> A person's influential power over another is based upon the person under the influence believing that the influential person possesses *something* (let us call it **S**) such as a trait, characteristic, information, expertise, knowledge, or status, or anything that is of value, that he or she desires. The intensity of this power is dependent on the degree of importance that the person under influence assigns to **S**.

Thus, as can be seen from this definition, the framework X-Be adopts a view of influential power that looks at the notion of influence from a perspective of human interaction. To implement this definition in concrete situations, one can use the principle of least interest (Waller, 1938) from social psychology to gauge the interdependence among individuals – the less interested partner in a relationship has greater power.

Consider the case of an employee at an organization who happens to believe that one of his supervisors has the ear of higher management, and thus exercises some degree of control over how he might attain recognition, a raise, promotions, and the like, all of which he would value greatly. This supervisor, as a result, wields a great deal of influential power over the worker – probably more than any one of the other supervisors. Because of the nature of this interdependence, the worker will have a tendency to try to impress her professionally. But, if he did not believe that she has the ear of higher management and/or he did not value raise and promotions, the power she could exert over him would be distinctly limited, as he would perceive nothing to gain abiding by her whims, and this will be the case even though she is his boss and has formal authority over him.

Most people experience the above views on influential power in their day-to-day lives. As a classical example, when you have a certain kind of beauty, you tend to have influential power over the others; we all know this. The following story was related to us by a friend of ours. One lady works for a famous bank as a part-time sales rep in the credit card division. Her performance in sales has been consistently in the top band, which is a rare case in a market of non-differentiated commodities like the credit card market. Her case has attracted the attention of other sales managers who want to find out what has made this sales rep so successful. The original goal of these managers is to learn from her something they could teach their own sales reps. Thus, they approach her and her supervisor and ask to be involved as observers in the sales rep's interactions with the clients. Once they are allowed, they spend a great deal of time observing the sales rep, what she says and does, and the way she works and interacts with her clients. To their disappointment, the findings are not anything of value that can be shared or used to teach their sales reps; it was just the pure natural gift of beauty that helps her be constantly a star in her company.

We do not claim that the above case brings anything original, as most people would have experienced situations like this one. But, the point we would like to make is that the more you have of something that is desired by others, the more influence you may have on people. Beauty, in its broad sense (education, intelligence, knowledge, good manners, passion, wealth, status, eloquence, and elegance are only a few examples of beauty), is a value that is naturally appreciated by humans and can be the source of a great deal of influential power. This is why a salesperson must dress up all the time and follow the standard guidelines that have been discussed extensively in various books on the subject of "Dress for Success." This might also explain the claimed finding about the positive correlation between being good-looking and the income level.

The discussion about influential power in this section started with the analysis of the influence networks within the purchasing organization, the goal being to point out some working handles and principles to help the seller address the issues of influential power among the people she deals with. When these principles are used to analyze how the key persons work together in a purchasing process, the levels of their respective influential powers (besides their formal authorities) can be assessed sensibly. Such customer knowledge will certainly help the seller to effectively position her sales activities and manage the selling process wisely. But, as has been presented in the above examples, the principles that underlie our views on the notion of influential power are general and apply also to the interactions between the seller and buyer. According to our definition of influential power, indeed, it is possible that the customer wields influential power over the seller, and this may depend on the nature of the supply and demand of the products and services in question. We should note, however, that a professional and successful salesperson never yields this power to the customer. Unsuccessful salespeople may lose ground if they commit gaffes such as the following:

1. Having little confidence in communicating with people who are not acquaintances or friends;
2. Creating key person hierarchies based only upon business cards, titles, clothes, the size, or location of offices;
3. Evaluating levels of influential power among key persons on the basis of these same superficial attributes;
4. Assuming, in the situations where the sales seems to be non-complex and where the interactions are taking place with one or a few individuals, that there are no other key persons or COLs involved in the business.

## THE CORE OPINION LEADER

The term "opinion leader" has been dealt with at length in much marketing research. Generally speaking, an "opinion leader" within a marketing context denotes those people perceived to be in possession of the greatest or most innovative knowledge of the product under consideration. They are accepted, trusted, and admired by the group which they lead in their buying behavior. In this sense, actors, models, pop stars, and other celebrities may be considered broad cultural opinion leaders. From that broad cultural perspective, they contribute to the formation of trends; they also inspire innumerable people (most of whom they very likely will never meet) to take up their money and head to the store.

Thus, an "opinion leader" may exercise her influence upon the purchaser even *in absentia,* in the form of a default value that is internalized in the customer's mind. But they may also be present and actively intervene in the purchasing process. This is more likely to happen when business is transacted between corporations and when the concerned transaction is a significant one. In fact, in such situations, the presence of the COL is rather critical for effective selling. Suppose, for instance, that a salesperson has communicated with all the relevant key persons many times over in order to sell a product, but none of them is willing to endorse the product during the meeting in which a supplier is to be chosen. The sale fails. A good salesperson seizes upon the COL and ensures their presence and outspokenness during the internal purchasing decision-making process.

The characteristics of COLs in the corporate world are as follows:

1. They must, first of all, be key persons (process-type, resource-type, and/or product-type).
2. They must have won the trust of the majority, if not all, of the key persons relevant to the sale in any given situation.
3. Their opinion must be very influential on supplier and product selection, official policy, and strategy design.

Some salespeople focus all their attention – and time, and energy, and rhetoric – on "general managers" or "chiefs," at the expense, perhaps, of those whom they really ought to be targeting. This sort of customer-interface structure is akin to public relations, but it isn't necessarily good sales sense. Concentrating entirely upon those on the highest official echelon will only guarantee influence in the case of those organizations operating under a management model that is paternalistic in the extreme, in which one or more members of the executive are entrusted with all major decisions or responsibilities. This power structure is not that practical, but a few organizations – governments, businesses, and families – operate as such. Most organizations, however, are reliant upon rather diffuse internal management, with delegated and individual responsibilities. The orders are rarely entirely autocratic. Thus, appealing to a single "power player" or a group of them might be of little use in securing a sale. This is not to say that public relations have no place under the aegis of sales, but they are neither its highest attainment nor the climax of the sales activity as a whole.

Also, in the context of the framework X-Be, salespeople do not limit themselves to a static identification of the key persons, because the reality is highly dynamic within organizations that deal with complex purchase processes. key persons would indeed vary depending on the actual PPP and on the specific issues to be dealt with in this phase. Also, it is rare that a key person has an absolute influential power throughout the whole purchasing process. The relative influence of a key person will fluctuate depending on the issues at hand. There are also those situations where a decision maker has responsibilities for a certain aspect of the business, but choose not to make decisions and, rather, rely on someone else to make these decisions for various reasons such as lack of knowledge and expertise, being afraid to upset other people who may have different views, less seniority in the current position, or simply having that personality that prefers "collective wisdoms" over individual decisions. There are also the situations in which the real decision maker is disliked by many people in the purchasing organization, in which case the seller must weigh whether to remain attached to this decision maker at the expense of a long-term business relationship with the customer company.

Because of all this, it is important for a salesperson to identify who the key persons are for a specific sale, assess their relative influential powers over each other on the key purchasing issues, and sort out the candidates for the core opinion leader role(s) at each phase of the purchasing process, and avoid making a blanket assumption about these major players in the company. To do this, salespeople could make use of the notion of influential power as it was defined earlier in this chapter and apply the principle of least interest to the relationships that they observe within the organization under various conditions and circumstances. Another general guide that salespeople can use for identifying and classifying COLs is depicted in Figure 3.2.

As described in this figure, a key person can be classified into one of the four categories, depending on his position and degree of influence over other key persons on specific issues in the organization: "Big Says," "Expert," "Lame Duck," and "Little Concerns." The best COLs that a salesperson can target may be among the "Big Says" who possess not only high influence because of the respect they have earned from others, but also an important position within the organization for making decisions on the issues that are relevant to successful selling. Good COLs may also be among the "Expert" whose formal positions are not that high but whose expertise cannot be excluded in making sound decisions. Salespeople should try to have the "Experts" on their side, especially in the sales of new, risky, complex, or essential products or solutions. As for the

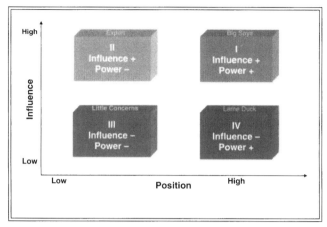

**FIGURE 3.2**  A General Guide for the Identification and Classification of Core Opinion Leaders (COLs).

"Little Concerns," salespeople should respect them as a valuable starting and/or contacting point for the selling process, and/or as a useful information source, but certainly not as COLs to strategically position the selling activities. Finally, regarding "Lame Duck," the best choice for salespeople is to avoid them or, otherwise, they may risk facing overwhelming objections and dislikes from others in general.

To conclude, the notion of value roles and the other concepts associated with it should be useful to salespeople in identifying those key persons who are in a position to influence the course of the purchasing process. Also, they are practical and easy to implement in concrete selling situations. They help focus a salesperson's attention on the relevant and appropriate messages that pertain to the process of customer value formation, communication, and exchange. Finally, the adoption of a definition of influential power that examines the notion of influence from the perspective of human interaction makes the analysis of the influence networks within the organization practical and pertinent to the (dynamic) identification of key persons and COLs. With such a successful identification, salespeople can allocate their efforts and time effectively, by targeting the right people in the customer organization for a specific sales objective. The above analytic knowledge of key persons and their relative influential powers could also be adapted to consumer selling when the notion of consumer's immediate social surrounding (CISS) is taken into account (more on this in Chapter 10). And this could be much valuable in the design of integrated sales interaction and communication programs to improve the connectedness and sustainability of exchange relationships of a company with its target market.

# 4

# VIEWS ON CRITERIA: BASE FOR JUDGING VALUE

In the previous chapter, we were concerned primarily with the issue of *to whom* one sells – those individuals whose perceived value are at play during the purchasing process, namely key persons and core opinion leaders. It is these people's value that the seller has to *endeavor to understand*, in order to be able to architect the final integrated product. The focus of this chapter will be on the process of how the customer-perceived value is formed, and the various strategies and tactics that are available to the seller to effectively deal with this process. The process of value formation is very intricate and can take different shapes depending on several factors including the nature of the customer needs, the situation where these needs emerge (new versus existing situation), the risks involved, and the key persons involved. Sometimes, we like to compare the intangible process value formation to the physical process of crystals formation. It would probably be beneficial for the reader to use the crystals formation process as a metaphor for visualizing what we will describe below about customer value formation.

The general consensus of marketing research is that the seller ought to be concerned with the customer's needs above all; the "Voice of Customer" has been a consistent emphasis in papers written on the subject in the past years, and many companies have even used this vague concept as a strategy. There are, however, many situations in which sellers fail to understand the customers' needs on the basis of the Voice of Customer. The reasons for such failures are various:

• the customers may not be able to clearly express themselves;
• the customers may not be clear about their own needs;

- the sellers may misread the implications and insinuations in the Voice of Customer;
- the customers change their minds due to new information that has become available to them.

Understanding how value is perceived by people (customers and others), and how it gets formed in their minds is a very tricky question. The sales community needs knowledge that is both principled *and* practical to help develop this understanding and make use of it in selling and sales management, just like the natural scientific community has physical sciences (chemistry, thermodynamics, solid physics, etc.) to approach the phenomenon of crystals formation. The X-Be framework attempts to build such knowledge for value perception and formation. For this purpose, it starts by implementing an important concept without which value formation cannot take place: *criteria* – the criteria that the customers use to judge value. Based on this concept, the X-Be element "Views on Criteria" is then introduced as a renovation of the tool of "Voice of Customer."

## THE CUSTOMER'S SELECTION CRITERIA – AN INSOLUBLE RIDDLE?

The concept of "criteria" has different connotations depending upon context, and its deployment is not limited to the field of sales and its management. But from the X-Be perspective, the most meaningful version of it is the notion of *selection criteria*. In the hands of a key person, selection criteria complicate each individual sale and render it unique. These criteria are by definition subjective, inasmuch as they are private or organizational, and tend to be subject to revision and interpretation. Indeed, if selection criteria were entirely objective and static, all sales activity would consist merely of mathematical or machine-logical operations, and there would be no social diversity of products or services. The diversity and changeability of individual and organizational selection criteria for value greatly colors the way sales should be pitched. All this ensures that there can be no such thing as focus-free, "one-size-fits-all" selling.

In the context of a free market, a person in possession of money has the option of putting that money toward the purchase of a variety of products and services. This presents a very large network of possibilities for the dispensation of the potential customer's resource. And though certain expenditures are essential (e.g., rent, electricity, water, food, etc.), there are myriad internal possibilities and combinations in all those media with differing customer values perceived by different individuals.

Can, thus, a customer's selection criteria for making buying decisions ever be usefully illuminated? The short answer might simply be: *the heart wants what it wants*. But that answer is fatalistic and is of not much comfort to the eager salesperson looking for an edge in understanding her pool of potential customers. The most important but often difficult step of effective selling, as most seasoned salespeople suggest, is to clarify why the customer wishes to possess the item in question at a given time. But how is a seller to approach this question systematically and sensibly? To address this question, the X-Be framework implements the concepts of "Views on Criteria," and, later in this book, "Buying Points" and "Selling Points."

## VIEWS ON CRITERIA (VOC)

The notion of "criteria" is central to human cognition. Criteria are there to help people with a critical feature of their cognition: the selective attention (this aspect is discussed in more detail in Chapter 11 of this book). One cannot make a meaningful decision, judgment, or perception of value without criteria (explicit or implicit). Because of this, a seller, when she interacts with potential customers, should endeavor to understand these customers' views on the criteria for judging value and designing or selecting the right sales offer for them; hence, the expression "Views on Criteria."

Understanding what the customers' selection criteria are is not an easy task. The X-Be framework proposes to carry out this task by having the seller look for the following two components in the course of her communication and interaction with the customers: Selecting Points and Selecting Rationales. These components are what make up the X-Be concept "Views On Criteria":

$$VOC = \text{Selecting Points} + \text{Selecting Rationales}$$

The selecting points are those factors, aspects, or qualities that are perceived by a key person as *relevant* to the situation in which the purchase need has emerged. Some concrete examples of selecting points are the price, some quality features, maintainability, after-sales service, and so on. Understanding what a key person's selecting points are is usually not enough, as it does not provide the seller with an effective handle on the process of value formation in the key person's mind. The seller must strive to address the "why" question – why the identified selecting points are *relevant* to the key person, and what their respective *degrees of importance* are to this key person; hence, the second component of the views on criteria: the Selecting Rationales. A Selecting Rationale refers to the feelings, beliefs, or logic that account for why the key person considers a selecting point as relevant and for the degree of importance of this selecting point to the key person.

We will discuss the concept of views on criteria and its implications for selling and sales management in more detail later in the chapter. But for now, we will account for why we have developed and deployed this new concept by indicating some of its advantages over older methodologies (e.g., "the voice of the customer," etc.) for analyzing similar scenarios:

1. Any judgment or decision must be made on the basis of some sort of selection criteria. Purchasing behavior is just a specialized kind of decision-making process, so the same rules apply. The customer's selection criteria for the satisfaction of need are among the most important factors at play during the purchasing process. It should follow that acquiring them should be the seller's primary goal during sales communication.
2. The customer's views on criteria can be acquired by means of communication – although this can be a challenge, and may never be accomplished perfectly.
3. The views on criteria could be mutable and evolving. In particular, the final shape of the customer's views on criteria could be a result of the *interactions* that took place between buyer and seller. Such an understanding is more realistic and much closer to capturing the reality of the buyer – seller relationship than the image of a customer's sense of purchase need and value being entirely his own and static.
4. The concept of views on criteria makes it possible to depict and account for more aspects of exchange behavior in a manner that is logical and reasonably close to reality (as we will see later in this chapter and in later chapters). The seller is thus afforded more conceptual "angles" to approaching the customer's value formation and exchange process.

In many situations (e.g., new, risky, complex, and important buys), a customer's initial views on criteria are protean impressions which, at any given time during the process of sales communication, may mutate and vary; priorities change subtly and fitfully throughout this process, even if the basic philosophical and socioeconomic underpinning on the part of the key person remains largely unaltered. The key person's final evaluative ruler of the customer value in a sales offer at time of exchange may be markedly different than that initial one, even if his general mood is the same. But, it is the views on criteria that key persons and core opinion leaders use to judge value and, therefore, whether a sales offer addresses their needs or not; so it is the seller's responsibility to oversee the changeability of the customer's views on criteria, and to design her sales offer according to the final shape of these views. We should note here that the seller may also be able to influence the development of the customer's views on criteria (just like one could influence the direction of crystals formation), by helping the key persons discover other values that may not have been visible to them. Indeed, not all customers' buying behaviors are always in their best interests; also the process of value formation does not take place on the customer side in a deterministic fashion, but it is rather a result of a series of social interactions with other parties including the seller, even in highly competitive markets where customers may have a big say.

By the time a purchase has been made, the customer has already (presumably, and perhaps only momentarily) decided that the sales offer in question will be of satisfactory value to him, and will satisfy the initial sense of need that gave rise to the purchasing behavior. What he purchased conformed to his "final" views on criteria, and exemplified them in a tangible way. And though there can be no doubt that the nature of the customer's initial sense of need might not have been that clear, perhaps even beyond his own comprehension – in the end, he accepted the offer, for reasons that seemed (at the moment of acceptance) logically, emotionally, and economically sound to him.

## VOC AND DEFAULT VALUE BEHAVIORS

In many other situations as in daily life, people are also reliant on default values – and demonstrate default value behaviors (or DVBs) – constantly, concerning almost all matters, both trivial and socially integral. Because the little decisions with which the average person is presented in the course of a single day are myriad, it is only reasonable to revert to a sort of social "instinct" so as to act and capitalize on one's limited supply of time in the complex modern dance. For every second misspent considering minutiae too deeply is at the expense of time that might be lucrative, pleasurable, or otherwise of value. Years of social training have allowed adult humans the benefit of bypassing certain analytical steps in banal, quotidian choices. And however disappointing the spoils of such "instinctual" decisions might be, they are not likely to be disastrous. More often than not they simply make things quicker and easier at no particular disadvantage to the person involved; they are habits, personal preferences, routines.

The "information age" has increased exponentially the value – in the business and personal dimension, in dollars and in pleasure – of each second, each minute, each hour. This fact makes particularly imperative our use of – and particularly voluminous our stores of – DVBs (Herbert A. Simon's (1984) popular concepts of bounded rationality, or mental shortcuts such as cognitive heuristics as suggested by researchers like Kahneman and Tversky (2000)). For all the brain's convolutions and astonishing versatility, it has its limits; and the incredible complexity of modern life tests those limits to the point at which "shortcuts" like DVBs become an effective strategy for living.

Default values are environmental and contextual. An early-rising New Yorker who is used to venturing to the corner coffee-shop for a cappuccino and cruller will likely be frustrated if he attempts to do the same while exploring trade opportunities in Lahore. A similar sort of default value frustration will be familiar to anyone who has traveled from a metropolitan area to a rural one, even within the same state. But as for our New York executive, successful marketing and selling, as well as social trend-making, have instilled in him the desire for a cappuccino and cruller as a default value particularly lucrative to the coffee-shop chain in question.

There are obvious advantages to any commercial enterprise in making use of customers' tendency to rely on DVBs. Brand loyalty is a good example of this tendency: logos such as Nike's, for instance, having become enduring, monolithic symbols of quality goods and vanguard fashion. The omnipresent Apple iPods of the first few years of the twenty-first century and their huge fiscal returns for their manufacturers and sellers bespeak what sort of rewards await the effective selling of the marketers who successfully shift the public demand paradigm: in this case, from "I want an Mp3 player," to "I want an *iPod*" (those interested in the psychology of marketing and selling should take particular note at how Apple's sales-plan skewed toward a younger target market, a market which is simply more susceptible chemically and developmentally to advertisement than an older demographic one might be). In such cases, brand identification becomes a predominant criterion for consumer purchase; default values can thus often represent the most vexing of VOC obstacles for a seller whose product or brand does not have the advantage of cultural hegemony; in such cases, attempts should be made to unearth and foreground the consumer's most practical and fundamental views on criteria for personal satisfaction, to emphasize the ways in which the seller's product can accommodate these values, and to relegate the glamour of brand identity to the realm of the "irrational" and the specious.

For many other businesses, however, customer loyalty is just too luxurious for the sellers to have. Deep down, customers are only loyal to their own interests. We, human beings, seem to get continuously "programmed" by many aspects of our own learning, which then means that our default-value behaviors will keep changing as we live on. As society continues to change, so do the customers living in it. This is why companies have to keep up with the changes of their target customers' default values to achieve continuous success.

## VOC, DVBs AND SELLING TACTICS

To a certain extent, all purchasing behavior involves some degree of DVB in the formulation and satisfaction of views on criteria. Broadly speaking, though, there are three general levels at which default values can influence a customer's views on criteria, namely: (1) the level of almost complete dominance (in the case of inessential or trivial items or services, usually in the area of less-costly and familiar consumer goods marketing); (2) the level at which default values are a factor but not the dominant one in the customer's behavior; and (3) the level at which default values are scarcely a factor at all (as is usually the case in the sales of new, risky, and important consumer goods, and in organizational sales involving many key persons and a complex initial sense of need). The following subsections will consider each of those levels in detail, but Figure 4.1 might be a useful guide for a quick and general understanding of the three selling tactics discussed below.

### Selling when Purchasing Behavior is Dominated by DVBs

Even in the case of familiar, inessential products and "impulsive" purchasing, where the customer is driven largely by default values and has no particular interest in substitution, there is still much the seller is capable of doing to bring about a sale. The seller must first adapt herself to the views on criteria of the customer, and then attempt to highlight the customer value of the sales offer in a way that is in line with the default value-driven VOC. That last step can be challenging – no doubt once the client's default values have been mined and analyzed, it might appear that

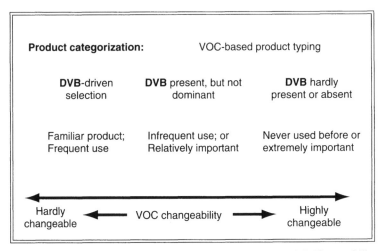

**FIGURE 4.1**   Product Classification in Accordance with VOC Changeability.

several of them are unfavorable to the sales offer one is attempting to provide. This may be particularly the case when brand identity was the primary influencing factor for the purchaser's sense of need.

In practice, when faced with purchasing situations that are dominated by DVB, the seller may have to choose from two different tactics:

- *Meeting the customer's criteria.* This tactic may work effectively if the relevant customer's default values are, in the overall, favorable to the sales offer at hand or if the seller has enough freedom to redesign her sales offer due to the very nature of the business. However, and since customer's default values may not always be favorable to the existing sales offer, salespeople who have to live with a rigid sales offer may have to do a great deal of work to generate a larger pool of leads so that they can meet their sales quotas.

- *Encouraging changes in the customer's criteria.* In selling to consumers, for instance, this tactic is often used by offering the customer irresistible trial offers. This may lead at least to some temporary acceptance of the sales offer, if not the immediate change in purchasing behavior. In some situations, this tactic may prove to be more effective when selling programs are focused on core opinion leaders. We should note here that there are three broad types of customer involvement concerning purchasing behavior: purchase involvement, product involvement, and program involvement; this tactic ("encouraging changes"), when it is focused on core opinion leaders, would work better if sellers manage to find a way to increase the levels of both product involvement and program involvement.

### Selling when Default Values are a Factor but not a Dominant one

This situation usually takes place in the case of an individual consumer, family, or business making a purchase of some importance (e.g., a major appliance). In such cases, default values are a significant but not decisive factor, and the seller will likely find the customer more disposed to accept direction to the best possible option. Also, customers will likely be more willing to discuss openly their criteria for value in the product, and the sort of features that might ideally satisfy them.

The tactics to be used in this situation are not much different from those suggested in the previous subsection. But since the purchase under consideration is of certain importance to the customer, the level of purchase involvement of this customer will be higher and his views on criteria may be influenced more readily by the seller; so there will be more room for interactions, and the effect of these interactions on purchasing behavior will increase accordingly. For this reason, the tactic *encouraging changes in the customer's criteria* introduced above will be helpful in this respect.

### Selling when the Default Values are of Very Little Significance

When an individual (or organization) regards a certain purchase or acquisition as crucial to his personal or social existence and development, default values tend to evaporate. The result is a purely "rational" approach to purchasing ("rational" refers here to the behavior of being agreeable to reasons in one's own conceptual framework, not necessarily the behavior of accepting commonly shared "right" reasons). In this situation the seller's relationship with her customer is likely to be comparatively open and cooperative, and it is very likely that customers do not even have clear VOCs yet; assisting them to develop and define clear VOCs could be beneficial for both sides. A sale could be made if the client deems the terms of it reasonable; the client's views on criteria will be devoid of promotional coloring, preconceptions, and preoccupations, and relate almost entirely to the strength of the integrated product being offered (remember the definition of the X-Be concept "Integrated Product": a set of VOC-endorsed Buying Points and Selling Points with certain deliverability).

Note that the sale has, in effect, started with *selling criteria* in the sense that the seller has assisted the buyer in developing and establishing the VOC for judging the customer value later on; then came the second part of the sale which is the exchange of the integrated product.

Default values will also be largely absent in the case of very new, innovative products of which the client has interest but no particular knowledge. In this case the seller shall have to *create* favorable new views on criteria in the time appointed to her interactions with the client. This activity largely takes place well before any given product has reached the public (or target accounts). As manufacturers interface tentatively with potential distributors (or target accounts) soon after (or during) product development, salespeople exercise a remarkable degree of influence over how the product is ultimately positioned. That initial pitch (which may, for example, consist in emphasizing a certain set of virtues) will often catalyze and characterize a product's entire public face. Many consulting services, complex production equipment, high-tech or new-tech solutions, advanced medicines, educational products and new entertainments have their successes in market dependent much more on the task of selling criteria than anything else. It is worth noting here that each of the two business philosophies of being market-driven or market-driving has its own merits when dealing with customer's views on criteria.

We should indicate here that it is not realistic to assume that all customers know what is best for them in every area and in any situation. This kind of assumption is not a reasonable one. It is against the reality of the limitations of cognitive capacity, the increasingly sophisticated division of labor, and the highly dynamic and diverse aspects of modern economies where domain-specific expertise and knowledge have become pervasive. Also, it does not take into account the huge costs and risks that the customers may face when they make wrong purchasing decisions.

Thus, in the situation where default values are of very little significance, the appropriate tactic, as suggested in the above discussion, could be named *selling criteria*. As the purchase under consideration is of importance to the customer, the level of customer's purchase involvement tends to increase dramatically and the customer's views on criteria may be subject to even more influence as a result of the interactions with the sellers.

## VOC, CUSTOMER VALUE AND SELLING STRATEGIES

We have returned often to the concept of "customer value" in this chapter, and come to the conclusion that clients are always seeking it when they make a purchase. It would also appear that it is through the perception and apprehension of "customer value" during the purchasing process that VOC are adjusted, adapted, shaped, and satisfied. But where is "customer value" to be found? What represents "customer value" in a sales offer? The answer depends on various factors, but it is not always the "product" with which people are familiar! Clear understandings of where the customer value lies will help a seller develop appropriate selling strategies for different sales situations.

## Intrinsic Value Strategy

If the customer's views on criteria primarily concern the product or service in question (because the customer believes that there are significant differences among the products or services available from various sellers), then it is true that customer value will be contained primarily in the product itself. In this case, the selling strategy should be geared towards demonstrating the intrinsic value of the product per se. Such a selling strategy, referred to as Intrinsic Value Strategy, tends to be successful in the situations of essential buys, e.g., costly technology products in industrial sales and health-care services in consumer sales.

## Extrinsic Value Strategy

If, on the other hand, the customer does not believe there are significant differences among the products offered by various sellers, and his views on criteria are primarily concerned with the *process* by which the product is procured, used and disposed, then it is in the *process* that customer value is to be found. (It is this kind of VOC makeup that impels customers to seek consumer products through different venues than stores – by mail-order, or the Internet, for example.) The corresponding selling strategy to address such a process-focused VOC calls for an emphasis on customer value that is extrinsic to the product and is thus referred to as Extrinsic Value Strategy.

## Relationship Value Strategy

And, predictably, if the customer's VOC are primarily concerned with the interpersonal or organizational benefits that can be yielded in the social or business relationships in question (because the customer goes for value that is beyond particular transactions, especially when the intrinsic and extrinsic values concerning these transactions are not much different across the competing suppliers), then it is in these interpersonal or organizational benefits that the customer value is to be found. This situation may need the so-called Relationship Value Strategy to generate sales. For instance, many virtually undifferentiated marketing offers (e.g., Sales of cars made by the same manufacturer) are actually differentiated by salespeople's personal relationships with the consumers, thus manifesting different sales results due to such different relationship values.

It should be noted that this selling strategy can sometimes compensate for disadvantages and weaknesses that may exist on the side of intrinsic and extrinsic value strategies. The extent and effectiveness of such a compensation depend on the cultural context (individualism versus collectivism) in which the buyer–seller interactions take place. For example, there are many industrial sales that had failed in some Asian cultures not because of business issues, but because of the high degree of interdependence that is favored in these cultures.

It is for the above reasons that we often use the expression "sales offer" (as opposed to "product") in this book when the notion of customer value is of concern in the context. And when discussing the customer's perceived value in a sales offer with certain deliverability, we refer to the notion of integrated product.

As regards the different purchasing behavior patterns such as low, limited, and extensive purchase involvement behaviors (Hawkins et al., 2003), we can illustrate their relationships, within the X-Be framework, to the concerned VOC in a logical manner as illustrated in Figure 4.2.

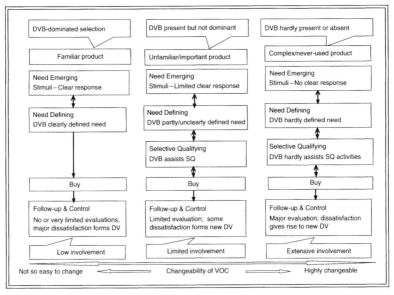

**FIGURE 4.2**   The Relationships Between VOC and Purchasing Behaviors (adapted from Hawkins et al., 2003).

It is worth noting that default values can be manifested in views on criteria in different ways. Default values might be primarily represented in certain selecting points, or in the concomitant selecting rationales – or they may dominate both aspects of a given view on criteria. All of this, and also situational factors such as deadlines to make a choice and customer personality, can impact and modify the purchasing behavior which customers use as an approximate working strategy to comprehend customer value. Of course, there are always strategies to consider when faced with impasses, as the case study in the next section will reveal.

## A CASE STUDY INVOLVING VIEWS ON CRITERIA

In the autumn of 1998, many Chinese domestic automobile manufacturers found themselves working in earnest toward satisfying the government's new emission standards (Euro-I equivalent), due to be implemented nationally on 1 January 1999. Research on the part of these companies revealed that the emission issue could be addressed by two means: either by working to develop an "open-loop" engine management system (EMS), or by employing a carburetor-plus-converter system. The latter would be very economical, but was understood as merely a temporary solution, which would not stand up to further tightening of emission standards (which was widely expected in light of the forthcoming 2008 Olympic Games). The carburetor-plus-converter system was also not in much use abroad. Those interested in EMS had taken the initiative and largely been in contact with the most powerful German-owned joint venture in China. On the other hand, some suppliers, proponents of the carburetor solution, had actively dispatched account managers and salespersons to pay visits to the manufacturers that were still undecided.

At the same time, the account manager in charge of sales at a different multinational supplier of EMS commenced small-scale market research, which climaxed in his targeting a number of minivan manufacturers as potential customers. Their overall annual production totaled about 400,000 vehicles, and all were producing product with a similar vehicle platform; all had expressed an interest in EMS in the hopes of expanding their market share. As well, none of them had managed to negotiate yet the foreign partnerships that might assist them in developing EMS for their minivans. From this list of potential customers, the account manager selected a company of affiliated factories (consisting of an engine plant and three minivan manufacturers, responsible for half the country's domestic minivan production) on which to concentrate his sales efforts. The account manager began making active customer visits, but soon encountered a roadblock.

Apparently, the core opinion leader of the affiliated companies, namely the owner of the engine plant, was leaning toward the German joint venture, having carefully reviewed all the EMS proposals and come to the conclusion that the account manager's company simply did not possess an adequate local development capacity and production base in China. These two selection points – local development capacity and local production base – were deemed by the owner of the engine plant unsatisfied, and soon the core opinion leader's lack of interest in transacting business with the account manager evolved into a disrelish at communicating with him at all.

In order to overcome the impasse, the account manager strove to deepen his understanding of the views on criteria of the COL and other Key Persons involved. Buying points and selling points would have to be isolated and promoted to the various relevant key persons and finally to the core opinion leader.

Table 4.1 illustrates the views on criteria of these key persons in terms of the selecting points and the associated selecting rationale for each.

**TABLE 4.1    Views on Criteria of Key Persons**

| KPs and COLs | Selecting Points (Major Ones Only – In Order of Importance) | Selecting Rationale |
|---|---|---|
| *Key Persons in Engine Plant* <br> Among them, there is a core opinion leader – the chief engineer of the plant | 1. Local development capacity | 1. COL believes that this is the key to meeting emission standards, improving engine function, and easy access to service – regarded as a most important selecting point |
| | 2. Development cost | 2. Low development cost is also very important for securing management approval |
| | 3. Local production base | 3. Guarantees timely supply, thus important for operation/implementation |
| | 4. Parts price | 4. An issue that needs to be considered, but not a major concern – one way of engineering low parts price is by involving competition, i.e. two suppliers |

**TABLE 4.1 Views on Criteria of Key Persons—cont'd**

| KPs and COLs | Selecting Points (Major Ones Only – In Order of Importance) | Selecting Rationale |
|---|---|---|
| *Key Persons in Minivan Plants* Among them, there are two core opinion leaders – the two chief engineers, plus two deputy general managers | 1. Quick availability | 1. Failure to meet delivery date may cause withdrawal from capital (Beijing) market, and success could provide competitive advantage in other urban markets, so this was the most important factor |
| | 2. Technical innovation (i.e., meeting emission standards) | 2. This may help relax the restrictions on the use of minivans in core urban markets, the capital city of Beijing in particular. For the purposes of image and prestige, local governments in the capital do not approve of many "low-end" vehicles on the road. So this point is very important. |
| | 3. After-sale service | 3. EMS system was new to the market, so after-sale technical support and service is very important |
| | 4. Price | 4. Not simply the price of the EMS components but how much the new system may cause overall vehicle price increase when replacing extant carburetor system |
| | 5. Quality | 5. Hoping for improvement in the reliability of engine performance with EMS, versus the carburetor system used on the existing vehicle platform |
| *Key Persons in Industry Administration* There are two persons – one of whom is in charge | 1. Quick solution to emission requirement | 1. Belief that EMS is the only solution to government requirement, and the key for minivan makers to survive in market, assuming emission standards are to be tightened in future |
| | 2. Future manufacturing cooperation | 2. Belief that cooperation will give rise to new and better technologies, and refinement of performance and price of EMS |

It was the account manager's in-depth understanding of these VOCs that led him to refine his sales approach, using the appropriate selling strategies and tactics (see the previous section) to effectively address the right customer value questions with those key persons and COLs involved. As a result, his company finally won the lucrative contract, and witnessed an unprecedented increase in sales volume and profit afterwards. This, coupled with the ensuing joint ventures and long-term cooperative manufacturing deals, led to considerable recognition and advancement for the account manager within his own company.

## MORE THOUGHTS ON VOC

The above-described case – in which the seller successfully isolated and shaped the views on criteria of several key persons for their values, thus persuading them to award the business – should attest to the centrality of selection criteria in the behavior of purchasers, especially in complex selling situations. Along with default values (with which they are inextricably linked), the initial VOC does serve the customer as a perceptual vehicle to sense and make sense of the purchasing value, but the lately recognized potential value can also switch the customer to a new perceptual vehicle in his value pursuing efforts. This interactive relationship between VOC and customer's perceived value justifies the notion of interactivism that is advocated in this book to understand why and how different interactions may take place between buyers and sellers. It is interesting that, in sales literature, there has not been a great deal of discussion about how customers make use of criteria under different circumstances, but there has been even less research on what these criteria might look like. Researchers on consumer behavior have discussed the circumstances where Affective Choice, Attribute-Based Choice, and Attitude-Based Choice might occur; and when talking about "decision rules," they might further elaborate on five commonly used decision rules such as disjunctive, conjunctive, lexicographic, elimination-by-aspects, and compensatory. However, in the ninth edition of their book *Consumer Behavior*, Hawkins et al. (2003) introduced the notion of "Evaluative Criteria" and defined it as "the various dimensions, features, or benefits a consumer looks for in response to a specific problem." In many dictionaries, the term "criteria" has been defined as established rules, standards, or principles, on the basis of which a judgment is made. However, it seems that few researchers had focused on the issues concerning the changeability of criteria, the mechanisms through which this changeability occurs and their effects on human interactions.

For our purposes, however, the concept of "criteria" is introduced to refer to the perceptual vehicle that a key person uses to sense and make sense of the value in a sales offer. This concept consists of two components: Selecting Points and Selecting Rationales. As far as our understanding is concerned, "criteria" serves the purpose of discerning what factors the key person thinks are *relevant* to the situation where a purchase need has emerged, as well as indicating the associated feelings, beliefs and logic for this relevancy and importance. The key person's views on criteria are shaped up by those factors (aspects or qualities) that have caught this key person's attention as relevant to his situation because of some reasons.

When a person faces a situation where he has to make a choice, this person will have to behave selectively: his attention will be directed in a *selective* manner to the internal or external stimuli; this act of "focusing the attention" should precede the act of choice making, as the stimuli must first be assigned a status in terms of relevancy, before the person even *consciously* realizes the existence of a criteria-related information processing operation being executed in his mind. Having said this, we do not deny the fact that a purchase need can be ephemeral, or even "irrational", in the sense that the person may be unconscious about the criteria-related information processing operations in his mind, or that he is going through these operations in a circular and/or highly non-linear fashion. But, what we would like to emphasize in our work on selling and sales management is that customers need to have some sort of views on criteria as a practical instrument to select or not to select a given stimulus as being relevant to their current situation. The name of the game of customer value seems to be "the criteria under use"; it is the VOC (explicit or implicit) that the key person holds that determines what value he could possibly see in a sales offer.

# 5

# BUYING POINTS AND SELLING POINTS: EXPRESSION OF CUSTOMER VALUE

Our discussion in the previous chapters focused on the first three basic building blocks of the working sales knowledge that we have developed to help sellers in their endeavors. This knowledge, which is embodied in the X-Be framework, is derived from various theories in the fields of human cognition, psychology, and behavior (as it will be explained later in Chapter 11) and aims at characterizing customer value in a manner that is both specific and practical. The three building blocks that we have introduced so far are as follows:

1. The PPP model, which is a working conceptualization of the process of value formation and exchange on the part of customer. This model allows the sellers to adjust the design and planning of their selling and sales management activities to the PPP that they happen or choose to be involved in.
2. The MAP model, which allows the sellers to identify the resource-type and product-type key persons. These key persons, along with the process-type key persons, assume various value roles in the purchasing process and possess different value preferences and influential powers. They are the ones who will discover and pursue (or facilitate the discovery and pursuit of) value on the part of the customer.
3. The key persons' VOC that are used as a base for judging value, and the default values of these key persons which may influence them in their judgments. The knowledge of these criteria and of the associated purchasing behavior patterns will further help the sellers understand how the customer perceives and pursues value, what type of value he deems important, and how he might identify this value with a certain sales offer.

When the seller implements these three building blocks and makes use of them to shape up her selling and sales management activities, she would have laid down a good foundation for her exchange-oriented communications and interactions with the customer. But a foundation is not an office tower, and there are a number of other elements that are necessary to get the structure to stand alone, tall, and stable – walls, beams, pillars, ceilings, and so on. And this, within the framework of X-Be, starts from the concepts of buying points and selling points, the expression of customer value in purchasing behavior – "what is in it" for a purchaser to act.

## THE NATURE OF CUSTOMER VALUE

Customer value has been a key focus in both business studies and practices during the past decade. To elucidate its meaning, various interpretations for it have appeared. For instance, customer value has been defined as "the difference between all the benefits derived from a total product and all the costs of acquiring those benefits" (Hawkins et al., 2003), and a total product refers to the entire set of characteristics associated with the marketing mix including the product features, price, communications, distribution, and services. Another concept referred to as "customer delivered value" was proposed by Philip Kotler (1996) in his work "Marketing Management: Analysis, Planning, Implementation and Control" in mid-1990s. There, it was defined as "the difference between the total customer value and the total customer cost," and the "total customer value is the perceived monetary value of the bundle of economic, functional, and psychological benefits customers expect from a given market offering. Total customer cost is the bundle of costs customers expect to incur in evaluating, obtaining, using, and disposing of the given market offering." Now, let us ask ourselves this question: how could a salesperson make use of such definitions to do her job on the sales floor? These definitions have roots in management accounting and address concerns that are not directly related to sales. Selling indeed is not just an accounting exercise, but a process of integrating value in a way that takes into account the dynamic aspect of customer cognition, psychology, and behavior.

For our purposes, and as we indicated in Chapter 1, we regard a customer as a value-chasing engine in a purchase process. So, we will study the concept of customer value as the driving force which drags the motion of this engine – the motion to purchase. A popular sales technique that is commonly used in practice consists in getting the salesperson to focus on "selling the benefits" to the customer, as opposed to selling just the features of the product. If the customer is happy with the identified benefits, and feel that they will address his needs, then he may act and buy the product. While such a rosy scenario tells us what condition is required to be able to sell, it does not show us how salespeople can make this condition satisfied, nor does it advise us about the extent to which these salespeople are working toward satisfying it – and that is where the notion of buying points and selling points becomes handy.

The salesperson should study the key persons involved and understand the evaluative criteria that they use to judge value – this will lead to the definition of the key persons' VOC, the concept of which was discussed in the previous chapter. On the basis of these criteria, the value that the customer is pursuing should then be elicited in terms of the X-Be dual concept of buying points and selling points, which reflect the personal and the socio-cultural factors that drive the purchasing behavior. It is by analyzing these points and addressing them (through the design of an adequate sales offer) that a salesperson can make her customer happy and thereby satisfy the abovementioned condition. In addition, and as will be explained in Chapter 8, by monitoring two selling status indices, attitude index and CI, which are based on these very concepts of buying points and selling points, the salesperson will be able to assess the extent to which she is moving toward making the customer happy and direct her activities accordingly.

The distinction between buying points and selling points is perhaps best illustrated by means of an example, so here is a simple one (see Figure 5.1).

Some months later, somewhere in the suburbs, a parent sits in his living room, clutching a wineglass wrathfully, as the television blares: "it's eleven o'clock. Do *you* know where your children are?" The parent clutches the wineglass tighter. "I told you an hour ago, *no!*" Two hours pass. Suddenly the door swings open, and Little Johnny stumbles in.

A nightclub owner has decided to spice up his once-trendy but now rather passé nightspot by renaming it *The Library*, taking on a literary-debauchery theme and, in the process (he hopes), attracting a younger clientele. Why might he have done so? Will it work?

**FIGURE 5.1**    Reviving a Nightclub with Buying Points and Selling Points.

The parent glares at his child and bellows hoarsely, "School was dismissed at three o'clock. It's one o'clock. That's *ten hours!* Where have you been?"

Little Johnny thrusts his leg out pertly and removes his coat – remarking casually, if a little unsteadily, "sure, school was out at three. But then I went to the library, and stayed there till it closed."

In a way, it could be said that the nightclub owner directly engineered this scene. Renaming his establishment *The Library* created a powerful selling point for his young patrons: upon returning home and being forced inevitably to account for their truancy to their parents, they are enabled to defend their actions by declaring (in all honesty) that they have been busying themselves at "the library" – a word with benign, in fact positive associations. The parents in question will thus be (hopefully!) appeased.

But in addition to placating the people to whom his young clientele are beholden, the nightclub owner must also strive to appeal to the young people themselves. So he provides trendy amenities and refreshments – the chance to see and be seen, and to drink and dance – and these purely personal benefits (buying points) were evidently attractive enough to entice Little Johnny to trade his leisure time and money for the chance to get at them.

Little Johnny's evening out, and his eventually having to justify it to a parent, vividly illustrates the dual nature of all human actions, which always have both a personal and a social dimension. Purchasing activity is no exception. The equal influence of both buying points and selling points on purchasing behavior reflects the reality of every purchaser being what might best be termed a social individual: no matter how personal the buying behavior, it will inevitably have to be justified, in one way or another, directly or indirectly, to someone else. Conversely, even a purchase that seems entirely driven by outside forces will always be characterized by the presence of some personal values, however sublimated.

---

**Buying points and selling points: a précis**

- Buying points and selling points are the expression of those characteristics of a considered sales offer, which motivate the key person to the motion to purchase.
- Buying points are implicitly or explicitly related to the VOC of the key person inasmuch as they are the attractive elements of the considered sales offer that motivate the purchase behavior on the individual level.

- Selling points are explicitly related to the VOC of the key person inasmuch as they are the attractive elements of the considered sales offer that help justify the purchase to those to whom he is beholden.
- Buying points and selling points always reflect the current VOC of the key person involved in the purchase process. Therefore, a change in the VOC will lead to a change in the buying points and selling points.
- The buying points and selling points of a key person can be the same, overlap, or be completely different.
- There are apparent buying points and hidden buying points.
- The identification of the buying points and selling points is essential for effective selling.

## BUYING POINTS IN CONSUMER AND ORGANIZATIONAL SALES

Buying points are all those characteristics of a promised sales offer (including the implications of making use of such a sales offer) that are considered to be beneficial personally to the individual key person, and thus foster the desire in this key person to accept it. Being intensely personal, they will necessarily differ from key person to key person; in other words, the same sales offer may boast a number of different aspects that will be perceived and weighted differently by each key person, even if ultimately everyone is in agreement that the product is desirable enough to purchase. key persons can all agree on the same outcome regarding the sales offer (say, for instance, the sales offer must be accepted), but they would have different reasons and different buying points to buy in the product. In any case, to the individual key person, buying points represent an impression of the positive consequences and contributions that the attainment of the sales offer in question would bring to his life and happiness. This is true for both organizational and consumer sales. In a consumer sales relationship, it is sometimes easier to perceive the effects of buying points on an individual purchaser's behavior – and thus to identify the buying points at play. But, in organizational and industrial sales, this often tends to be more difficult, mostly because the contexts are usually themselves complex.

One may wonder how we could talk about buying points in the case of organizational sales, when all key persons work and buy for an organization, not for themselves. A basic principle that has been adopted in the X-Be framework is that a key person does not lose his individuality after he joins an organization. You would not believe that a key person will support and actively advocate for a sales offer that benefits the organization but damages his own interests, would you? After all the bulk of economic theory is based on the assumption that people are selfish. The robustness of this assumption has long passed the acid test, and is still reliable when dealing with individual people, whether they are working for a certain organization or not. Because of the implicit nature of buying points in the context of organizational sales, we would like to provide a convenient shortlist for those who still think that selling to organizations comes down to selling only organizational benefits.

A convenient but certainly not exhaustive list of buying points in organizational sales:

- Improvement of one's performance
- More recognition by others
- Contribution to promotion
- Gaining respect and gaining bonus
- Demonstration of professionalism
- Good for self learning
- Contribution to one's achievement
- Strengthening relationships with significant others
- Consolidating authority or power base
- Protecting one's turf
- Change in boring routines
- Image of a smart decision maker
- Demonstration of leadership

The fact of the matter is this: different key persons are working in different situations, coming from different departments, rising from different backgrounds, having different KBs, at different stages of the career ladder, and part of different internal and external social networks, and so on; all these facts could lead them to recognize different personal benefits, even if the tangible features and operational benefits of the sales offer are actually the same for the organization. A seller who has a good understanding of this issue will certainly put herself in an advantageous position. And while the sellers should help the key persons recognize their buying points in a sales offer, they should avoid crossing the ethic lines when they face a situation where some hidden buying points are in breach of the code of conduct specified in their company's or in the customer's documents, though many hidden buying points do not pose ethical issues.

Thus, if a certain sales offer will somehow help a key person strengthen a positive self-image or give him a chance to demonstrate leadership, then this will be a buying point for him, which may motivate him to think positively about the sales offer. Now one may react and say that some key persons have their personal goals completely aligned with their organization; this is of course possible, and in such a case, these key persons and the whole organization would have the same criteria to judge value, that is, the same VOC; the key persons would feel rewarded personally by pursuing the organization's objectives such as, for instance, market share increase, technological advancement, and so on; these key persons' buying points would then be correlated with the organization's objectives. But, of course, there is the other extreme case where personal agendas exist that are totally against the organization's goals; in such a case, the features of these agendas will also constitute buying points for the corresponding key persons. Sometimes, these key persons will have great difficulties sharing what these buying points are with other people and with salespeople. When this happens, we refer to the buying points as hidden buying points. The issue of hidden buying points will be discussed more in Chapter 8.

In summary, thus, the notion of buying points is not unique to individual consumers; it is also applicable to the context of organizational sales. It is the seller's job to understand what the customer's buying points are and how her sales offer could address them, so that the key persons can be effectively motivated to accept this offer.

## BUYING POINTS AND PURCHASER'S ATTENTION

In a consumerist society – in which every citizen is inundated almost from birth with every imaginable variety of advertisement – individual consumers quickly become inured against the hyperbole and grandiloquence of promotional language and wary of obvious attempts at manipulation. The result might be termed "audience apathy" – a sense of skepticism and financial self-preservation. In a sense, and especially in retail sales, "audience apathy" is the veil through which buying points must penetrate in order to precipitate a motion to purchase, if the seller manages to attract the consumer's attention.

Piquing and maintaining the consumer's attention is essential, particularly in today's attention economy, and it is the nature of human attention to be drawn to that which is novel and unusual, as opposed to what is more quotidian and unremarkable (We will discuss the nature of attention in Chapter 11). Organizations that sell new and unusual products or services can actually benefit from "audience apathy," particularly if their wares are sufficiently different from those of their competitors, if the differences in question might represent unique buying points to a particular sector of the population, and if the sellers in these organizations are shrewd in communicating these unique buying points to the target market. In other cases, where the products or services being offered are more of an everyday nature, with less variation from outlet to outlet, it is up to the seller to creatively communicate and interact with the customer, observe when the consumer's interest has been piqued, and identify what aspects of the product might have piqued it. The attention economy requires seller's creativity – just the creative way to communicate a similar product may render different buying points and will certainly help these buying points penetrate the "audience apathy."

## BUYING POINTS AND INFLUENTIAL POWER

In Chapter 3, the term **influential power** was defined as such:

> A person's influential power over another is based upon the person under the influence believing that the influential person possesses something (let us call it **S**) such as a trait, characteristic, information, expertise, knowledge, or status, or anything that is of value, that he or she desires. The intensity of this power is dependent on the degree of importance that the person under influence assigns to **S**.

It is thus a sort of power distinct from (although occasionally overlapping with) formal internal hierarchies, and uncovering it might require a bit of interpersonal "detective" work. Ultimately, though, the necessity of isolating and exploiting this power in the name of a successful sale has been underscored. But it is important to note that just because a person with influential power has been identified within the network of key persons, there is no guarantee – regardless of how much attention is lavished upon this person or how much effort is expended in the interest of his or her amity and complicity – that he (or she) will act as direct advocate for the salesperson during the purchasing process.

The formula for the degree to which influential power is exercised in a given sales relationship predictably relates to buying points is fairly obvious; it is in fact identical to the formula which dictates the degree to which the power exists in any other relationship: just replace the something **S** in the above definition by "buying points" (i.e., make **S** = "buying points"). When a key person with influential power is attracted to the buying points identified with the features of a sales offer, the more important he deems those buying points, the more likely he is to implement his power in favor of the salesperson. This may be mitigated by the absence of sufficient selling points (see below in next section), but otherwise, buying points are among the most important catalyzing factors for influential power to act in favor of the salesperson, and thus should be the obvious center of any sales activity, regardless of whether the target of this activity is the key persons in organizational purchasing process, or the consumers and their associated CISS (consumer's immediate social surrounding). Once an individual key person with influential power has been convinced that a product is worthy of purchase – even if it is for entirely self-interested reasons – he will be motivated to exert his influential power on other key persons in the purchase process.

However, and as it will be explained below in the following section, the salesperson's work on the question of buying points should not be at the expense of the selling points. Selling points are just as important as buying points and the salesperson should dedicate the same efforts to each of them.

## SELLING POINTS, COMMUNITY, AND THE MOTION TO PURCHASE

The mantra which circles at the center of any discussion of buying points is that they are often subjective, private, and personal. But human beings, as a general rule, are never truly independent, entirely individual, sequestered from all others; they are basically social creatures. For this reason, citing those private, not always express buying points, as the sole contributing factor to the motion to purchase would be an incomplete image of the way business is truly transacted. Although purchases that are acts of pure individual agency do exist, there are very few of them in the real world; many purchases are indeed made by individuals beholden to a chain of corporate command, or simply to society, community, family, and their underlying culture. At all times, the purchaser craves the understanding, acceptance, approval, respect, and admiration of others so as to assure his social status and interpersonal happiness or harmony. Selling points are any aspects of the sales offer which would qualify the purchase to those people, the (implicit) approval and recognition of whom the purchaser seeks; they are the elements of the sales offer that make the purchase of it socially or culturally attractive, rather than personally attractive. We shall refer to this meaning of the expression "selling points" as the "X-Be sense." This meaning is a 180 degree U-turn from the traditional one. It helps sellers refocus their attention on the customer and on the value he

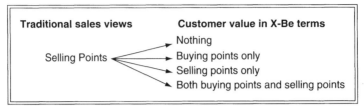

**FIGURE 5.2**   Traditional Sales Views Versus Customer Value as it is Expressed in X-Be Terms.

is chasing. Identifying selling points and tailoring them to the purchaser at hand requires the seller to step outside the confines of what might be termed the sales offer's "internal vocabulary," to view this sales offer not as a discrete artifact to be contemplated in its isolation, but rather as a functional element of the purchaser's life, and to sell accordingly.

The notion of selling points in the X-Be sense is pervasive in both consumer and organizational sales. In the former, one of the powerful aspects of branding is to provide social recognition through the use of branded products; this social recognition sometime constitutes, for the consumer, a selling point more than a mere buying point in the X-Be sense of the term, that is, a social and cultural justification for his buying behavior. In the latter (organizational sales), on the other hand, it seems to be the norm that any key person needs to justify his buying behavior to other people in his organization – he will do that by means of his selling points in the X-Be sense as well.

Finally, we should point out that the traditional meaning of the expression "selling points" has no valid place in the X-Be framework primarily because it is too general to account for what customer value really is. But for those who feel it is hard to give up this old tradition at once, we provide Figure 5.2 for necessary caution when thinking about selling or communicating with this old concept.

## BALANCING THE SELLING POINTS AND BUYING POINTS

Like buying points, in the interest of a successful sale, selling points must penetrate the monotonous noise of product positioning and advertisement, as well as the delicate veil of default values. The mission, the logical end, of both, is the same; and this congruity serves to emphasize the fact that the apprehension of buying points and selling points is by no means necessarily sequential. From the discussion above, one might have come to the conclusion that a key person may only begin to recognize his selling points after an appropriate period spent dazzled by his buying points. This is rarely the case. In fact, most customers weigh both factors simultaneously if not necessarily equally, and the process of value assessment on a sales offer is one which involves much internal thrusting and parrying, of weighing the personal dimension against the social dimension. A simple dilemma of this sort might be the case of a person attracted by an expensive car who resists purchasing it because his family might resent such an ostentatious and prodigal expenditure. Here, possession cost is a selling point variable – a negative one. Obviously, this variable is contextual: were the person beholden to no-one regarding his finances, the cost, and its implications of status would be a hallmark of what is often termed "conspicuous consumption" and a social boon – a positive selling point of the buying behavior, in other words.

Individual purchasers and purchasing groups vary greatly along the lines of the degree to which their self-image arises from the opinions of others, and how much their happiness or security is predicated upon their responsibilities to others. And even between the poles, those purchasers and purchasing groups shift about, being rather Protean entities; the extent to which buying points are subordinate to selling points (or vice versa) is entirely situational. Items for private use (razors, underwear, meals, etc.) might be purchased entirely on the basis of buying points; items for public display (business clothing, art, charitable donations, etc.) might be purchased entirely on the basis of selling points. But in many cases, buying behaviors are motivated by the customer values represented by both buying points and selling points perceived in a sales offer, and this is especially the case in industrial selling.

*A thought exercise:*

*– Bought what?*
*There may arise sales situations in which the seller is the sole buying point and/or selling point – this is to say, when a purchase is made entirely out of admiration, affection, trust or even pity for the seller. Can you think of a case when this might occur? Recall our broadly inclusive definition of what constitutes a "sale" earlier in the book.*

## SELLING POINTS AND THE USE OF INFLUENTIAL POWER

Whereas buying points alone constitute the device that inclines key persons toward the motion to purchase, it is the selling points that will likely be used by these key persons to exert their influence within the organization on the purchasing process; this seems to be especially true in the case of COLs, but other key persons may behave like that as well. In other words, selling points empower key persons and COLs to exert their influence over others gently and intelligently, rather than wield it authoritatively (which, by the way, does not work well). A seller who advances a sales approach that concentrates on only buying points (however attractive and appealing they may seem to be to the involved key persons) at the expense of selling points does so at her own peril. The more important the buy, the higher the number of involved and affected people, and the more sweeping will be the social repercussions of the purchase. And this is especially the case when selling to organizations.

## MORE THOUGHTS ON BUYING POINTS AND SELLING POINTS

As was pointed out earlier in this chapter, a number of key persons within a purchasing collective may possess dissimilar VOC, and thus perceive entirely different buying points and selling points in the same sales offer, even if they are equally inclined to purchase. But, in other cases, buying points and selling points can be difficult to distinguish. For example, when a number of key persons are evaluating a product, and all of them perceive and value more or less the same buying points (and are aware of their consensus), then any one of these key persons may deem his own buying points to be his selling points as well, because they are the buying points for the rest of the group. In other words, any buying points that are shared amongst members of a purchasing collective can also be considered the selling points for each individual within that group. That is to say that selling points can represent, in some cases, nothing more than shared values of the organization or community in which the key persons live or work. For a seller to find out whether a buying point also serves as a selling point for a particular key person, the seller needs to check if this key person will publicize this buying point among the other people involved in the purchase process.

In general, if one's buying point is also the others, this buying point can also be his selling point; if one perceives something in certain a selling point that is personally beneficial to him, then this selling point is also a buying point for him; if one has some hidden benefits in a sales offer, then these benefits are referred to as his hidden buying points, and such buying points rarely overlap with his selling points.

Just like VOC, buying points and selling points can evolve and vary as the customer moves through the PPP; because of this, they could be elusive. While this can be frustrating, it does have some positive implications for the ways in which the seller can deal with impasses in sales communication; such impasses occur, for instance, when the customer's VOC are unfavorable to the offer. So, if the seller finds that the key person occupies a PPP that gives rise to VOC not conducive to an exchange, the seller may encourage the key person to mentally move to a later phase and discuss the possible buying points and selling points that he may not be able to foretaste with his current VOC for selecting an offer.

An example scenario might unfold as such. A company that builds and distributes major appliances is looking to contract out part of its manufacturing division to a third-party company. But upon meeting with a salesperson representing a predominately domestic manufacturing company (MC), the key person discusses the issues regarding the qualifications of potential suppliers, and has clearly expressed such a view that the ideal supplier ought to have international networking capabilities, which MC has yet to cultivate. The salesperson immediately recognizes two things: first, that the key person is mentally in the phase of ND; second, that the key person's concern regarding the 'international networking capabilities' as a selecting point (which is one component of the VOC) indicates that his VOC may not be favorable to her company. Whereas the seller acknowledges that her company lacks the capacity for international networking, she remains firm in her conviction that this perceived deficiency has no bearing on her company's ability to provide the services that will best satisfy the customer's demands at an irresistible price. So, the salesperson may encourage the client to look at the value of this irresistible price she is able to offer, together with the other attractive values her company could provide in terms of this key person's buying points and selling points, at which point the key person might opt to assess suppliers on the basis of their other virtues, which could be just as relevant and important to him (the key person would have now moved, mentally, into the SQ phase). The salesperson can thus highlight those characteristics (in terms of buying points and selling points) that distinguish her sales offer to the customer, and by doing so, she might be able to reshape the key person's VOC which had initially placed her at a competitive disadvantage.

The above example does also illustrate the interactive relationship between VOC and customer value (represented by buying points and selling points) and how the latter may impact the former; indeed, enough interests in something may make people change their views. However, any effective selling does require the seller to first understand the customer's

VOC for judging value, before thinking about changing them. In any case, the ownership of the (changed or unchanged) VOC always rests with the customer, even when the change is induced by the seller.

## CONCLUSION

While the solitary and social aspects of human beings have previously been highlighted in different subject areas, we are here to make use of this knowledge to develop working concepts in the context of selling and sales management and characterize the notion of customer value. Thus, the concepts of buying points and selling points, which were introduced in this chapter, not only provide an adequate description of this notion, but they also afford the seller effective and practical tools to do their job. As the readers will indeed see in Chapters 6, 8, 9, and 10, these X-Be concepts help establish an entire new and useful selling and sales management knowledge system in a logical and parsimonious manner. Combined with the other X-Be building blocks, they give a rise to a powerful methodology for managing sales opportunities, constructing sound judgments about customers, generating accurate sales forecasts, designing and planning sales events, and many other tasks.

But, for now, an important question needs to be addressed: if those buying points and selling points that are of great importance to the customer have been identified with the characteristics of a sales offer, will the customer buy in? The answer to this question, within the X-Be framework, requires the concepts of deliverability and integrated product, which will be introduced in the next chapter.

# 6

# DELIVERABILITY AND INTEGRATED PRODUCT: TOTALITY OF A PURCHASE IN TERMS OF VALUE

In this chapter, we introduce the fifth building block of the X-Be framework, which refers to "Deliverability and Integrated Product." To do so, we first look at the existing definitions of product and discuss their limitations in the field of selling. Then, we introduce the concept of "deliverability" to handle the customer-perceived buying risks and objections. Finally, we define the meaning of integrated product or simply product in the X-Be framework and discuss its implications in selling, as well as the value elements for its successful development. We also present a case study to illustrate our ideas.

## LIMITATIONS OF THE EXISTING DEFINITIONS OF THE CONCEPT OF PRODUCT

Marketers have tried to enrich our understanding of the notion of product by introducing the concepts of "customer value" and "customer value hierarchy." Different "product levels" have been introduced in marketing textbooks, going from the level of "core benefit" to that of "augmented product." Each level tends to add more customer value. There are also many classifications of products such as, nondurable goods, durable goods, services, convenience goods, and specialty goods for consumer marketing and materials, parts, capital items, and business services for industrial marketing.

Marketers have also attempted to define precisely what the term "product" refers to. Many of these definitions consider a product as anything that is offered to a market to satisfy a need or want. It can be a physical item such as a piece of furniture, a core service tendered by human beings such as consulting work, or some combination of the above such as a shoeshine. There have also been definitions of the concepts of "need," "want," "demand," and so on. While such definitions could be useful from a marketing point of view, they tend unfortunately to be ineffective for the job of selling and sales management. They provide the seller with no specific instructions, guidelines, hints, or clues as to how she can get involved effectively and successfully in the process of value formation and exchange on the part of the customer. Marketing concepts tend to focus on the end result of the process of exchange between the seller and buyer ("product = anything that is offered to satisfy a need or want"), while selling is about all of the interactive actions that take place throughout this process, including, but not limited to, the actual exchange. This is why many of the insights that are valuable on the marketing side provide little information on the way business is actually transacted and, as a result, they are hardly useful for sellers in their day-to-day activities.

A more sales-oriented definition of what a product is is based on the technique of "features, advantages, and benefits" (FAB). While this definition tends to facilitate the sales, the corresponding sales pitches rarely reflect how a sale succeeds or fails and do not provide a comprehensive view of how the customer judge value and make buying decisions. Consider the case of a government seeking options for providing power to a major city (it is presumed in this case that the city's electrical infrastructure is operated by private interests, which is becoming increasingly common in North America). The municipal government presumably does not merely sign the contract for the lowest price and the highest yield; they might seek instead stability of supply, minimal detriment to the local environment, insurance of constant output, and maintenance. Purchasers do not always intend to have a proverbial "beginning" and "end" for the product they want to acquire; sometimes "peace of mind" is as valued a commodity as the item actually changing hands. Something as intangible as a commitment to future emergency service may be the single most important factor in convincing a purchaser of the merits of a given supplier. The real question here is about how to work out, with the customer, a "product" that helps the key persons and COLs achieve their respective personal and social objectives that might associate with the purchase in question, and not about pushing an exiting product or service onto them. And, it is in this respect that the existing definitions of the term "product" tend to be not so useful in helping sellers with their job.

Also, at various occasions in this book, we have presented a number of sales scenarios in which the nature and identity of the "product" has changed significantly during the course of interactions between the seller and buyer. This change has almost always arisen in response to information communicated (deliberately and otherwise) by the customer. This is equally true for organizational selling as it is for simple retail or noncommercial exchanges. Clearly, there are many exchanges – commercial and otherwise – that manifestly involve "products" but, because of the highly **dynamic** nature of the interactive processes that underlie them, any of the above attempts to define the term "product" as a static notion corresponding to segmented demographics will take away such a dynamic and interactive nature of the exchange process; it will also necessarily impose certain limitations on our understanding of this process and, consequently, diminish the effectiveness of (personal or non-personal) selling.

Thus, although no one doubts the centrality of the "product" to the business of selling, the nature of this abstraction, as it relates to the seller's job, has nonetheless yet to be fully and satisfactorily described. This represents a major theoretical chasm for the study of selling and purchasing behaviors, a chasm which extends to the very foundation of any selling and sales management framework, and renders perilous any attempt to construct a practical selling strategy atop it.

In the X-Be framework, we propose another way of describing the notion of product. We indeed base the definition of this notion (referred to, in the X-Be framework, as "Integrated Product") on the previous X-Be working elements, in a logical and integrated fashion. This definition takes into account the highly dynamic nature of the cognitive, psychological, and behavioral characteristics of this value-chasing engine that is the customer. By doing so, we equip the sellers with practical tools that help them in the field carry out their selling job effectively, that is, interact with the customer for a mutually satisfactory exchange.

We will discuss the X-Be definition later in the section of "The Concept of Integrated Product," but before we do that, we need to explain a bit more the X-Be concept of deliverability.

## THE CONCEPT OF DELIVERABILITY

When customers go through the phases of the purchase process, they could engage in many meetings, sales events, and formal and informal conversations with the potential sellers. From the customers' perspective, each of these interactions is accompanied with risks of failure to achieve the expected result from the interaction in question. These risks include, of course, the buying risk that is associated with the final step where the actual exchange would take place. The more complex, costly, or valuable the purchase, the more likely that the customers take the risk factors seriously; for instance, issues such as warranties, quality control, logistics, and previously satisfied customers will all be concerns for the industrial customers; company's public image, reputation, words of mouth, and post-sale service will all be concerns for the consumers. In general, a trustable level of assurance on the part of the seller will be essential in bringing to fruition an exchange. Keen purchasers reasonably expect a satisfactory delivery of the buying points and selling points in a sales offer if they are to make a risky commitment to it and to its provider.

A common manifestation of these risks is the so-called customer objections. Because of their very frustrating nature, customer objections and how to overcome them have been for a long time a core subject in the discipline of selling and sales management, as it is illustrated in many sales books and textbooks. But why customers throw out objections to sellers? As one can imagine, there could be many different answers to this question. For instance, customers could use objections as a tactic to get more value, but they can also throw out objections because they are not sure of the value in the sales offers, or they simply do not believe in the sales pitch and/or in the sellers at all.

How does the X-Be framework deal with these issues?

Earlier in this book, we subjected to deconstruction the various factors which drive a customer's interest in a sales offer. These factors ultimately revealed themselves to be the customer-perceived values specifically related to certain characteristics of a sales offer in terms of personal benefits and social justifications in the eyes of others (present or not at purchasing time). These were called the buying points and selling points, which must be (implicitly or explicitly) consistent with the identified VOC. All of these aspects are ultimately individual, and the eminent domain of the key person is targeted throughout all phases of the purchase process; the seller must mine and understand them (i.e., buying points, selling points, corresponding VOC) and adjust her sales techniques accordingly. But to what extent can this deconstruction of the customer's motion to purchase be helpful in making sound judgments about the customer's commitment or action to actually buy? Apart from whether the relative significance of buying points and selling points (as the net benefit in the transaction) is perceived to match the customer's expectations, which will be discussed in Chapter 6, the action of actually buying also depends on the customer's perceived deliverability upon the buying points and selling points, which is related to the perceived buying risks, customer objections, and customer satisfaction. To succeed and win the sale, the seller must convince her customer that she and/or her sales offer can deliver the promised buying points and selling points.

In the X-Be framework, the concept of deliverability is defined as the extent to which a key person perceives the "contents" (i.e., the identified buying points and selling points) of the possible exchange could be delivered.

Customer-satisfying deliverability (upon the identified buying points and selling points) could be among the most influential factors that can bring about a sale. Therefore, it is critical that sellers engage in effective communications with their customers about this question of deliverability. For this purpose, the fifth X-Be building block, "Deliverability and Integrated Product," provides the sellers with practical tools and empowers them in their involvement in the process of value formation and exchange on the part of customer. It also gives them an insightful understanding of what selling is all about; as we will see below in the section of "Further Thoughts on the Integrated Product," "selling" will be expressed as a function of three of the X-Be building blocks.

Now that we have introduced the concept of deliverability, we can move to the discussion of what an "Integrated Product" is.

## THE CONCEPT OF INTEGRATED PRODUCT

The identity of a product is as multifarious as that of the customer. The item, or service, itself, is simply the most visible element of the product; when that "peace of mind" (see the foregoing case of a government-seeking options for providing power to a major city) reflected in the above sense of buying risks is woven into a purchase decision, the mind of customers becomes with the deliverability upon the identified buying point and selling points in a given sales offer. And this is why when talking about customer value in selling and sales management, we prefer the concepts of buying points and selling points, as they could be isolated in terms of the purchaser's behavioral motivators which drive him to act from his respective personal and social perspectives. Such a technical treatment is not only of operational value for the actual selling work (i.e., the interaction with the customer – the salesperson's job), but also of managerial value for sales management as we will see in the development of the selling status indices (Chapter 8) and the uses of such indices to manage sales opportunities and sales forecasts (Chapter 10).

With the concept of deliverability as introduced above, we can now introduce our definition of product in a way that reflects the dynamics of the cognitive, psychological, and behavioral characteristics of the customer as a value-chasing engine:

> *Integrated product*, or simply *product* within the X-Be framework, is a *set of VOC-endorsed buying points and selling points with certain deliverability.*

If this deliverability is satisfactory to the customer at purchase time, the exchange may take place; if it is not up to the customer's satisfaction after purchase, then the customer will be dissatisfied. In any case, the customer value in a sales offer amounts to the integrated product. It is this product and only this product that is actually sold as far as customer-perceived delivery of value is concerned. Let us now illustrate how this definition of product could provide sellers with directions and powerful guidelines for their effective participation in the process of value formation and exchange on the part of customer.

In order to make a sale, according to the definition of integrated product, a seller will have to integrate the customer-perceived value into her sales offer. To do so, she may, first of all, have to find, verify, or even help establish the customer's VOC which equip him (i.e., the customer) with an evaluative base. On the basis of these VOC, she then may purposefully interact with the customer to find out what buying points and selling points he wants to see in a sales offer and also purposefully choose and relate the VOC's selecting rationales to convince him about the satisfactory deliverability upon these buying points and selling points. And if she wins the deal, she will have to make sure that deliverability is fulfilled at least as expected or more, to sustain a satisfactory customer relationship for future business.

This dynamic can be illustrated by means of any number of common, real-world examples. Here's a simple one:

*Example: At the electronics shop*

1. *A customer enters an electronics store* and expresses an interest in purchasing a television.

2. *The seller engages the customer in conversation.* She attempts to discover *why* the customer wants a television at this point in time, what place the television will occupy in the customer's home or workplace, and what the customer hopes to get out of the experience of owning a television. The seller also hopes to find out what the customer's attitudes are with regard to various brands, models, styles, and sizes of television.

3. *The seller suggests particular models* that she believes will satisfy those VOC of the purchaser that she was able to determine in step 2.

4. *The purchaser reacts to the seller's suggestions.* He emphasizes that he wants something quite *small* and preferably portable. The seller introduces the purchaser to the smallest model in the store.

5. *The purchaser reacts again.* He wants something small, yes, but also comparatively inexpensive. The smallest model, he says, is a little pricey. The seller then suggests a different model – slightly larger, but a good balance of low price and small size.

6. *The purchaser reacts a third time.* The low-cost model appears rather fragile. The seller's response is twofold: first, she stresses that the return rates on this model of television are quite low; secondly, she mentions that an extended warranty is available, for a nominal extra charge.

7. *The purchaser balks at the extra cost of an extended warranty,* and seems unwilling to make a purchase, maintaining his wariness of the unit's fragility. The seller suggests that the store has a policy offering a 30-day money-back guarantee, no questions asked.

8. The purchaser, who recalls what his colleague, an electronic engineer, told him before (if an electronic device works fine during the first few weeks, it will likely be fine for many years), becomes satisfied and agrees to complete the transaction.

Although our example is concise and thus somewhat simplified, it nonetheless contains all the elements we have been discussing in this section and demonstrates how all of them ultimately aspire toward the finalization of the integrated product at purchase (steps 7 and 8). The process of sales communication begins with the seller attempting to identify the purchaser's VOC (steps 1 and 2) and making suggestions (step 3) in the hopes of helping to develop them. Four times – steps 4 through 7 in this case – the purchaser feels the need to react to the direction the exchange relationship was taking, and four times the seller attempted to change course, and make more suggestions, in order to get the purchaser to reveal more of his evolving VOC. In the course of these interactions, the seller identifies the VOC (size, price, and durability), as well as the mix of buying points/selling points that the purchaser is looking for (small size, low price, and very durable). She also tries to address the purchaser's objections and sense of risk by attempting to prove the deliverability upon the identified buying points/selling points (steps 6 and 7). In the end, the seller was able to guarantee a satisfying deliverability to the purchaser through the "30-day money-back guarantee" policy. This process of sophisticated, bilateral interaction, carefully heeded by the seller, is similar to the sort of interaction that takes place on a much grander scale in organizational settings.

## FURTHER THOUGHTS ON THE INTEGRATED PRODUCT

In the previous section, we showed how the concept of product can be defined on the basis of the X-Be elements and explained how this definition can be usefully implemented to provide the sellers with directions and guidelines for their interactions with their customers. Here, we would like to define the meanings of the following concepts within the X-Be framework for operational purposes: (1) purchase need, (2) selling (the interaction with the customer for a mutually satisfactory exchange), and (3) exchange relationship.

### Purchase Need

Instead of defining a need as a basic human requirement, a want is a learnt need to a specific thing and a demand is an affordable want, what else can we have as a refined definition that is informative enough to sellers in their daily work? Within the X-Be framework, a purchase need can be defined as a set of VOC-endorsed buying points and selling points in a certain hypothetical sales offer. The implications of this are straightforward: a purchase need can be uncovered, verified, or even created by simply looking at the customer's VOC (by analyzing the existing ones or creating new ones) and addressing the relevant buying points and selling points.

### Selling (the Seller's Job)

What is selling and what is the role of sellers? In the X-Be framework, we define selling as a function $f$ of the customer's VOC, buying points and selling points, and the deliverability of these points:

Selling $= f($VOC, buying points and selling points, deliverability$)$.

This equation, to a certain extent, inverts the causal reality of value production. It directs the seller to concentrate her efforts on the task of uncovering the VOC, integrating the VOC-endorsed value in a sales offer by purposefully designing or selecting its characteristics to respond to the customer's personal (buying points) and social (selling points) objectives with regard to the purchase, and proving to him that a satisfying deliverability on both the buying points and selling points will be ensured. The integrated product that is designed as a result of this work belongs, in the end, to that individual customer with whom the seller was interacting. From this perspective, the X-Be framework is consistent with the emerging agent-based modeling methodology. The foregoing equation also suggests to us to abandon the "one-size-fits-all" sales approach, whereby a product is said to contain all needed "FAB" that inherently appeal to particular "demographics." Of course, we do not say that we cannot learn from the past to improve our effectiveness in the future, but we believe that the complexity of the modern economy calls for a deep customization of the selling approach.

## Exchange Relationship

How does an exchange relationship look like? As far as the customer's assessment of deliverable and delivered value is concerned, the exchange relationship can be depicted, within the X-Be framework, in a geometric form as follows (see Figure 6.1):

What this figure tells us is that the exchange of value is based on the deliverability; the contents of the value are the buying points and selling points, which stem out of the customer's VOC.

Finally, we should note that some more reasons as to why we base the exchange behavior in selling and sales management on concepts such as VOC, buying points, selling points, and deliverability will be explained in later chapters of this book. In Chapter 8, we will introduce the Selling Status Indices which are based on the foregoing concepts, and which help in assessing the effectiveness of selling. In Chapter 9, we will turn our discussion to competition and explain how it too can be expressed in terms of VOC and customer-accepted deliverability. In Chapter 10, we will expand

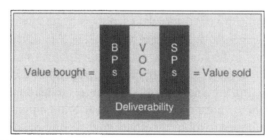

**FIGURE 6.1** Exchange Relationship Described in terms of Deliverable and Delivered Value. BPs, Buying points; SPs, Selling points; VOC, Views on Criteria.

our discussion to detail how the methodology introduced in this book can be applied to manage sales opportunities and develop sales forecast.

For now, though, let us turn to a case study of how one large, well-established company (which we'll call Z) succeeded in winning a significant sale by implementing X-Be (Sheng et al., 2005).

## INTEGRATING CUSTOMER VALUES INTO A SALES OFFER – A CASE STUDY

Our story concerns Z, a glass manufacturing company located in a major city on the upstream of the Yangtze River. For many years it has specialized in the production and sale of coffee-colored bottles for liquid medicine. Its market share approaches 40% across the nation, the second largest in the medicine-bottling industry. However, in recent years, changes in market demand have pushed coffee-colored bottles out of vogue. More and more pharmaceutical companies prefer white-colored bottles, so as to better showcase their increasingly palatable-looking concoctions, especially for "over-the-counter" medications. Z was ready for the change from the start, having very quickly implemented the capacity to manufacture white-colored bottles. For the sake of peak efficiency and low costs, they also draw up plans to begin phasing out their coffee-colored bottles. Only one obstacle remains.

One of Z's strongest business relationships is with a company we'll call S Pharmaceuticals. S is a major pharmaceutical company with a significant market share, and thus a valuable ally for Z. But because S almost exclusively produces medicine requiring a prescription, they are not too concerned with the aesthetics of their products and are happy with the coffee-colored bottles they have been using for many years. So happy are they with their secure market position and the efficiency of their operations that it is said they might be reluctant to accept any change. Z very much wants all its clients to switch to white-colored bottles, but cannot afford to lose S. So their current objective is to convince S of the advantages of white-colored bottles. The salesperson in this case will be one Mr. Zhang, the regional manager for Z in South China, long responsible for dealings with S.

Over at S, business relating to bottle acquisition is handled by the purchasing department. The director in charge of the department is one Mr. Li. He is one of most senior managers at S and commands universal respect and admiration within his organization. But because he is one of the company's most senior managers, he plans to retire in the middle of the fiscal year.

From the start, Mr. Li has been an almost imposingly energetic nego-tiator, with an abiding dedication to the professional image projected by his department. His personal life has been closely tied to his professional life; his wife is another highly ranked and senior individual in the company, a process designer who intends to retire along with him. Overwhelmed with the responsibilities of their work, the two have found themselves unable to take much vacation time in recent years and are looking forward to the leisure time their retirement will afford. In particular, they long to see the Three Gorges together – a famous tourist destination on the upstream of the Yangtze River, coincidentally quite near to Z's headquarters.

Mr. Zhang's personal rapport with Mr. Li is strong. Still, although Mr. Li has expressed a polite willingness to consider a switch to white bottles, he has given no indication that he is interested in doing so, making any changes to their current supply relationship. In response, and in the hopes of swaying him, Mr. Zhang has several times invited Mr. Li and his wife to come upstream to tour Z's newly renovated facilities, and, while in the area, to take some time to explore the Three Gorges. He has even offered to cover the costs of such a trip, with all the amenities. But S has a very stringent ethics code, which prohibits its staff from accepting any gifts or "goodwill gestures" from potential or current business partners. Strict discipline will be applied in the case of any infringements. Obviously, neither Mr. Li nor his wife intend to blemish their faultless records of professional service so near to retirement, lest such a blemish negatively impact their pensions and retirement benefits. So Mr. Zhang's offers are flatly (but graciously) refused.

But – as Mr. Zhang has discovered – the pharmaceutical company has other internal regulations as well, and not all of them are so restrictive. For example, in the interest of professional development, and improving the company's visibility and prestige on the national stage, S encourages its employees to participate in certain outside-the-workplace activities, such as academic conferences on issues related to the attending employee's field. With this in mind, Mr. Zhang approaches his company's marketing department with a new proposal. The proposal is evaluated for cost-effectiveness and quickly approved.

One month later, a small-scale technology conference, sponsored by Z, is held at a resort near the Three Gorges. Its focus is on the relationship between quality control and process technology in the production of white glass bottles for medicine. Several speakers – some associated with Z, some independent researchers – make presentations. Among the speakers are both Mrs. Li and Mr. Li. The former has been invited to make a featured presentation entitled *Issues in the bottling process related to the quality of the bottles being used.* Mr. Li presents some well-received opening remarks on the effects that the quality and stability of bottles can have on medicine production. The conference is well attended, and once over, there is universal agreement among attendees that many interesting and productive ideas were presented.

With the conference at an end, the participants are invited on a tour of the Three Gorges. Mr. Li and Mrs. Li seem particularly delighted by this. But neither of them is quite so delighted as Mr. Zhang. For, upon returning to work the following week, Mr. Li recommends to his superiors that *S* make the change to white bottles. He offers as justification some of the ideas put forth by presenters at the conference. Heeding their senior manager's recommendations, the boardroom gives Mr. Li the go-ahead to sign a long-term supply contract. Mr. Li does so, as a last professional act just before he and his wife embark happily upon their retirement.

Let's examine more closely how Mr. Zhang achieved this unqualified success. As we have noted throughout this chapter, a successful sales relationship is one in which the purchaser's values are effectively and comprehensively integrated into the final offer. Which of Mr. Li's values did Mr. Zhang accurately detect and successfully integrate into his final offer? Recalling our earlier equation, we will explore the exchange in terms of VOC, buying points, and selling points and customer-satisfying deliverability.

## Views on Criteria

In Chapter 7, we will discuss some of the resources that might have been available to Mr. Zhang to enable him to gain insight into Mr. Li's VOC and into the internal regulations of his company. In the meantime, here are Mr. Li's relevant VOC for this exchange relationship, expressed in terms of selecting points and the according selecting rationale:

| Selecting point | Selecting rationale |
| --- | --- |
| 1. Product quality | Required, because safe and effective liquid medicine production requires high-quality bottles |
| 2. Supply stability | Required, because stable medicine production requires reliable and consistent access to bottles |
| 3. Competitive price | Required, to keep costs low and medicine prices competitive |
| 4. Anything else that helps to strengthen a sense of professionalism | Reflects well on Mr. Li, his department, and his company |

## Buying Points and Selling Points

As we recall from the Chapter 5, buying points and selling points arise from the purchaser's VOC and represent, respectively, benefits perceived in the sales offer for the purchaser's life as an individual entity and benefits perceived in the sales offer for the purchaser's life as a social entity. As well, it is important to remember that buying points – personal benefits – can be either apparent or hidden.

So, what was in this integrated product for Mr. Li?

| Buying points (Personal benefits) | 1. Apparent buying points<br>– Demonstration of professionalism (obtaining for the company a good quality product, with a stable supply, at a competitive price.)<br>2. Hidden buying points<br>– The opportunity to tour the Three Gorges with wife<br>– Strengthening the interpersonal relationships (conference) |
|---|---|
| Selling points (Purchaser's justification for his buying behavior in the views of significant others) | – Good quality, to ensure production safety<br>– Supply stability, to ensure reliable production<br>– Competitive and feasible price – required in order to ensure the boardroom will approve the expenditure<br>– The promotion of professional development and research (by means of the conference) |

## Deliverability

At the start of the exchange relationship, the impasse in negotiations perceived by Mr. Zhang seemed to stem less from any problems related to customer-satisfying deliverability than from Mr. Li's sense of need not according with the product being offered. Still, it is significant to note that, to Mr. Li, the primary buying point at that juncture – a tour of the Three Gorges – seemed undeliverable, being prohibited by company regulations. That sense of undeliverability precluded Mr. Li taking an active interest in negotiations. But as the exchange relationship evolved, the scope of the integrated product expanded; more and more buying points and selling points emerged, and their deliverability became more and more a significant factor. By the time the contract was signed, deliverability assurance had been provided mostly by two means: the first was the impressively professional atmosphere of the conference, and the persuasiveness of the ideas presented there; the second was Mr. Li's feeling of trust in Mr. Zhang as a negotiator and in Z as a company. This trust stemmed partly from

Mr. Li's long-term business relations with Mr. Zhang and with Z, but was doubtless strongly reinforced by the experience of the conference as well. And the conference also engendered a way to ensure direct and ethical delivery of the initial hidden buying point, a tour of the Three Gorges for Mr. Li and Mrs. Li.

## FINAL NOTES ON VALUE INTEGRATION

In the above example, and throughout the last few chapters, we have noted the incredible diversity of "value elements" – classes of buying points and selling points – that can be leveraged to come up with a successful integration of the product (in the X-Be sense). In consumer marketing, for example, different brands have been created to satisfy different personalities of different consumers; the easy access and availability of many consumer goods through different channels and outlets has provided a level of convenience that is valued by many customers; in some service industries, the promptness of the service provided has given consumers a great deal of spare time for them to spend on something else; in some developing countries, the promise of a high ROI on various educational products, especially those targeting children, have driven parents mad in their spending on education.

Similarly, in industrial marketing, there are so many elements that can be as valuable for a successful integration of the product to be exchanged. In the list below, we propose a classification of these elements into five major categories:

1. The sales organization's general profile: size, R&D capabilities, investors, location, public image, position in the industry, financial status, business scope, and client base (demographics, distribution, etc.).
2. The sales organization's support infrastructure: sales support and management, manufacturing, logistics, after-sale service, training, insurance, warranties, product-specific R&D, and updates/upgrades.
3. Available and applied human resources: the various relevant key professionals – their passion, cooperation, experience, and past success.
4. The product itself: its performance, price, functionality, efficiency, quality, durability, operation, technological currency, security, reliability, and eco-friendliness.
5. Any other factors that could be valued by the customer.

And it is up to the seller to select the most appropriate combination of these value elements and include them in the design of the integrated product. Ultimately, the aim of any act of integration is to foster confidence in the customer that the considered sales offer does include the wanted value with a satisfying deliverability. A set of integrated features, services, and any other factors could become part of customer value, in a purchase situation, only when the key persons and COLs perceive them to serve their personal (buying points) and social (selling points) objectives with some certainty, that is, with a satisfying deliverability. In this respect, it is important to note that a number of different key persons and core pinion leaders, in the same organizational purchase process, may hold significantly differing values, stemming from their differing areas of specialty and positions within the company. They will be attracted to different types of buying points and selling points as they tend to be rewarded differently within the company, and their VOC will reflect the nature of the sector in which they work.

Once the appropriate buying points and selling points have been identified, the sellers must focus on the deliverability question to ensure a successful integration of customer value. Deliverability is directly connected to the business philosophy of customer satisfaction and brings a great deal of long-term benefits to the sellers and the sales organizations. Selling is not merely getting orders, but cultivating and maintaining sustainable business relationships. If a seller under-delivers the promised customer value, the customer will be dissatisfied; if she delivers her promise, customer will be satisfied, and if she delivers a little bit more than what customer had expected, the customer will be delighted.

One way to help a seller ensure the deliverability upon the buying points and selling points is to specifically identify these points. The more specific they are, the clearer the seller will be about what to deliver. But sellers must be careful not to become overweening; the quest to successfully integrate customer value into the sales offer with impressive features suiting the customer needs must always be within the realm of possibility, and all promises must be honored. For these reasons, it is crucial that the sellers keep in mind the following two fundamental principles for carrying out a successful integration:

1. Specificity: The buying points and selling points being integrated must be specific and individual to the values of the key person (i.e., they must accord with the key person's VOC and phase of the purchase process).
2. Deliverability: Promises will not do. All buying points and selling points promised in the sales offer must be delivered exactly as promised, at the level and time promised.

For the seller to specifically identify the buying points and selling points, and understand the level of deliverability expected by the customer, she should get actively involved in the process of value formation and exchange on the part of customer, through interactive communications aiming for mutually satisfactory exchanges. These interactions can take various forms including highly pro-active one to one personal involvement, involvement via other non-personal means, or combination of both. However, the essence of any selling process of any kind remains unchanged: integrate the deliverables in terms of customer value into sales offers. What tends to differ from customer to customer is the nature of these deliverables and the way they should be integrated, which requires the involvement of a salesperson whose job is to produce the finished integrated product on the basis of actionable customer knowledge in terms of the VOC, buying points, selling points, and required deliverability. This is why we introduce the SALES – the Simple Algebraic Language to Engineer Satisfaction of both parties (buyer and seller), which can be used to effectively "calculate" what customer value exists in a sales offer.

# 7

# APPROPRIATE COMMUNICATORS AND NETWORKED RESOURCES: FACILITATORS OF VALUE FORMATION AND EXCHANGE

In the previous chapters, we focused the discussion on a particular exchange process and the X-Be building blocks that are used to approach such a process. But, before the salesperson gets to work on a specific process, she has to deploy a great deal of effort to know the industry and business community in which her company operates, collect relevant customer information, and find leads and qualify them. To do all of this, she will have to interact with many people and get involved in myriad sales events and activities. This chapter introduces the sixth building block of the X-Be framework that helps dealing with these issues: the appropriate communicator and networked resources.

In the next section, we discuss the salespeople's roles in their organizations. In the Section "*WHY WE COMMUNICATE*," we describe a case that motivates the need for third parties in effective customer communication. In the Section "*THE APPROPRIATE COMMUNICATOR*", we present the concept of appropriate communicator, and then in the remaining sections, we discuss the notion of networked resources and how to manage them.

## SALESPEOPLE AND THEIR ROLES

Because of the nature of their job, salespeople have to be involved in many activities. They have to find leads, qualify leads into potential customers, plan sales calls, communicate and interact with potential customers, close deals, and ensure that a better after-sales service is provided. To do all this in an effective manner, salespeople need a great deal of actionable information to guide them in their activities. Without such information, they would end up just speculating, which is never a good approach to success. It does not matter what type of media (Internet, e-mails, teleconferences, face-to-face, etc.) salespeople would use to communicate with their customers and with the wider community in which they operate, but they need to be able to collect quality customer information to help them direct their efforts and participate effectively and efficiently in the process of value formation and exchange on the part of the customers they want to pursue.

While some customer information such as company's background, industry type, past purchasing behavior, or financial records might be obtained in a relatively easy manner, the most critical customer information for the success of the seller's work and for effective sales management is certainly not easily available. This critical customer information often includes aspects such as who the key persons and COLs are, what the current stage of the purchasing process is (for the company as a whole and for the individuals), what the VOC, buying points and selling points are, and what the expected deliverability upon the last two is.

Obtaining such critical information is a major challenge that salespeople face on a regular basis, and can handle effectively if they have enough knowledge about how to bridge the social gaps facing themselves with an appropriately netted social web for continuous sales. The increasingly complex nature of our modern economies leaves us with no other option except to develop an effective and integrated sales communication system that is constantly supported by an integrated sales organization.

And yet, many salespeople remain obsessed with the idea of being the sole "author" of their successful sales and of managing on the basis of only their own knowledge, charisma, and sales skills to close deals. While personal sales skills are necessary for any salesperson, relying solely on them for selling in modern economies may not lead to success all the time. Time and again, many salespeople who adopted the "lone-wolf" attitude and thought would be successful with just their own skills did not manage to convince their customers to respond to their enthusiasm. The reason behind this is very simple: the salesperson is not the "right person for the job," all the time. She is not always the expert-polymath who can answer all of the customer's questions, dispel all his doubts, and convincingly articulate all the business rationales – this is especially true in the case of the sales of complex industrial products (e.g., costly production systems, business services and strategic solutions). Thus, the way we view the role of a salesperson in an organization has to change.

In the X-Be framework, salespeople are called upon to act as coordinators, directors, and managers for an integrated customer communication – but never sole, autonomous actors: in addition to their own communication with customers, they need to give structure to sales, get the right people involved in the customer communication whenever there is a need for that, take lead to position themselves and thus their company on the social webs of potential customers, collect, use and manage the use of relevant customer information, particularly the critical one, to win sales. By doing so, the salespeople transform their companies into integrated sales organizations that promote concerted efforts on the part of all departments.

## WHY WE COMMUNICATE

When people get together, forming relationships and exchanging information, it is reasonable to assume that they are doing so because they perceive the potential for gaining something of value from those relationships. The corpus of sociological research attests to this (e.g., Blau, 1964) – as do a number of everyday examples: marriage, student – teacher relationship, friendship, and so on. In any case, the impulse toward communication – the active or passive exchange of information and values – almost always seems to stem from the desire to exert some sort of control over the direction of these relationships, so as to ensure the greatest dividends for the individual communicator. These dividends can be intrinsic to the relationship (security, pleasure, happiness, etc.) or they can be extrinsic (economic gain, recognition, power, etc.). Regardless, the act of forming relationships can generally be understood in terms of the pursuit of benefits – that is to say, the unflagging human pursuit of that which is perceived as being of value.

Naturally, this applies to exchange relationships as well. In these relationships, the seller is directly concerned with delivering value to the customer; but in order for this to happen, the customer must first feel that the seller has something of value to offer. And in order for the customer to feel this way – especially in complex or organizational sales – a stable and conducive communications relationship must first be in place. Establishing one is thus the seller's necessary initial goal. Let's consider a typical case involving a business-to-business sale – this one excerpted from our working files, except the real names of the people involved.

> Relationship selling has been a popular topic for years, but its extraordinary value may be heart-felt more dearly in a society where people appreciate interdependence than otherwise. In Chinese culture, for example, virtually every salesperson has rich mundane experiences or different versions of Guanxi stories to tell, even though he or she may

not understand why various relationships work in society as a sociology scholar and how to systematically build and sustain a rewarding social web for continuous success like some PR pros. Chao is just such a kind of salesperson who has prospered with relationship value in China.

Chao started his business career as a salesman at a small private valve company in Wenzhou of Zhejiang Province. He now owns and manages a successful business in Shanghai, the biggest and fast-growing economic engine in Asia. Currently his company employs more than 200 people, manufacturing and selling different valves for industrial and civil use. Even today, he is still often involved personally in many sales situations to cope with ever-intensifying competition.

Back in 1995, Shell, a renowned global petroleum company, was building a sea-fed oil depot in Tianjin, one of the most important harbor cities in North China. The project was jointly owned and financed by Shell and its two local partners, one of which is CAOSC, the Chinese monopoly engaged in the national jet fuel distribution service business at virtually every airport across the country. The project itself was strategically important to Shell not only because it marked its "real" reentry to China in a business sense at that time, but it was then believed to help lock it into the future jet fuel supply business for Beijing International Airport, which is now one of the busiest airports in the world. Shell took this project seriously and sent its dedicated team for the on-site project management. Eventually a subsidiary of Zhongjian (hereafter Zhongjian), a local construction company won the tender as a wholly responsible project contractor on the condition that Chiyoda, a Japanese company, must be employed as a consultant to supervise the work of TJCI, an inevitable local design institute with which Zhongjian had partnered to bit for this project.

Like many oil projects, various valves are needful, which was why Chao appeared in this case. Representing ZJV, a local small valve manufacturer, he noticed, at the beginning, that he could not even stand a chance to get an appointment to meet any decision maker involved in this project from the various parties, Zhongjian, TJCI, Shell, or Chiyoda. Unlike those sales reps selling the products of big names such as General Valve and Orbit Valve, Chao just could not find a single door opening to his company. Just nobody wanted to see him at all in the first place – this, unfortunately, happens times and again to so many salespeople (novices or veterans) today, especially when they are facing new customers, working in SMCs (small or medium companies) or selling hardly-recognized brands. Such a hard life is not unique to Chinese salespeople but an unavoidable nightmare everywhere in the world, as stated in a published case, "the worst part about being a salesperson is feeling like a big fat nobody. You make calls, you send e-mails, but no one answers." (Melanie Warner, 2001).

Chao managed to survive his initial difficult time and eventually won the deadly wanted business from this Shell's project, and the deal also helped elevate his company's profile – ZJV has become a valve supplier for Shell's project in China. What magic did he conjure up on the winning path?

After many unsuccessful attempts, he engaged with Mr. Hu, a man he knew a long time ago. Mr. Hu was working as a liaison for the public affairs of North China on behalf of the local government of Zhejiang Province, where Chao was born and grew up. Mr. Hu had a friend, Mr. Wang, who was working in TJCI (the local design institute) as a design engineer for the Shell's project. Because of this, Chao was introduced to Mr. Wang. Chao's meeting with Mr. Wang opened up the door for another meeting with Mr. Jiang, the project manager of Zhongjian (the main contractor). And coordinated by Mr. Jiang, Chao was able to meet the core opinion leaders, two expatriates engaged by Shell from Singapore to manage the project construction. During various meetings with these key persons, Chao demonstrated not only the unique value of his products and services for their project, but impressed everyone with his understanding of their businesses, his honesty in answering tough questions, and his ability to provide prompt feedbacks from his company. With these diligent efforts, Chao was finally awarded the valve supply contract after the key persons' inspection tour of his company, which was also well organized and accompanied by Chao personally.

Chao's efforts paid off immensely well beyond this particular contract. Not very long later, he was contacted by Mr. Zhang, the deputy project manager from CAOSC in this project, for many other valve businesses in its various storage tank projects at different airports.

One might read this case as yet another exciting story and go for a superficial understanding. For instance, he may congratulate Chao for his individual achievement and might be impressed by Chao's "thick skin" spirit and his own sales skills demonstrated during the meetings with various key persons, which included the ability to understand the needs of the different parties involved, to demonstrate the unique value of his products and services, to respond to the requested feedbacks, and to organize the customer's inspection trip.

But such a superficial reading of this case adds very little to our sales knowledge. All that we seem to conclude from it is that sales skills (attitude, tenacity, perseverance, professionalism, probing, presenting, etc.) are what a salesperson needs, and that Chao's case is another interesting story that illustrates this fact. As we all know, the sales literature is abundant with cases and stories like this one, and the analyses like the above reading have hardly helped the sales community. As a result, many salespeople still blindly try to make use of anything they can think of to attract the attention of the target KPs, especially those at the high levels of the hierarchies. By doing so, they tend to waste a lot of their valuable time and efforts (telephone, Internet, socializing, etc.) and leave little resources for the actual work of selling.

One moral of this story, which many sellers often tend to overlook, is this: selling can often be pretty exhausting for customers too! So inundated are they with the clamor of sellers demanding communication (ringing phones, crowded in-boxes, and a teeming office) that their attention is often scarce, not to mention capricious. For with potential sellers constantly tapping at their shoulders, they are well within their rights to reject any given seller's request for communication!

But there is something in the above case that is even more fundamental to selling and sales management. Let us point out. The initial technique failed for Chao, but note how, in this example, he then seized upon the network of communications resources that were available to him: first, he contacted his "liaoxiang" (fellow-townsman), a trusted person by the *TJCI* design engineer who had proven connections to the contractor company; that engineer's connections were necessarily in a better position to be in touch with another key person, the contractor's project manager who acted as a *communication facilitator* to help with the needed communications with Shell's expatriates from Singapore. The result was a series of meetings with various key persons and core opinion leaders seconded from various parties involved in this sea-fed oil depot project.

Clearly, there is a communication network in this case. The willingness of other individuals to communicate with Chao has helped him build the communication relationships that have led to the success. So an adequate interpretation of what has caused the required communications to flow in this case might be like this: the initial communication facilitator (the fellow-townsman, Mr. Hu) perceived something of value that motivated him to introduce Chao to Mr. Wang (the design engineer from the local design institute), and Mr. Wang perceived something of value to introduce him to Mr. Jiang (the project manager from the main contractor), and Mr. Jiang perceived something of value to coordinate Chao's communications with Shell's expatriates, and Shell's project team perceived something of value to offer Chao communication opportunities.

So a major success factor in the field of selling, especially in today's highly competitive environment, is to establish the communication relationships with individual customers based on the existence of some-thing of value that will motivate them to authorize the seller to interact with them. This is even more true in the case of organizational sales. Indeed, many organizational businesses are developed and maintained mostly by those salespeople who are good at building and managing appropriate communication relationships. Within the scope of these salespeople's relationships, there are often some other people who, at times, may be even more helpful (than the salespeople themselves) in the process of customer relationships development and management. Thus, a very important part of salespeople's work is to develop, coordinate, and manage various communication relationships that can supply them with people who would be helpful when they are needed. So, it is essential to think about who else – other than just the salespeople – could act as *appropriate communicators* in the eyes of customers.

## THE APPROPRIATE COMMUNICATOR

Often, as was the case our example of Chao, above, a third party may be called upon – a third party armed with the particular expertise or trust or anything valuable to the key persons – to advocate persuasively for the value of the communications requested by the salesperson. This third party may emerge from within the sales organization; in B-to-B sales, for example, he or she may be an engineer, a sales manager, logistics engineer, quality controller, or a financial advisor, while in B-to-C sales, he or she could be a satisfied consumer, an after-sales service person or one of those people who are well connected to both potential buyers and the seller. But the individual in question may also come from elsewhere, being a particularly skilled unaffiliated person, or a supporter from the purchasing organization, or an enthusiastic grandma in the community of consumers. Regardless, this person's role is to act as an effective facilitator for certain sales communications, to move along the purchasing process and the process of value formation and exchange. In some cases, he or she may also be called upon to create occasions for communication when communication relationships between the seller and the buyer cannot be built directly by salespeople. In the X-Be framework, this person is termed an appropriate communicator.

An appropriate communicator could be selected on the basis of var-ious aspects such as the nature of communication at hand (technical or commercial in terms of required expertise) and the interpersonal attraction factors (proximity, familiarity, similarity, or personality). In what follows, we suggest issues to consider in identifying an appropriate communicator:

## Sensitivity to the Purchaser's Values

The essence of selling is about integrating the customer value into a sales offer. Open and effective communication relationships may take place if the key persons feel that someone is sensitive to their values. For the appropriate communicator, this entails an intimate knowledge of those aspects of the sales offer in question that the key person might value according to his VOC, including the relevant buying points, selling points, and expected deliverability that distinguish an integrated product. In many cases, salespeople do have good knowledge about the integrated product, so they can effectively play the role of appropriate communicator, but in some other cases, someone else may have a better position to know what a customer desires; this person can be an appropriate communicator if salespeople could engage her in the communication relationship with the customer. It should be pointed out that the appropriate communicator might even be in a position to help salespeople engineer an integrated product when they have been unable to do so. She accomplishes this with particular intimacy to the customer's VOC, the buying points (sometimes the hidden ones), the selling points or a keen understanding of the capacities and limits of the sales organization.

## Relationship to the Key Person

A key person may have his own social circles to which salespeople are not related, and it is not realistic for salespeople to be directly related to any (potential) key person before their selling. However, if salespeople could have a relayed association with the key person by someone they know, then this intermediary may help them build up the required communication relationships with this key person. These intermediaries could play the role of appropriate communicator, and, in some cases, they go even further to help broker deals in our commercial world, especially in cultures that favor interdependence among people. In many industries, the personal touch can be particularly needful, inasmuch as it can distinguish one integrated sales organization from the competition. The valuable advice here is that salespeople should develop and manage social networks that incorporate those people who could help broaden their future business horizons and enhance their existing relationships effectively and efficiently. How these social networks should look like and how to measure their effectiveness will be discussed later in this chapter.

## Expertise in the Field Related to the Communications Impasse

People often tend to the opinions of various experts and, in many cases, believe in them. This tendency seems to be increasingly common as life is getting busier and labor market is getting more segmented. Expertise in the field at hand also plays a significant role in industrial purchases. Although all salespeople should be expected to have a certain working grasp of the knowledge that underpins their work, sales staff in B-to-B industries are not necessarily engineers – nor are they technicians, researchers, or designers. And there will necessarily be questions they cannot answer – and too, questions to which they may have answers, but only in a narrow, incomplete way that would convince few and satisfy fewer. Too, whereas salespeople are often instructed to make use of the jargon of the marketing department people (who are, generally, not technology expert either), they often have a rather tenuous understanding of the technical aspects of their company's products and highlighting extraordinary features in hi-tech terms could be a challenge. This would also be largely unconvincing to the key persons who are on the technical side of the customer's organization. For instance, a customer's chief engineer would likely be far more comfortable having his technical concerns assuaged by a person who contributed to that aspect of the product's development. People trust experts – especially charismatic ones. This applies to many industries; antiques and collectables, for example, are far more convincingly appraised by specialists than by non-specialized dealers. Regardless, sales organizations that ignore their experts and leave selling to salespeople alone imperil their ability to handle complex or specialized transactions. Such transactions often call for appropriate communicators with sufficient expertise in the fields dealt with in sales communication relationships, which are usually developed and managed by salespeople.

## Status

People are inclined to communicate with those whose status is similar to or above theirs. This often causes difficulties for salespeople to reach the "nerve center" of the purchasing organization, as, in many cases, the buying decisions are much dependent upon the communication relationships with those key persons whose status or authority is well above that of the salesperson. Because of this, some companies have practiced the so-called Like-rank Call policy which helps their salespeople to engage their managers with appropriate status or authority in developing the required communication relationships at various levels of a customer company.

This customer communication policy can be implemented in a much better way if it were to be applied by salespeople using the more general notion of appropriate communicator in a given sales process. Unfortunately, however, many salespeople seem to be either too shy about getting their management to help with their sales communications or they simply do not know how to make their management act as an appropriate communicator in their sales processes. But, to be fair, this cannot be blamed on the salespeople, but on their management who often forget that their careers are dependent on the performance of their sales force. The fact of the matter is that, in most companies, there are only two kinds of people whose incomes are mostly commission based: salespeople and top management – so, in this sense, the performance of salespeople should be the priority of the company's executive.

There may be some other parameters that sellers could use to identify and select their appropriate communicators. But, in any case, sellers should not overlook the important roles that these communicators can play in the process of communication and interaction with customers. In modern economies, indeed, selling has become increasingly complex, and sellers are often faced with highly intricate social webs on which individual customers net so many different (business and other) aspects that are of value to them.

## NETWORKED RESOURCES

In the previous section, we described situations in which third parties, which we term appropriate communicators, can be called upon to help with the effective communication and interaction in a particular exchange relationship. From this section on, we will be turning our attention to the "big picture," namely, how a seller can improve her chances of success in all her sales endeavors, across all sales processes, by developing social networks (referred to as *Networked Resources* in the X-Be framework) that ensure consistent access to appropriate communicators and quality customer information.

Scholars from various fields may differ over the precise meaning of the word, but no one doubts the centrality of relationships to our day-to-day lives. As human beings, we are, fundamentally and critically, dependent upon one another. Indeed, it can reasonably be said that our lives essentially consist of the formation and maintenance of relationships with one another. Earlier in this chapter, we attempted to provide a basic account of why and how relationships form by describing the process in terms of the perception and exchange of value; this provides an effective transition into the world of selling.

Whether we are operating in an economy that values individualism (as in the United States or Western Europe), or one that values collectivism (as in China and other Asian countries), where a particular word, *Guanxi*, exists to describe the notion of relationship in a much more comprehensive way), we are reliant on our relationships with others to survive and prosper. In the last few decades, researchers have become increasingly aware of this, and the result has been a deluge of material attempting to investigate the issue. This is why concepts such as "Relationship Marketing," "Relationship Selling," and "Customer Relationships Management" have become very popular in the field of sales and marketing.

The X-Be framework leverages the notion of relationship in a way that is different than the approaches built on these concepts. Throughout their careers, salespeople develop networks of contacts that they use at various occasions. Some of these contacts will be best at obtaining customer information and identifying leads; others will be more useful in the critical task of facilitating effective communication and interaction with the customer in various stages of the purchasing process. The X-Be framework terms the totality of a salesperson's useful relationships as her networked resources. The networked resources are highly important to the salesperson's job herself as well as to her managers and organization. Indeed, as it is the case in many fields like sales, *"knowing whom is as important as knowing how"*.

A few important questions arise now with regard the concept of networked resources; they are as follows:

1. What should be the size (that is number of contacts) of a salesperson's networked resources, and how should this size be managed?
2. How can we assess the effectiveness and efficiency of a salesperson's networked resources?
3. What should be the structure of a salesperson's networked resources?
4. Who should be in a salesperson's networked resources?

These questions are addressed in the next section.

## NETWORKED RESOURCES MANAGEMENT

### Size of the Networked Resources and Sales Performance (Questions 1 and 2)

Many salespeople tend to think that the more contacts they have in their networked resources, the better it is for their sales job. But, this belief is true only to a very limited extent. The relationship between the size of a

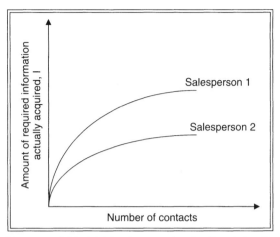

**FIGURE 7.I**   The Law of Diminishing Returns for the Correlation Between I and the Number of Contacts in a Salesperson's Networked Resources.

salesperson's networked resources and the usefulness of these resources is not of a proportional nature. In the X-Be framework, we propose to measure the usefulness of the networked resources by the "*amount* I *of required information that was actually acquired when it was needed*" and the size of networked resources by the number of contacts. It has been our experience that the correlation between I and the number of contacts follows a law of diminishing returns, as illustrated in the Figure 7.1. At what might be called the "point of saturation," the information, insights and aid provided by various networked resources will begin to either overlap, or decrease as the quality of relationships cannot be maintained due to the increase of the contacts, and, therefore, the rate of increase of I tends to decline. In addition, the shape of the correlation between I and the number of contacts differ from salesperson to salesperson, as has also been illustrated in the Figure 7.1. Some salespeople would reach the saturation point for I at a higher level, while others may not exceed a certain threshold and, therefore, their networked resources will not be as effective. Thus, to assess the effectiveness and efficiency of a salesperson's networked resources, it suffices to monitor, over a long enough period of time, her number of contacts, the amount of information acquired when it is needed (to assess effectiveness), and the amount of time it takes to obtain this information (to assess efficiency).

## Structure of the Networked Resources (Question 3)

The discussion in the above subsection focused on just one characteristic of a salesperson's networked resources: the number of contacts. But, how about the structure of these resources? There are two parameters that a salesperson should take into account to structure her networked resources:

1. The business nature of the industry in which the salesperson operates in terms of the total number of potential customers.
2. Typical buying behavior of the customers in terms of their involvement in the purchasing process.

Let us discuss both of these parameters.

*The business nature of the industry*: In highly consolidated industries, such as the OEM sales of automobile parts, aircraft, communication systems, medical equipment, and so on, the number of potential customers tends to be limited, and qualifying leads will generally be not so difficult especially for those dedicated account reps. In such industries, the account reps should be concerned with selecting the right density for her contacts in the industry in which she operates. Networked resources with a density that is close to 1 would mean that the salesperson knows almost everyone in the industry, which would of course be very costly to maintain. But, with a too low density, the salesperson would not have enough contacts to do her job effectively. The members who make up the salesperson's networked resources should of course be drawn from the right pools of people who are active in the industry (see subsection below), and the salesperson will have to plan for frequent contacts (meetings, visits, phone calls, etc.) with these members. Because of the consolidated nature of the industry, the key for success is often not about having a large pool of contacts for prospecting, but rather a limited number of well networked influential people. Such a type of networked resources is much more productive for the seller to get the needed critical customer information on the target accounts, procure solid referrals and supports, coordinate various in-depth customer communications, and manage the use of corporate human resources to generate the customerized integrated products that are required for the targeted sales.

If, on the other hand, the salesperson operates in industries that are less consolidated, such as insurance, consulting, housing, and so on, she faces a large number of potential customers, and she may have to spend a great deal of time to find and qualify leads. Because of this, the structure of the required networked resources in this case will be substantially different. Indeed, the salesperson should be concerned with selecting the right *distribution* of her contacts across the industry in which she operates. Like the previous case, the members who make up the salesperson's networked resources should also be drawn from the right pools of people who are active in the industry (see subsection below); but, because the number of these members will likely to be large, they will be contacted less frequently than the previous case.

*Typical buying behavior of the customers:* In the sales situations of extended purchase involvement of customers, the salesperson should focus on selecting the right density for her networked resources which will be composed of highly frequently contacted members. But, in the sales situations of low or limited purchase involvement of customers, the focus will, on the other hand, be on the wide distribution of the networked resources, the members of which will be less frequently contacted on one-to-one basis. However, the seller could still improve the connectedness and effectiveness of the dispersed networked resources normally required for the sales in the situation of low or limited purchase involvement. This is based on such an observation: it seems that the seller's networked resources consisting of the contacts knowing each other tends to be more effective for closing the sales; while those of the contacts not knowing each other help more in identifying more potential customers (better prospecting). So it may be advisable for the seller to help the members of her networked resources to know each other in certain clusters by certain kinds of 'community-joining efforts'. Such efforts, for instance, can be some organized corporate events, managed internet forum or any proper social activities that are of value to different clusters of the dispersed contacts. Doing so will help the seller to increase the connectedness and effectiveness of her networked resources. Salespeople can do better to cover even larger market. They could carefully select a small number of influential members from the widely dispersed networked resources, and entertain these selected with honored regular programs (program involvement) to increase their product involvement, thus make them the better-qualified core opinion leaders in the purchasing behavior of those they can influence effectively.

## The People in the Networked Resources (Question 4)

There are, in essence, two distinct "pools" of people from which **networked resources** can and should be drawn. The first pool pertains to organizational (specifically industrial or B-to-B) selling; the second, to consumer sales. In organizational selling, with emphasis on the limited number of well connected influential people to effectively manage target accounts, the pool of potential networked resources is more or less as follows:

1. key persons and COLs within potential purchasing organizations;
2. otherwise active people – especially experts (writers, critics, consultants, researchers, etc.) – in the industry;

3. people in the sales organization whose jobs are closely related to either sales;
4. satisfied customers;
5. other individuals who are closely associated with one or more of the above categories.

For consumer sales, the pool is quite different, because the success often depends more on effective prospecting than that in industrial selling:

1. "opinion leaders", in the marketing sense;
2. activists or otherwise highly influential people in the target community;
3. otherwise active people (experts, writers, consultants, critics, researchers, etc.) in the community/industry;
4. satisfied customers;
5. other individuals who are closely associated with any of the above categories.

The lists we have provided here are by no means exhaustive or especially detailed, but they are a start.

## MORE ON NETWORKED RESOURCES MANAGEMENT

In addition to the principles discussed above, here are some more advices that salespeople could find helpful for the management of their networked resources.

1. The salesperson should classify the members of her networked resources by their respective influential powers ("influential power" was previously defined in Chapter 3). As discussed previously in this book, the influential power of a person is determined by "something" that this person possesses and that is valued by other people; this "something" refers here to the customer information you value for your sales job. The salesperson should plan her contacts and meetings with these members using the 80/20 principle or other appropriate classification methods. It should be noted that this planning is not specific to a certain sales process or sales opportunity, but concerns those casual contacts that should take place on an

on-going basis to maintain an excellent communication relationship with the members. Of course, if it is possible to align the contacts for specific sales goals with the casual ones, it is even better. In reality, however, it is often the case that salespeople need to initiate contacts with other people much earlier than they could enter something specific such as a possible sales opportunity or a sales process. This is particularly true in societies where personal relationships are critical for success. For instance, the business practices in Asian countries, where the Chinese culture of "Guanxi" ("Guanxi," a Chinese word, refers to a set of complex sociologic and interpersonal values entangled with business intercourses) is predominant, are very different from those in western societies. It should be noted indeed that many good businesses had unfortunately failed in Asian regions mostly because of the culture of "Guanxi."

2. The salesperson should integrate the appropriate messages into each and every contact or sales event that she plans. Messages can be classified into three different categories: those for social intercourse (e.g., greetings for birthday, New Year, and Christmas); those for business communication (e.g., regular mail-outs of customer information, product information, industrial conference, company seminar information, and corporate events); those that are intended for a specific exchange (e.g., attractive price, promotional try-outs, and new value-added service). It should be noted here that the purpose of conducting social intercourse is to facilitate future business communication.

3. The salesperson should assess the effectiveness and efficiency of her networked resources and the corresponding activities (meetings, phone calls, conferences, etc.) to maintain them on a regular basis. The effectiveness can be measured by the amount of useful customer information that was acquired when it was needed, and the efficiency by how much time was saved in obtaining this information, thanks to the existence of the networked resources. All salespeople and sales management should carry out these assessments to evaluate the performance of the existing networked resources and adjust the planning of their sales events and contacts with customers; by doing so, they will improve the overall quality of individual-based and team-based networked resources and outperform the competitors who may have little knowledge about how to develop and manage effective networked resources for continuous business success.

Below (see Figure 7.2) is a précis that summarizes in the form of questions the main points that have been discussed above regarding salespeople's networked resources:

---

◆ How many important people do you know?
◆ Who is important to your current and future success?
◆ How well do you interact with these important people?
◆ Do you meet them on a regular basis?
◆ How do you do it?
◆ How do you judge the quality of your work?
   – Information received
     » Usefulness: do you often get useful information from your contacts?
     » Timeliness: do you often get it timely?
◆ What approach do you use to manage your networked resources?
     » Ad hoc approach?
     » Systematic approach?

---

**FIGURE 7.2**    Networked Resources for Continuous Success.

## CONCLUSION

The main purpose of this chapter is to highlight the important role of third parties and the invaluable relationship resource that they provide for both the seller and purchaser during the process of customer communication. Other people could indeed be actively involved in facilitating the sales process, besides the seller and the key persons who collectively represent "the purchaser." From a seller's perspective, developing a network of all the relevant and important individuals who could either act as valuable communication facilitators in a given sales process, or simply as resources to share customer information and help finding leads and qualifying them, can greatly improve the performance of the seller and her organization. To capture and conceptualize these notions, we introduced the concepts of appropriate communicator and networked resources, which constitute the sixth building block of the X-Be framework. By implementing the ideas of this building block, salespeople will be able to transform their companies into integrated sales organizations that promote concerted efforts on the part of all departments, run integrated customer communication systems, and deal with the challenges of uncertain and complex customer relationships effectively.

# 8

## SELLING STATUS INDICES: MEASURES FOR MONITORING THE VALUE INTEGRATION PROCESS

In previous chapters, we discussed the various parameters that need to be abided by a salesperson and sales manager in the course of integrated planning and executing sales activities; these centered primarily on communication and interaction with customers. We also introduced the first six basic elements of X-Be as follows:

- A working model of PPP for the phases of the purchase process – a process of value formation and exchange on the customer side.
- A working model of MAP and its components for identifying key persons and their capacity for and demonstration of influential power as it affects value formation and exchange on the part of customer.
- VOC – the value basis by which key persons measure the value of a sales offer.
- Buying points and selling points – specific manifestations of the customer value in a sales offer as purchase behavioral motivators.
- Deliverability and the Integrated Product – the sum and consummation of all the above buying points and selling points combined with customer's consideration of buying risks.
- Appropriate communicators and networked resources – those people who facilitate value formation and exchange in the sales process and advocate on the part of the seller for the virtues of the sales offer, and the social network which connects salespeople and sales organization for continuous businesses.

The principal goal of our reading thus far has been to enable a salesperson and a sales manager to systematize and oversee the process of selling itself, with an emphasis on the purchaser's reward-oriented behavior motivators in terms of customer value, VOC, buying points, selling points and deliverability. This chapter will aid the salesperson and sales manager in evaluating and managing the status of selling as it is in process. As we have pointed out in Chapter 1, a process can only be controlled if its progress can be monitored. And yet the current body of sales knowledge provides no effective means for monitoring the sales process effectively, leaving salespeople with no reliable barometer but their own feelings and intuition based on vague and often bias-prone social cues – "gut instinct" in the end. It is naive to let sales staff believe that effective sales communication is either a talent in certain individuals or a skill that can only be acquired after years of work in the field. Yet, for whatever reason, salespeople and sales managers insist upon striving in the dark without any desire to develop a logical framework – a framework that allows salespeople and management to parse the selling process, and its underlying mechanics. For selling, like every other activity, requires its practitioners to follow through a number of steps from beginning to end.

Certainly, subjective feelings are of some use in so fundamentally interpersonal an activity as a sale, but they remain unreliable, and in many cases confusing, unless some sort of order is imposed upon them. X-Be establishes this order by introducing a set of measures by which the salesperson's ambiguous feelings can be solidified into active engagement and control. These measures, selling status indices, are built upon the customer's reward-oriented behavior; indeed, the first one is related to the discussion of **WHY WE COMMUNICATE** in last chapter, and the other two are based directly on the X-Be concepts of buying points and selling points, discussed earlier in Chapter 5.

Selling status indices provide salespeople and sales management with an effective tool to evaluate the progress of the selling process, to evaluate the probability of closing a deal, and further to evaluate the repeatability of business in an established exchange relationship. They also provide a means of effectively gauging communication and interaction with customers. The indices afford the employer and the employee a set of straightforward criteria by which communication and interaction with a customer – where it is now and where it's going – can be evaluated. While these indices are rooted in theoretical psychology and sociology, they provide practical and working concepts that efficiently translate feelings, thoughts, impressions, and expressions into a unified and meaningful picture of customer-interfacing success, one that indicates what techniques have been successful and which ones should be renovated, even as the sale is in progress.

## THE RELATING STATUS INDEX

The relating status index describes how conducive a salesperson's relationship with a key person is to the sale itself. In our conversations with experienced salespeople and sales management about this issue, the authors have found that many admit that they are unsure of their relationship with their customers and want meaningful and easy-to-use measures by which they might evaluate whether a relationship is working toward a sale or is merely frivolously cordial. For some salespeople seem to have a good "rapport" with their customers, yet they are unable to secure sales and are simply at a loss as to why.

A typical tale related by one salesperson went as such: To facilitate the closing of a deal with an important customer, the salesperson's company managed to win the son of a very influential key person (within the customer's organization) to his side, and the cause of the sale. The salesperson was confident as such that he would succeed, but in the end was surprised to find that he didn't. He could not understand what had happened; his product offered better value than other competitors' products, and as far as customer relationships were concerned, everything seemed promising, with all the benefit of the father – son relationship at hand. So what had gone wrong?

The salesperson's reasoning was flawed, because he misjudged the status of his relationship with the customer, overconfident as he was in but one interpersonal advantage. "Relationship marketing" and "relationship selling" have long been cardinal areas of interest for people studying sales and marketing, but aside from repeatedly emphasizing the importance of this topic, most references actually contain very little substance from which salespeople may learn, and very little direction as to how to make effective use of relationships in general.

To dislodge the vagueness and ineffectiveness associated with relationship selling, X-Be provides salespeople and sales management with a working real-time measure of success potential, termed here the relating status index. The relating status index is defined as a measure of **the amount of useful information** (i.e, information beneficial to the selling process at hand) received from a key person during or after interaction with him or her. As such, not only can the relating status index be easily calculated by any salesperson while communicating and interacting with the key person, but it can also provide an effective measure of his or her current selling relationship with this key person.

### Relating Status Index and Relationships

In the course of daily life, people form and participate in myriad relationships, in private life and in public, at home and at work; they find, invariably, that good relationships facilitate communication, cooperation, edification, and pleasure. These factors in turn help them to enhance exiting relationships and build new ones. Salespeople are no different, having a particularly vested interest in establishing favorable business and private relationships with their customers, present and future. And most people seem to have a fairly good idea of which of their relationships are beneficial and germane, and which are not. But are the subjective social cues truly an effective means of gauging a selling relationship? After all, many salespersons and companies make extensive use of such cues in attuning their sales efforts. But these sellers are often misled. A great many salespeople mistakenly take a considerate or enthusiastic-seeming customer to be one with whom they share a privileged relationship; in many cases, however, they find themselves to be in error, and the sale is lost to someone else.

There are good reasons to define the relating status index as the amount of pertinent information that the salesperson has received from a given key person. The advantages of this definition are as follows:

- It gives rise to a more objective index. Social cues can be elusive and obscure; but a salesperson always knows whether information gleaned from a key person is useful to the sale at hand.
- It can be deployed by any salesperson, skilled or otherwise, easily, involving as it does plainly observable factors to which sales judgment may be anchored.
- It is goal-oriented and is concerned with some of the most important elements of any sale: information that is useful for achieving the goals of the selling process.
- It is directly concerned with the logical goal of most salespeople, namely, the uncovering of undisclosed, scarce, "trade secret," and hard-won facts and opinions from the customer – that interpersonal "Rosetta stone," that secret, the revelation of which just might guarantee a sale.

It should also be noted that the relating status index is conservative. According to the definition of this index, a key person who provides very limited information would be classed as among those with whom the salesperson shares an unfavorable relating status. A salesperson may thus decide that this key person constitutes a detriment to her selling work, but this is may not be the case because key persons providing limited information are often marginal ones and tend to have limited influence on the final buying decision. Through communication with other key persons, and awareness of other aspects of the matter at hand, a salesperson will be able to resolve the issue of whether a key person is truly marginal, or if it is her relating status that is unfavorable.

## Relating Status and Trust

In sales situations where the implications of communication tend to affect both parties in terms of their own respective interests, what might be termed a "communication filter" develops between what the communicator thinks and what he or she says (as per the Figure 8.1). A direct consequence of this filter is that a person's thoughts and expressions of them differ considerably, and in most cases, the amount of deliberation underpinning all his or her actions, gestures, and word choices will be greater than what is immediately evident. There are several reasons why a communication filter may develop; among them is lack of trust.

Trust is another important factor that influences the selling process. An individual's success in selling is predicated upon the degree to which she is trusted by those around her. In fact, if a salesperson cannot win the trust of others, the sale is doomed to failure. Therefore, a trust-level gauge is of the essence in evaluating a sales relationship. But, since the relating status index has been defined as a measure of the amount of useful information a salesperson has gained from a key person, this index

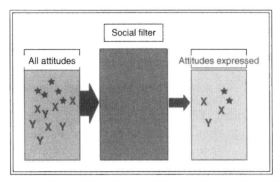

**FIGURE 8.1**    Communicating Filter Between What the Communicator Thinks and What He or She Says.

also reflects whether the key person trusts the salesperson or not. In other words, the notion of trust level is implicitly recorded as a part of the information exchange measured by the relating status index. The more the key person expresses, the more information transcends the "social filter" (which may be organizational or personal), the more the seller is trusted.

## The Relating Status Index and Occasions for Communication

When the relating status index was defined above, we considered the amount of information that the salesperson received from a given key person as if it were a single lump sum. But, as explained earlier, a sale proceeds through several phases – namely, the phases of the purchase process – all of which boast their own predications and environmental customs. The information a key person is able to reveal in a given occasion for communication varies with these phases and with other factors such as the involvement of other key people. Therefore, the responsibility of a salesperson is to find (or perhaps create) the appropriate occasions for communication with the respective key persons and to collect from them whatever useful information particular to a given PPP that might be offered. The occasions for communication are particularly important in some culturally enriched societies (e.g., China) or organizations (e.g., those crowded with managers whose authorities are not clearly defined). If a salesperson cannot find or create such occasions, she may not achieve her objective of gaining useful customer information for sales. Indeed, whether a salesperson is able to find or create an appropriate occasion for communication with a key person bespeaks her entire relating status with this person. The relating status is reflected not merely in the amount and degree of usefulness of the information that has been collected from a key person, but also in the key person's willingness to find himself in situations in which this information may be disclosed.

Occasions for communication will be further elaborated upon later in the chapter. For now, though, we provide four anchor points, as demonstrated by the Figure 8.2, by which a salesperson's relating status with a given key person may be gauged.

Most conducive sales relationships will commence in the PR stage and progress from there. Those which commence in the critical stage are often salvageable but should be considered more challenging than most. Indeed, those factors which placed a customer in the critical stage should be diagnosed; competition is almost certainly involved, or a discrepancy in default values. A customer in the partner stage, by contrast, may make for an effective networked resource for sales in the future.

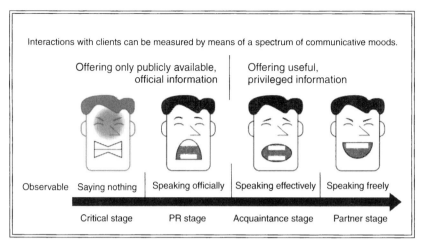

Interactions with clients can be measured by means of a spectrum of communicative moods.

| Offering only publicly available, official information | | Offering useful, privileged information | |
|---|---|---|---|
| Observable  Saying nothing | Speaking officially | Speaking effectively | Speaking freely |
| Critical stage | PR stage | Acquaintance stage | Partner stage |

**FIGURE 8.2**    Four Anchor Points to Gauge Relating Status with a Key Person. PR, Public Relations.

## Relating Status Index and Networked Resources

As explained in previous chapters, the term "networked resources" refers to the sum of all people from whom a salesperson is able to gain information pertinent to the sales for now and for future. We have argued that this is not only an important asset for salespeople, but for sales management as well: any company with an interest in rendering its sales apparatus more efficient and expeditious should develop, maintain, improve, manage, and invest in this important asset. The importance of this concept can also be seen from the perspective of the relating status.

Within industries and even across them, many businesspeople maintain relationships and contacts; invariably, these relationships are intended to lubricate the exchange of information. These relationships also contribute by enhancing business level and cordial understanding of businesspeople among themselves – understanding of particular talents or limitations, and areas of interest and expertise. Also, this networking presumably enhances the individual salesperson's relating status with others who may find themselves some day in the position of key persons in some purchase processes. On the other hand, a favorable reputation, a history of successful sales and satisfied customers will enable a salesperson to build a capital of trust that can be transferred and leveraged to achieve more sales.

A salesperson's relating status with the sales-related people from her own company is also important to her selling work, as some of these people may be helpful in playing the role of the appropriate communicator at different PPP as discussed. For continual success, a salesperson needs a systematic means of effectively managing networked resources as discussed in Chapter 7. With relating status in mind, salespeople and sales organizations should establish sales-positioning priorities, by considering estimated total sales figures and integrating sales-related information contributed by a member of the networked resources. Doing so will uncover where there are gaps in the seller's knowledge and where improvements may be made in her sales approach in specific cases and in the future.

## THE ATTITUDE INDEX

In the field of psychology, the term *attitude* refers to a person's mental and behavioral disposition toward something or someone. There is a great body of research and discussion of this subject in the field, and interested parties can consult any one of the innumerable introductory psychology textbooks available. For our purposes, various attitude indices have been adopted in social studies and market research. But as regards the relationship of attitudes to behaviors, psychologists have found that, though the relationship is not necessarily entirely causal (which is to say, broad, object-nonspecific attitudes do not necessarily give rise to objective and predictable behaviors – as per LaPiere, 1934), there is nonetheless a degree of consistency between attitudes and behaviors, and a causal relationship does begin to emerge as the object of an attitude becomes more specific (Fishbein & Ajzen, 1975).

In Chapter 1, we defined the attitude index in X-Be as a measure of the degree of importance that a key person assigns to each of his or her buying points and how important the purchaser deems these buying points in the grand scheme of things. To calculate this index, we will adopt a scale that consists of three discrete levels of value: *essential* buying point, *desirable* buying point, and *minor* buying point. As will be discussed below, this definition is not only relevant to selling, but is also easy for salespeople to evaluate especially when used in tandem with the relating status index, and the degree of observational attention to each buying point and behavioral cues the key persons involved have paid toward their overall buying points in a sales offer.

### The Attitude Index and Buying Points

As noted in previous chapters, buying points are what arouse and drive a key person to the motion to purchase. When individual key persons have realized that a product or any other element of an integrated product can provide them with personal benefits that are compatible with their individual VOC, their buying points may be considered satisfied. However, key persons have different attitudes toward each of their buying points, and assign to them differing levels of significance and value. How a salesperson might evaluate these discrepancies of value is of central importance. Providing that the salesperson enjoys a good relating status with this key person, the latter will share his views about a given buying point on appropriate occasions: for instance, the key person can express his preference for a certain feature of a sales offer, or point out that those features of the sales offer may yield dividends to his work performance. Such buying points are open ones, for the key person may be willing to express his or her views about them (as long as there is a favorable relating status between the salesperson and this key person). The problem, however, is that there are many situations, especially involving organizational purchases, in which key persons are unwilling to divulge some of the buying points they seek to satisfy, for various reasons (including but not limited to corporate secrecy and the privacy of specific key persons), despite a good rapport with the salesperson. These are referred to as *hidden* buying points, for the key person considers them to be private. The next sections will provide a method to identify the extent to which a key person favors these hidden buying points.

## The Attitude Index and Hidden Buying Points

In organizational purchases, it is often buying points that, for whatever reason, are not divulged, and thus are not satisfied, that are the most common cause of unexpected sales failure. In fact, key persons in corporate settings are probably less likely to personally make use of purchased products or are only responsible for managing people who use them. If these key persons are not clear about what personal benefits they might gain for themselves from making a purchase, then the sale might be lost. Hidden buying points often involve the personal interests and subjective feelings of key persons. The ability to acquire knowledge about them is one crucial talent that distinguishes excellence from mediocrity.

Let us use a real case to elaborate this point.

From the latter half of 2001 to April 2002, one multinational auto-parts company anxious to enter the Chinese motorcycle market experienced some difficulty in getting sales underway, for the following reasons:

- The company was new to the motorcycle market, at least in China.
- Before the company even arrived, there were already five companies selling comparable products in the region for a

considerable amount of time; two of the companies developed products (jointly with their Chinese customers) that were available in the Chinese marketplace, while the other three were competitive multinational companies.

- On the whole, the product provided by this company was not any better than the products sold by its competitors.

The account manager in this company was instructed to target as customers the two most influential motorcycle-manufacturing companies in China. After initial customer visits, the account manager got the impression that one of her two targeted customer companies had already signed a product development contract with a foreign supplier and that the other one had been negotiating with four suppliers (off and on) for almost two years. After a systematic analysis of the two companies, evaluated in terms of their respective phases of the purchase process, key persons, COLs, VOC, buying points, and selling points, the account manager still found it difficult to identify the specific buying points important to the COLs.

But, looking into these two cases, the account manager found that the COLs in these two different customer companies were both very young and relatively new to their current positions. Obviously, this information would be useful in deducing the buying points unique to these COLs. After all, the account manager thought that people who are new to their jobs could have a stronger desire for management recognition – so intent are they to prove their worthiness to executives, with an eye perhaps to reinforcing their position within the company and paving the way for further advance.

With this in mind, the veteran account manager visited the two COLs and did not even discuss joint product development or buy-sale issues; she discussed career life experience instead. From these conversations, the account manager got the impression that talking about life experience, professional development, and advancement might improve her personal, and thus, sales relationship with the customers. During these free chats, the account manager noted, among other things, that the COLs were somewhat apprehensive about the abilities of the engineers under their supervision to adjust to and implement new technologies. But above all, both COLs sought to demonstrate their talents and abilities to management, and they could best do so by providing the most impressive overall integrated product. Since products from the various suppliers were not that different, the account manager made the deliverability upon this hidden buying point as part of the integrated product, the crux of her sales pitch (one may thus refer to this hidden buying point in question as "boardroom appeal").

She was able to deliver upon the hidden buying point by promising to install a thorough and systematic training program for engineers working under the COLs' leadership. Of course, this training service could have been proposed by any of the salesperson's competitors. But what made this integrated product distinct was the account manager's ability to communicate its virtues; she explained, in detail, proposals and arrangements for the training of their subordinates and articulated the implications of and correlations between the proposed training program and the contributions that the two COLs could make to their companies and even demonstrated the ability to deliver with a selected motorcycle equipped with some development-in-progress parts from Taiwan in an organized gathering of the engineers, the COLs and the their top management in the customers' companies respectively. A short time later, the account manager felt a relaxation in the communication process. Not only did she gain useful sales information from the two COLs, but she was also offered better comments and suggestions for the training of their employees. The account manager successfully won the five-year exclusive development and supply contract from both customers. Also, she developed an open, friendly relationship with the two COLs. The very private nature of these relationships made the account manager feel even more confident that her success came from proper intuition, knowledge, and handling of hidden buying points.

Though the buying points that may arise from the strengths of the product itself might bring some success factors for winning sales, one must always be mindful of the fact that less overt, more personal buying points may play even greater part in a sale, especially in competitive environments when the product itself has no obvious unique advantages. Effective understanding and handling of hidden buying points is usually the key to successful selling. This is especially true in the case of a homogenous product field or, in terms of X-Be, one made homogenous by the VOC of particularly influential key persons. Homogeneity usually comes as a result of a common product concept, or industry norm – and in this case, what a salesperson truly sells is an integrated product that incorporates both express and implicit buying points.

## The Attitude Index and the Detection and Verification of Hidden Buying Points

### Finding Hidden Buying Points

However obvious it may seem, a good starting point – but it is merely that – for the detection of hidden buying points might simply be the process of common reasoning by which the tacit motives of others are usually gleaned – investigation and trial and error. Like a detective in a mystery novel, the salesperson notes contextual "clues" and attempts to stitch together a comprehensive – if piecemeal – portrait of the purchaser's value system. The salesperson considers first the professional situation of a given key person, then his or her personal situation; whence comes an early impression of the latter's VOC. And, as noted earlier, VOC are a fairly sound foundation upon which to erect buying points, hidden or otherwise.

The presence of hidden buying points can be suggested by a number of interpersonal cues during the sales process. If a key person seems to be supplying confusing or contradictory information regarding the integrated product he has in mind, it is very likely that his (implicit) VOC contain certain elements that he is reticent to reveal. Similarly, if the key person seems entirely unresponsive to the buying points and selling points tendered by the salesperson, regardless of how personally, professionally or socially attractive they may be to a person in the client's position, the presence of an unfulfilled desire – however covert and unexpressed – should be evident. If no amount of cordial exchange and keen product positioning can improve a seller's relating status with a given key person, the seller must immediately begin the quest to unearth the client's most covert desires and values. As with all sales activity, the seller's ensuing "detective work" is a subjective and communicative exercise. The resources available to a seller frustrated by a taciturn client are admittedly limited: firstly, other key persons, specifically ones with whom the seller has a favorable relating status, and ones who are also privy to the attitudes and values of the key person presenting the sales challenge. Other accessible persons – networked resources – who are not necessarily key persons, can also be assets. All expressed VOC on the part of the purchaser should be considered. The implication of this method is, of course, that a buying point unexpressed to the seller must nonetheless be expressed to someone else. This may not necessarily be the case, and uncovering private motives and inclinations is always at least tricky, but humans are social beings, and the public dimension is the only one in which business can be transacted and social exchanges evaluated; and indeed, as expression is the only gateway from thought to objectivity it is all that should be under consideration in a systematic framework. In most circumstances, however, at this point a seller should at least have some minimal impression of what is impeding the sale and which of the purchaser's concerns remain unaddressed.

**Verifying of Hidden Buying Points**
The hidden buying points that may have been detected above are ultimately, though, mere speculations, or assumptions, and may not reflect a

key person's actual buying points. Here, we provide a method for verifying whether hidden buying points have been properly apprehended. Let us start with Daniel Katz's (1960) functional approach to the study of attitude. He (Katz) argues that the attitudes of human beings serve a certain practical function, namely that a person's attitudes are situational, being predetermined in order to gain the greatest personal, physical, and emotional dividends in any given situation. In other words, people are usually more attentive to those matters that may prove beneficial to them (Katz, 1960).

Therefore, if a seller tactfully broaches the various topics in which hidden buying points seem to be embedded (based upon earlier discussions with networked resources), the purchaser is more likely to respond favorably to those topics actually pertinent to her. The seller should be keenly aware of changes in the key person's word choice, expression, and other indicators of attitude, in evaluating whether a hidden buying point has been piqued.

Another method for which a seller might opt to gauge the client's attention may be described by some as the "teacher's method." It takes its sobriquet from a common scenario. Consider how teachers check whether students have been attentive to their explanations: they single them out to answer questions about the explained concepts; students who were attentive will provide correct answers. And though a seller's position is hardly all that much like a teacher's, the teacher's method can be re-engineered into an effective means of communications management (the skill of *"pace setting (ii)"* as it was termed in the Section *ON SELLING SKILLS* in Chapter 10): it can help a salesperson monitor a key person's attention and glean his or her hidden buying points in the process. The goal of this attention test is to quickly turn the conversation to the objective conditions corresponding with those hidden buying points the seller needs to verify.

This can be achieved by simply asking the appropriate questions after a certain lag phase. This lag phase should be measured from the time the key person and the seller engaged in a discussion that the latter believes to be related to hidden buying points. With incisive questions, the seller can invite the key person to express his or her own views, to comment on whether the seller's buying point suggestions would better facilitate the decision-making process. The best approach might simply be the "silent treatment," which is to say, waiting for the key person to respond on his or her own accord. If the answers offered by that key person happen to be consistent with those gleaned in previous conversations, with this key person or with his or her peers, and if he or she suddenly shows interest in the seller's suggestions, the hidden buying points under consideration can be considered confirmed.

## Attitude and Relating Status Indices

Concerted application of the attitude and relating status indices greatly improves the effectiveness of a person's interpersonal sales approach. A good relating status index allows salespeople to gain information about a key person's attitude index and vice versa. Such a relationship between indices reinforces the fact that the essence of selling is, after all, communication and interaction among people to reach a mutually satisfactory exchange. Useful information from a key person can help a salesperson better understand the key person's buying points, increase the precision and effectiveness of his or her sale position, and obtain reliable information regarding the key person's reading on the attitude index. Thence, directed by an appraisal of this attitude index, the salesperson can deliberately and meticulously work toward satisfying the particular buying points that are of interest to the individual key person. This will result in an improved relating status; a salesperson who has ingratiated herself with the customer will be all the more likely a recipient of privileged information and, thus, access to hidden buying points.

## Attitude Index and Occasions for Communication

The attitude index is related to occasions for communication even more closely than it is to the other indices. This is because people generally only make public their opinions and attitudes on occasions on which doing so may be beneficial to them. Once again, this should remind salespeople to take initiative and purposefully select occasions that are appropriate in the eyes of the client. An aptitude for developing appropriate communication occasions is an important part of any salesperson's interpersonal apparatus. Also, the ability to create communication occasions reflects the general relationship between the salesperson and the individual key persons.

In the actual selling process, we suggest that salespeople choose an occasion where they can obtain their client's complete and undivided attention. Generally, this works best "one on one" – seller to customer. Doing so facilitates the intimacy of communication and gives the seller a chance to understand the client's buying points and obtain useful information about his or her attitude toward these buying points.

Finally, we would like to emphasize the following point. As far as the exchange behavior is concerned, the working assumption is that the individual key person acts as a *value-chasing agent*. The more important the buying points are to the key person, the more he (as an individual) is inclined to buy the corresponding sales offer. And the attitude index is here to indicate the extent to which a key person, as an individual beholden to no-one, may be attracted to the buying points integrated into the sales offer.

## CONFIDENCE INDEX

### On the Implications of a Specifically Defined Confidence Index

Most companies rely on their salespeople to estimate the probability of success for a sales transaction. In companies where a high process control is implemented, executives and sales managers rely on salespeople to provide a specific degree of confidence toward sales opportunities: 25%? 50%? 75%?

And why not? Aren't these salespeople, after all, closest to the customers? Their judgment should, therefore, be the most accurate. But salespeople generally find it hard to assign a specific degree of confidence to each of their sales opportunities in a systematic manner, especially at certain precarious points in the purchasing process. For no salesperson's intuition is infallible, regardless of how long she has been in the business. While it is all right – or at least not detrimental – to rely upon one's subjective feelings in evaluating a sale-in-progress, the challenge is that there is no standard social psychology framework by which these feelings might be systematized and evaluated consistently and reliably. In order to ease this kind of unreliables, many B-to-B companies turn to the "statistic logic" of sales funnel or pipeline without considering its intrinsic problems (discussed in Chapter 10). The end result of an entire enterprise operating on the hunches and assumptions of its agents is nothing more than management chaos. But that is not all. Other negative consequences result from this irrational way of handling the confidence issue including the following:

1. When a sales opportunity is overestimated and lost, blame is almost always directed at the salesperson. This can lead to depressed morale and an unproductive work environment.
2. Generally, salespeople become very conservative in estimating the probability of their sales success, even though doing so is not necessarily good for selling and sales management.
3. When a sales opportunity has been lost, management is usually unable to isolate the actual "deal-breaking" factor in the salesperson's explanations, which are often geared to clear the latter of responsibility.

X-Be resolves these issues by introducing a third selling status index that enables salespeople to reach an objective judgment about the success of a sales opportunity and guides them to the expected result of their selling efforts. We call this measure the CI.

X-Be defines the CI as a measure of the extent to which a key person has acknowledged, overtly, the selling points (regarding the seller, her sales offer, or her company) either by words or by deeds. The rationale behind this definition is twofold:

- It makes reference to an overt act, objectively apprehended; thus, this definition is easy to implement.
- People usually make public their attitudes when they are confident about a salesperson or a sales offer's features to be their own social justification (i.e., their own selling points) of their purchasing behavior in certain social setting. In addition, once an opinion or attitude is a matter of public record, it is difficult to contradict or retract it (recall the "escalating commitment" phenomenon). As a result, the more positive and public a key person's attitude is, the more confident a seller can be about the success of her sale.

Generally speaking, salespeople can only achieve a breakthrough (with regard to the CI) after gaining favorable results with regard to the relating status index and attitude index. As well, key persons are often reticent to make the sort of public declarations that might boost a seller's CI. There are three reasons for this: uncertainty at the rationality of selling points, concern regarding their deliverability, and the scarcity of occasions for communication and attitude declaration. Let us consider these three problematic factors in sequence.

## The Confidence Index and the Rationality of Selling Points

It is very important that key persons see their selling points as rational. This is because people in general tend to take very seriously the subjects about which they are willing to make public declarations. They feel comfortable expressing their attitudes toward these subjects only when they consider them to be reasonable for themselves, but often in the views of significant others. This requires the salespeople to consciously project and articulate (for the key persons) the rationality of the selling points during the selling process. The techniques described earlier in this chapter for the recognition of hidden buying points may be useful to the seller in establishing what key persons deem "reasonable," and thus deliverable.

## The Confidence Index and Deliverability

In previous chapters, the concept of *deliverability* was introduced as a contingent element of the integrated product. One main objective of developing and promoting the integrated product within one's organization is to make key persons believe in the seller's and/or sales offer's ability to deliver upon the buying and selling points, while adding necessary features to the actual product or service practical to its installation, use, or maintenance. Usually, key persons need to psychologically eliminate (risk aversion behavior) as many deliverability obstacles to delivery as possible before they are willing to publicly express a positive attitude toward the selling points under consideration. A salesperson must strive to put an end to these misgivings in order to attain a positive CI.

Some activities that can ease the minds of key persons regarding deliverability include inviting them to visit the company, submitting samples, demonstrating how the product works, and offering positive referrals from satisfied customers. Salespeople should also ensure that their staff is networked, coordinated, and informed. This is crucial because selling activities usually involve many other staff, departments, or perhaps the entire company. All the relevant people and departments need to prepare and get ready to participate in all sales activities.

## The Confidence Index and Occasions for Attitude Declaration

As with the other two indices, salespeople need to learn how to manage and bring about the sorts of occasions that can help them gain favorable CI ratings early on in their relationships with key persons. The current phase of a company's purchasing process should not deter a salesperson from becoming the first to gain a favorable CI rating in each phase. In this respect, the outstanding performance of a highly professional salesperson would make others seem like mere playmates. To achieve a favorable CI rating, a seller must be proactive and seek appropriate occasions in which key persons can make declarations of opinion. This may commence with an intimate, "one-on-one" exchange, evolve into an intermediate state involving a few others, and finally climax with a public proclamation. Recall from our earlier discussions that purchasers are rarely able to contradict themselves after expressing an opinion publicly; public record is inflexible and monolithic – escalating commitment.

In some cases, however, a seller may be lucky enough to encounter key persons who are willing to buy something right after initial contact with that seller, her company, or their product. It will be to the advantage of the salesperson's company to arrange for a public airing of that purchaser's positive purchasing attitude at the earliest possible opportunity – with, of course, the understanding that the company and seller be able to deliver upon the buying points and selling points which initially secured the sale.

In any case, selecting and arranging the appropriate communication and interaction occasions (to gain favorable ratings as per selling indices) is one of the most important responsibilities in the career of a professional salesperson. And appropriate platforms must be arranged to facilitate these occasions.

## CONCLUSION

It should be obvious at this point that a "knack" for forming and maintaining conducive sales relationships is neither some innate old-guard salesperson's talent, nor something that necessarily always comes with experience. On the contrary, it is the product of two overlapping interpersonal skills, which can be acquired by anyone if need be. Firstly, the seller must be keenly sensitive to the purchaser's VOC and value points in terms of buying points and selling points, the respective deliverability, and her impressions of both the sales offer and the salesperson; secondly, the seller must actively engage in facilitating the communication of the integrated product and impressions – by engineering the sorts of situations in which the potential customer may be most inclined toward self-revelation, trust, and comfort for the sake of his own value pursuing purpose. The indices provided in this chapter at once emphasize the importance of the former and act as an impetus to the latter: they force the seller to be attentive to the customer – to her attitudes and confidence on the matter of the exchange value and, as well, to her trust in the seller – but also to take note of whatever factors might hamstring a given sales approach, and to strive to remedy them. By focusing on the customers' ever-shifting, multifarious values in terms of their value-pursuing cognition, psychology, and behavior in a purchase process, a seller contributes to the personalization of customer value in a sales offer (integrated product); this is where salespeople assume the role of integrating value and engineering satisfaction – a truly client-centered sales activity that distinguishes an integrated salesperson from one who strives blindly with "instinct" and "luck."

# 9

# DEALING WITH COMPETITION: AN APPROACH FROM THE PERSPECTIVE OF CUSTOMER VALUE

Competition permeates the life and work of anyone involved in an exchange process such as selling. To help manage it, several theoretical frameworks have been developed for the minute parsing of those factors that give rise to it. Among the most influential of these theories in business studies are the *five forces framework* of Michael Porter (2004) and the concept of *Core Competence* of Pralahad and Hamel (1990). There are also other perspectives on the same issues, including one on technology (Meyer & Utterback, 1993), one on resources (Wernerfelt, 1984) and one on appropriate knowledge (Kogut & Zander, 1992).

The above competition theories are concerned mostly with the positioning of the organization at the strategic level and, as a result, they are not helpful to salespeople who tend to focus on microscopic issues of the relationships and interactions between the organization and its customers. There are no practical methods for translating the strategic analyses of these competition theories to recommendations that would be useful at an interpersonal level where salespeople operate. For the purpose of selling and sales management, we propose a new working approach for analyzing and managing the competition issues that salespeople face in the course of their jobs. This approach is practical and easy to use. It characterizes competition in terms of the abilities of the considered sales offers and their respective providers to deliver the customer value. Our intention is to re-focus the study of competition on the customer's perception, which is the one that ultimately determines whether and where a seller could win a sale. This new approach, as readers will learn in this chapter, will not only enable salespeople and sales managers to effectively assess their respective sales performance in a competitive environment, but will equip both with a truly integrated framework that will help them analyze in a systematic fashion their selling and sales management. The integrated nature of the approach is reflected in the logical relationships that are established between the X-Be elements, as discussed throughout the previous chapters, and the concept of competition which is, often, presented as an isolated subject in other frameworks. Such an approach to handling competition also helps ensure that a seller's positioning in a competitive environment remains, in the end, a system of value positioning, which is consistent with our earlier account of the construction of the integrated product for the sales offer. This is especially true in high-competition sales situations, when your product is not much different on its own intrinsic merits from the competitors. As well, a practical tool for competition management will be presented to aid a seller in evaluating the overall competitive position of an existing sales offer in a target market.

## A NEW DEFINITION OF COMPETITION

The majority of people working in business environments have at least some basic understanding of how competition affects their work. Competition is colloquially regarded as having two constituent elements: a competitor (which is to say, a similarly equipped and skilled seller or sales organization who targets the same market as the seller in question) and a competing product (which is roughly or wholly equivalent to the one being vended by the seller in question). But the head-to-head military nature of this definition imposes unnecessary boundaries on a seller's management of competition and could be misleading; the seller may indeed become absorbed in the analysis of the differences between her product and her competitor's, or in the disparities of experience or networking between the two competing parties. But no customer has ever abandoned a prospective purchase on these bases. Also, the above definition of competition implies that, if you are the sole supplier of a particular product or service, your only concern should be whether your potential customers are themselves competing with you, that is, whether they have the internal resources to solve the perceived problem or not; if they do not have these resources, then you should be able to sell very easily to them. But this reasoning is not correct; there could very well be other factors that act as obstacles against your sales work; for instance, the customers' perception of their problems could be of such a nature that they think that your product or service is totally irrelevant to their needs. The colloquial definition is, therefore, necessarily incomplete as far as sales is concerned. It may also be misleading, as it tends to distract sellers from what should really be their main focus – the customers' VOC which are the major factors that determine whether a sale is won or lost. What a competitor does is and should be considered secondary, as it will impact your sales work only if it succeeded either in providing more value to the customer than your own offer or in changing the customer's VOC, leading to a change in the customer's bases for judging of value.

X-Be proposes a fundamental renovation of the concept of competition that is similar in some ways to our earlier reconstruction of the term product; indeed, it is built, to a certain extent, upon it. The overall result might be termed integrated competition.

Integrated competition is the sum of all the factors that impede a customer's recognition, acceptance, deployment, or employment (or continued utilization) of a sales offer. Such factors, which will be referred to within X-Be as the **impeding factors**, can always be linked to a set of VOC-endorsed buying points and selling points that, in the perception of one or more key persons, the seller has difficulties delivering to the satisfaction of the latter key persons.

As can be seen in this definition, the presence of competitors and competing products or services has not been included in a head-to-head military fashion, as this was the case in the traditional definition of competition. Rather, it is its possible influence on the customer's buying decision that is incorporated into our definition, and this incorporation has been done from the customer's point of view, not the seller or competitors (which is consistent with the overall customer-centric nature of the framework X-Be). Hence, the existence of a directly competing product is just one source, among others, of impeding factors that compete against a sales offer in satisfying the VOC of the key persons. It should also be noted that a factor that influences the sales process – for good or ill – can ultimately be viewed as a reflection of the customer's personal/organizational values and social context.

Competition can thus arise at any time, before and even after (in the case of a service or supply contract) signing and closing a deal. It is the salesperson's responsibility to identify all those factors which are obstructing her efforts to position the sales offer at hand, maintain her sales relationship with the client, and trace the causes of these obstructions. To help the salesperson do so, the framework X-Be provides practical and easy-to-use tools to detect and manage these factors. Indeed, the extent to which an individual impeding factor may impact the selling could be measured by the attitude index, the CI, or both, depending on whether the impeding factor acts on a buying point, a selling point, or both. By implementing these indices and the other X-Be concepts, the salesperson should ultimately be able to evaluate her ability to surmount the factors mitigating the sale, and thus be aware of her competitive position. The following section provides more details on this.

## COMPETITIVE POSITION

To judge her current competitive position in a sales process, and improve it if it is not as strong as it ought to be, a salesperson could follow the following steps:

1. Identify the possible impeding factors in the sales process. While she carries out this identification, the salesperson should keep in mind the above definition of the terms "competition" and "impeding factors."

2. Evaluate the impact on selling of the identified impeding factors. The salesperson could successfully do so by using the attitude index and CI that she has recorded with each of the key persons involved in the purchase process, provided that she enjoys a reasonable relating status index with each of these key persons individually.

   In many cases, however, it may be unnecessary or time-consuming to check what the impeding factors are for all key persons involved. In such cases, the salesperson could proceed a bit differently, but still remain effective. Once she identifies the possible impeding factors, it might be enough to just address the question of which key persons are likely to side with the identified impeding factors. It is not unusual to find out that these impeding factors would resonate more with those key persons with whom the salesperson's relating status index is as poor as being at the "critical stage" or at the "PR stage" (definitions of these stages have been presented in Chapter 1 and discussed in Chapter 8).

3. Assess your overall competitive position in the purchase process. The salesperson could do so by checking on the respective influence levels of those key persons with whom she has a good relating status index (say, the "acquaintance stage," or "partner stage" – definitions of these stages have also been presented in Chapter 1 and discussed in Chapter 8). Once she has done so, the

salesperson can assess her overall competitive position using the following logical rules:

a. You are in a relatively good competitive position if you have a good relating status index with those key persons whose influence levels on the purchase process are high, and these key persons believe that you, with the sales offer at hand, can successfully deliver their VOC-endorsed buying points and selling points.

b. You are in a worrying competitive position if the influence levels of those key persons with whom you have a good relating status index are not so high, although they believe that you can, with your sales offer, successfully deliver their VOC-endorsed buying points and selling points.

c. You are in a poor competitive position if even those key persons with whom you have a good relating status index do not believe you can, with your sales offer, successfully deliver their VOC-endorsed buying points and selling points.

d. You are in an unclear or mixed competitive position if none of the above is the case.

Unfortunately, it is this last type of competitive positions – mixed competitive position – that salespeople often face in the course of their sales process. However, the analytical method outlined above using X-Be's indices can still be useful in guiding the seller to specifically parse the impacts of the identified impeding factors. It can also help direct her to the real concerns of the key persons in the purchase process and get her to think about how to deal with these concerns. In the next two sections, the selling strategies and tactics discussed in Chapter 4 are employed to shed some light on the mixed competition situation.

## STRATEGIES IN MIXED COMPETITION

In any state of competition, the focus of a salesperson's efforts should be the VOC of the key persons involved. This is especially true of a state of mixed competition, since that is one in which a sale can potentially be secured as long as sufficient effort is made to attune the integrated product to the customer's values. Intimate awareness of a key person's VOC is central to establishing which expressed and tacit VOC-endorsed buying points and selling points this key person thinks you have problems delivering, and often working out just what these buying points and selling points are is the trickiest part of doing business in a competitive environment.

Thankfully, though, there is a bit of a shortcut in practice. For, as veteran salespeople will note, most sales seem to occupy one of three value criteria categories – categories that start at a center (the product itself) and expand outward. To each one of them corresponds a different methodology for managing one's competitive position.

1. **Intrinsic Value Strategy – Sales centered on the intrinsic value of the product or service itself.** This is the simplest sort of value positioning, and the sales situations it might represent can run the gamut from medical services in a private clinic to jewelry to complex proprietary technologies. IBM, for example, has long stressed the effectiveness of its product in solving customers' problems. If the customer's VOC indicate a foremost interest in the quality and dependability of the item changing hands – "a good, solid product" – over and above any social or organizational factors involved in the purchase, then the competitive position should be improved by ensuring the deliverability upon those virtues of the product in question that are relevant to the key persons' buying points and selling points. As a matter of fact, this scenario is also and often identified in the sales of those products that are associated with "revolutionary" technologies or that contribute to dramatic changes in social trends when they are successfully introduced in the market.

2. **Extrinsic Value Strategy – Sales predicated primarily to the values of the purchasing process or environment.** When the products offered by various sellers are not too different from one another or not different at all, then the intrinsic value of the product or service in question is likely of little consequence in influencing key persons to make a motion to purchase. Rather, their foremost interest (and the most salient of their VOC) could be in the rapidity of execution, convenience of administration, courtesy of auxiliary service, pleasantness of purchase environment, or any values that are primarily embedded in the process by which a product is provided, used, and disposed. Represented by this mode of integrated product in terms of customer value are, among other things, bank services, Internet retailers, commodity goods, and the like. As a result, improving one's competitive position in situations such as these would necessarily follow from ensuring the deliverability upon the

customer's buying points and selling points, as they relate to the purchaser's needs of an environment and process of exchange that is as convenient and efficient as possible.

3. **Relationship Value Strategy – Sales lubricated primarily by interpersonal or organizational relationship.** In this case, the current product or service to be exchanged is, in actuality, something of a "pawn," a token that indicates the development of an interpersonal or organizational relationship, and the fostering of connections and networked resources. These sales tend to be broad or strategic in the sense that the customer is seeking values that are external to a particular transaction of goods or services. An example might be the office items sold periodically to the buyer with whom the salesperson has a good personal relationship. These sales arise from a network of patronage or personal relationship, or what is termed 'Guanxi' (a Chinese word for relationship, representing a set of complex sociologic and interpersonal values entangled with business intercourses). The relationship value strategy can be more effective in the following situations: (1) there is not much difference among the sales offers (including their purchasing, using and disposal); (2) selling in the culture that favors much interdependence among people; (3) there is a strategic reason for a purchasing organization to partner with the sales organization. In any of these cases, the seller could work more effectively than otherwise by leveraging the relationship values.

In all likelihood, a competitive sale involves some combination of two or all three of the above categories, but one presumably prevails, and that should be a strategic path upon which the seller directs her efforts to understand buying points and selling points that drive the (purchaser's) key persons (or at least the most influential of them) to the motion to purchase. By doing so, the seller will be able to examine and analyze the effective ways to strategically integrate the customer value into the customer-centered integrated product and, as a consequence, cultivate a strongest and long-term competitive position for herself and her company.

## TACTICS IN MIXED COMPETITION

Necessarily, though, in most free market environments, a situation of mixed competition is also an opportunity for the seller to refine her sales offer into a customer-centered integrated product, impress her customer, and ultimately beat the competition. As long as it has not been established clearly that the seller is in a desperate competitive position, there is still a chance for this seller to win the deal, and she ought to work hard toward achieving that goal. To do so, and as discussed in Chapter 4, she can make use of different tactics depending on how strongly the key persons feel about their VOC and the degree of their involvement in the purchase process:

- The "selling criteria" tactic:
  If the VOC have not yet been established, and the key persons are still not sure about them, then the seller must find ways to become active in the process of "co-defining" what the criteria will be; in doing so, she can point out some of the important values or combination of values that were not fully appreciated before, and make sure that the final list of criteria for the purchase is satisfactory to both parties (the buyer and the seller). This situation may happen when the product or service to be purchased is crucial or new to the company and may allow the seller to offer relevant expertise for the definition of the VOC when there is an extended involvement of key persons in the purchase process.
- The "changing criteria" tactic:
  If, however, the VOC have, to a certain extent, already been defined, and the key persons are relatively clear about them, but still willing to seek external opinions about some specific purchasing issues (which is typically the case for a medium level of purchase involvement), then the seller can use this customer's purchase involvement to interact with the key persons involved, strengthen those criteria factors that are beneficial to both parties, and encourage changes in the key persons' criteria so that they could see something better than what they had in mind.
- The "meeting criteria" tactic:
  But, if key persons' VOC are hardly changeable, then the seller might want to simply deliver more of the values that the key persons are looking for according to their existing VOC.

The seller can also work on the relevant buying points and selling points of her offer, to manage a mixed competition situation. She can "tune" the presentation of these points to the needs and desires of the key persons, to the point that the newly customized integrated product becomes irresistible and the meddling voices of the competition and their impeding factors are muted. That being said, if customizing an integrated product to a particular key person requires an extraordinary amount of effort or capital, pursuit of that sale might not be worthwhile. This issue will be addressed later in this chapter, in the section titled "Is the deal worth winning". In any case, a state of mixed competition should be seen as a challenge to the seller's knowledge about the customer's situation and about its key person's purchase needs in terms of their respective personal and social-cultural objectives. And the efforts to procure the relevant customer information will help the seller refine her sales offer and align it with the values sought by the customer. Here are some interpersonal tactics that will most likely equip neophyte sellers with the necessary skills to succeed in mixed competition situation:

1. Leverage anyone (key persons and others) with whom you have a relating status index at the acquaintance stage or partner stage and who might be able to provide some of the relevant and needed information.

   No matter what actions the seller wants to consider taking in a mixed competition situation, the most critical customer information that is required for the design and planning of these actions consist of the VOC, buying points, selling points, and the corresponding deliverability requirements of those key persons with whom the seller has poor relating status indices. Hence, it is this type of information that the seller should look for.

2. Leverage anyone (key persons and others with whom you have a good relating status index) who could act as an appropriate communicator in the eyes of those concerned key persons, in order to facilitate the communication with them.

   In addition to being the main players in business, key persons are also social beings who could be influenced more by their acquaintances and other people who possess "something" deemed valuable by these key persons. This is the reason why the seller may consider using appropriate communicators to interact with the reluctant key persons. She should try to select such communicators from the group of individuals who have a formal or informal authority over the latter key persons, or who have anything (such as information and expertise) that is valuable to these reluctant key persons. In practice, this tactic could go as far as leveraging the customer's broader social relations that could provide support to the seller (e.g., the customer's key suppliers, the customer's customers, and other interested parties).

3. Improve the relating status with those key persons in PR stage and critical stage.

Covering the key persons with whom your relating status is in the PR or critical stage is not an easy job, but it can be crucial for your success, particularly in the mixed competition situation. The best among all options to improve your relationship with these key persons is to understand and address their real concerns. You might be able to do so by collecting the needed customer information and involving appropriate communicators. But this could become a difficult situation for the salesperson when the real issue to be addressed is related to some hidden buying points of these key persons. This is why we discussed in the previous chapter how to identify and verify hidden buying points.

The tactics discussed above are intended to help a seller to effectively communicate and interact with her customers, especially when she is faced with a mixed competition situation. However, in the course of planning and taking actions, the seller might also want to consider the question of efficiency; she should allocate her time and resources to the endeavors with high return. Thus, it is usually legitimate to put in more efforts in the interaction with those key persons who are most influential and who could provide sufficient information and support for the success of the sales operations.

Having said the above, one should not be misled to believe that you can sell anything to anyone. As was indicated throughout this book, X-Be is not about teaching sellers how to "sell ice to Eskimos." X-Be is about the creation and exchange of real and long-lasting value, not deceiving the buyers and aiming for short-term gains at customer's expense. Its purpose is to reveal the fundamental scientific facts about the behaviors of the buyer and the seller. And, based on these facts, X-Be provides businesses with effective and efficient tools to carry out successful selling and sales management tasks, innovate and strengthen their internal production systems, and build sustainable value-adding relationships with their customers.

## ASSESS THE OVERALL SALES COMPETITIVE POSITIONS FOR DIFFERENT SALES OFFERS

The above discussion has focused on the analysis of a seller's competitive position in a specific sales process, but the concepts could also be expanded to cover the assessment of the overall competitive position of a particular sales offer of the company in the market. In this section, we present a brief discussion of X-Be's method for dealing with this issue.

When we look at a specific sales process, we focus on one single customer or a target account with a specific sales objective. For the seller to beat the competition, she carries out a detailed study of the VOC of the key persons involved and designs a customized integrated product for them by leveraging other resources inside and outside the seller's company. However, when the focus is on the overall assessment of a particular sales offer in the market where the seller's company operates, it is the whole industry that needs to be analyzed. The seller can then collect the list of the relevant VOC that prevail in this industry, and the corresponding customer's expected deliverability upon typical buying points and selling points. These data can then be organized in a tabular format as in Table 9.1. The customer-satisfying deliverability can be measured using three possible discrete values: "High," "Medium", and "Low." The cells of the table are then filled up by the salespeople and their co-workers using appropriate descriptors of the position of the company's sales offer compared to that of the competitors; such descriptors could be "Ahead of Competition," "Similar to Competition," "Worse than Competition."

Detailed discussion of this method is beyond the scope of this book. We just indicate, however, that the seller's company has to develop effective ranking systems that define the meanings of "High," "Middle", and "Low" in a way that reflects customers' buying decision making. Customers tend indeed to exhibit different selection behaviors in the purchase process depending on the type of the purchase to be made; for instance, some customers may rely on their feelings; others may make use of their knowledge regarding specific attributes or of general attitudes and intuitions (or any combination thereof). Thus, the seller's company should take into account these behaviors when designing the foregoing ranking systems. In addition, if the rankings are quantified, the seller's company could end up with an effective management tool to assess the salability of its integrated products and compare them to the competitors' sales offers. And this could also help in making reasonable assessments of the relative merits of product concepts and bundles developed through marketing efforts.

A main point we want to make here is that the basic building blocks of X-Be can be implemented to describe and manage many different situations at different levels where exchange is involved. As was explained above, this is the case when the focus is on a company competing in a specific sales process, or on a product to be sold in a particular market, but the ideas could also be extended to describe the exchange behavior of employees, units, and departments within a company. More research

**TABLE 9.1  A Template for Assessing a Sales Offer's Competitive Position in the Market (the Items "Price" and "Technical features" are Added Just As Sample Examples)**

| | VOC | Deliverability (Customer-Perceived) | | |
| --- | --- | --- | --- | --- |
| | | High (ahead of competition) | Medium (similar to competition) | Low (worse than competition) |
| Often mentioned selecting points | Often mentioned selecting rationale in the target market | | | |
| Price | 1. Low price is a must<br>2. ROI<br>3. Best ratio performance/price | | SP: Our price is often used by key persons to justify above average performance | |
| Technical features | 1. Gain technological advantage<br>2. Production efficiency | BP: Our advanced technical features make key persons look smart pros;<br>SP: Features are often used by key persons to "sell" their buying behavior | | |
| Overall competitive position | | 1. List of those frequently mentioned features which are often associated with customer's key BPs<br>2. List of those frequently mentioned features which are often associated with customer's key SPs<br>3. List of those costly or not so desirable features which are neither BPs nor SPs for customer | | |

Abbreviations: BP = Buying point; ROI = return on investment; SP = Selling point; VOC = Views on Criteria.

work on this can be carried out using various agent-based modeling and simulation methods which are, however, beyond the scope of this book. For now, we will briefly touch upon an important decision that salespeople and sales managers have often found very difficult to make.

## IS THE DEAL WORTH WINNING?

Of course all of the above strategies and tactics are only relevant if the costs (in terms of not only money, but also other elements such as time, reputation, ethics, and so on) involved are outweighed by the immediate or ultimate dividends of a sale. Sellers and sales organizations should be aware of when to "cut their losses" and bring a stop to high-loss deals that satisfy no one including the customers for their long-term interests. Some of the warning signs that a seller is being too conciliatory to a high-competition environment include the following:

1. Delivering upon the customer's buying points and selling points and/or overcoming the impeding factors would be prohibitively expensive (well beyond the pail of usual business costs); this could include developing a support infrastructure or instituting a variation in standard design.
2. Delivering upon some of the hidden buying points would require some sort of ethical transgression.

Though going about any of the above processes might bring about the immediate consummation of a deal, they could also compromise a sales organization's corporate or solvent status. And, in a high-competition environment, where reputation is of paramount importance, any deal that seems lucrative at first but which promises to put a seller at a competitive disadvantage in future is worth abandoning.

## CONCLUSION

Competition management is, like other aspects of selling, based on a system of winning battles for customer information to direct the sales actions. The following should, therefore, always be among priorities for salespeople:

- communication with all key persons, and especially with the most influential ones;

- effective, intuitive, and open exchange about the VOC of these key persons;
- clear, concise, and persuasive presentation and personalization of the integrated product.

It is important, however, to keep in mind that so many "inputs" (stimuli) that the salesperson receives from her environment do not represent information – certainly not the actionable information that a salesperson can use directly and effectively for her selling activities. As suggested by various researchers in the area of social psychology and cognition, social cues are often fundamentally ambiguous, and person perceivers, as a salesperson often is, are prone to certain errors and biases in their judgments, particularly in a mixed competition situation. This is why we developed the X-Be framework with clear logical foundations that help salespeople make a good sense of those ambiguous and bias-prone sales situations and derive sound and actionable customer information to do their job. This has been our basic approach to the study of selling and sales management, and competition management is no exception.

# 10

## PUTTING THE ELEMENTS TOGETHER: A ROADMAP FOR EFFECTIVE SELLING AND SALES MANAGEMENT

In this chapter, we put the elements of the X-Be framework together to formulate different roadmaps for selling to organizations and consumers. In particular, we focus on how sellers could apply those elements to conduct and manage their sales communications and interactions with their customers in an integrated manner. We also discuss other sales-related issues that can be analyzed and effectively resolved within the X-Be framework. These issues include management by objectives (MBO) in sales, sales opportunity management, sales forecasting, selling skills, personal and non-personal selling and combination thereof.

### SELLING TO ORGANIZATIONS

Selling to organizations is often characterized by multiple and complex communication relationships with various key persons and COLs on the side of customer. Because of this, the challenges and difficulties that salespeople and sales management face in the course of planning, implementing, and managing selling activities tend to increase dramatically when they deal with organizations. Those people who operate in the B-to-B area often feel, in their day to day work, that many consumer marketing concepts and instruments are completely powerless in handling organizational selling.

The typical features of a complex sales process, such as the ones that occur in organizational selling, could be summarized as follows:

1. Customers are usually involved in formal purchase processes of some kind.
2. The number of people involved on the customer side in a particular purchase process is often more than two – typically several or even more people who may have different concerns or interests over the same purchase.
3. Typical sales cycles are much longer than those encountered in the area of B-to-C selling – for instance, months or even a year or two in cultivating new businesses for industrial goods are very normal.
4. Once the deal is closed, either the single purchase order is significant in terms of dollars, or the continuous re-buys as stipulated in some sort of framework agreements are significant in terms of dollars, or the business relationships established are significant regardless the size of the current purchase order.

To deal with such complex selling situations, salespeople could be much more effective if they have a sound roadmap to effectively assist them in setting up meaningful action plans for targeted sales, evaluating the current sales status after executing each of the planned actions, and making decisions about what to do next, all in a systematic fashion. In this chapter, we put together all of the building blocks we have discussed in this book to formulate an effective roadmap for selling in such complex sales situations. This roadmap is epitomized in the tool presented in the Table 10.1 [A Customer Needs Management (CNM) System for Selling].

This tool is not difficult to use for planning sales actions, describing and analyzing the relevant snapshots of the current sales status, and making decisions about what to do next in your sales process, if one already understands the meanings of the building blocks we have discussed in the previous chapters of this book. In the next few sections, however, we would like to expand more on how the X-Be framework can be used in organizational selling and present an illustrative example as a concrete implementation of this framework.

## Integrate Relevant Customer Information to Construct Sound Judgments

Perhaps the most challenging task in selling to organizations is reading the thoughts and feelings of the key persons on the customer side. This task

**TABLE 10.1  A Customer Needs Management (CNM) System for Selling**

Account:  Product/Buy Time:  Units/Sale:  Account Rep:  Date Updated/Serial

Number:

| Key person/COL | | PPP of individuals | Views on Criteria | | Customer value | | Appropriate Communicator | Date of Sales Call (or Event) | Selling Status | | | Deliverability Issues |
|---|---|---|---|---|---|---|---|---|---|---|---|---|
| Name | Level of influence | | Selecting Point | Selecting Rationale | Buying point | Selling point | | | RI | AI | CI | |
| | | | | | | | | | | | | |
| | | | | | | | | | | | | |

The general assessment on current sale:                    Assessor/Date

1) The PPP of the account

2) The general Relating Status

3) The general confidence index

AI, Attitude Index; CI, Confidence Index; COL, Core opinion leader; RI, Relating Status Index.

is even more critical in the case of the COLs. Before, during and after her communications and interactions with a key person, to be effective, the salesperson needs to be clear about these selling issues: (1) what customer information is relevant and critical to his selling activities; (2) how to get it; (3) how to integrate the diverse and unrelated information received from this key person to make sensible inferences about the customer's real views and intentions with regard to the purchase at hand; (4) how to verify the validity of her inferences, and (5) what to do next. Salespeople often find it very difficult to do all these tasks with a needed confidence, but the X-Be knowledge will help with all these difficult selling issues in an integrated and logic manner. For instance, the X-Be elements incorporated in Table 10.1 will help with question (1); the Selling Skills outlined later in the section of "**ON SELLING SKILLS**" in this chapter will help address question (2), the intrinsic logic among the X-Be elements will help answer question (3), the applications of the three selling status indices will help handle question (4), and the identifying of the discrepancies in the answers to above 1–4 questions will help the seller build a clear perspective and structure in what to do next demanded in question (5). Therefore, salespeople can perform their selling activities effectively during the planning and executing of each and every sales call (events). It is in all these respects that the CNM tool (see Table 10.1) becomes very useful for effective selling and sales management.

Each time the customer information is collected, the X-Be logic will help salespeople analyze it, distill it, and integrate it to form reasonable judgments about the current status of the sale and the nature of the next steps to be taken. Salespeople need to be rational about the reasons behind the customer's behaviors, even when they seem irrational. In the following, let us just illustrate how a seller could, after each sales call (or event), use the intrinsic logic that links the X-Be's building blocks to integrate the collected customer information and convert it into reasonable judgments about a key person's value-pursuing behavior, and about the overall status of the sale. If a salesperson thinks that a key person's VOC are concerned with logistic issues, but her inferences about this key person's buying points and selling points have nothing to do with these issues at all, then these inferences are probably unfounded because the buying points and selling points represent the customer perceived value which must be compatible with the key person's VOC. If the salesperson believes that she has convincingly addressed the key person's concerns about the deliverability upon the significant buying points, she will have to ensure that the attitude index that she had previously inferred is a favorable one, as the attitude index is a reflection of the importance of the buying points in the key person's eyes – the logical rule that underlies this reasoning is as follows:

$$\left(\begin{array}{c} \text{Deliverability upon} \\ \text{the significant} \\ \text{buying points is addressed} \end{array}\right) \Rightarrow \left(\begin{array}{c} \text{Favorable} \\ \text{attitude} \\ \text{indicator} \end{array}\right)$$

If the salesperson believes that she has succeeded in convincing the key person about the deliverability upon the significant selling points, but the CI with this key person seems to be low, then she has to find out the reasons behind this discrepancy; this is because the CI should go up, when the key person is comfortable with the insurance that the salesperson provides regarding the deliverability of the significant selling points:

$$\left(\begin{array}{c} \text{Deliverability upon} \\ \text{the significant} \\ \text{selling points is addressed} \end{array}\right) \Rightarrow \left(\begin{array}{c} \text{Favorable} \\ \text{confidence} \\ \text{indicator} \end{array}\right)$$

If the salesperson makes inferences from the information that she has collected and constructs judgments stating that a key person is mostly favorable to her products and/or services, but latter finds out that her relating status index with this key person and with the others who know him well are only in the critical stage, then the salesperson's judgments and inferences are probably nothing more than wishful thinking.

In conclusion, and because of the intrinsic logic that underlies the X-Be framework and its building blocks, the CNM system for selling presented in Table 10.1 provides a powerful tool for salespeople to analyze their interactions with their customers and to make correct inferences about key persons' thoughts and feelings. This intrinsic logic, combined with other information such as the respective levels of influence of the customer's key persons on the buying decision-making process, will help construct reasonable judgments about the seller's competitive position, the next steps to take, and the overall progress of salespeople's work.

## Setting Up the SMART Objectives for Each Sales Call (or Event)

In complex sales situations, winning the purchase order depends on the achievement of the objectives of each sales call (or event). But this further depends on the salesperson's ability to set up the appropriate objectives for each and every sales call. Setting up these objectives can be done using the well-known principle of SMART objectives (S – Specific,

M – Measurable, A – Achievable, R – Realistic, T – Time). But, for a managerial principle to be effective, it must be supported by domain-specific knowledge to allow its successful implementation. Otherwise, the principle would remain just a set of abstract statements that look neat at the theoretical level, but have no practical application. Thus, when the principle of SMART objectives is used in financial or operation management, for instance, there has to be a good framework to represent knowledge in these management areas. This is also true in the case of selling and sales management. Suppose, for example, you want to initiate a sales call (or event) to familiarize yourself with a targeted account, you need to set up a SMART objective for this call. With the help of the concrete elements of the CNM System for Selling, you could easily define such an objective by responding to the following questions:

**S (specific)**: What is the current phase of the PPP (individual PPP or corporate PPP)? Who could be the key persons and COLs involved in the current phase, their respective VOC, buying points, selling points, or their expected deliverability on the buying points and selling points, or the impeding factors which could endanger your sales efforts?

**M (measurable)**: What is, in terms of the X-Be elements, the amount of information that is to be collected in the sales call, and what should be the degree of details?

**A (Achievable)**: Does the current relating status indices with the key persons make it possible to get the customer information you want to obtain in this sales call?

**R (Realistic)**: Could other members of your networked resources act as appropriate communicators and facilitate the communication to get more of the needed customer information?

**T (Time)**: What is the earliest possible time for the key persons, yourself, and/or appropriate communicators to get together?

In the area of selling and sales management, there is a question that is pretty simple but important and often difficult to formulate and answer specifically; it is this: how familiar are you with the targeted account? Within the X-Be framework, the formulation of this question becomes precise and straightforward: *to what extent have you filled up the table of the CNM System for Selling* (Table 10.1) *and how confident are you about the information you have entered for each X-Be element?* Addressing this question also becomes precise and systematic within the X-Be framework, thanks to the intrinsic logic that underlies this framework and the bonds among its elements.

The high degree to which the X-Be framework makes selling and sales management precise and systematic is not specific to this question, to the principle of SMART objectives, or the task of constructing sound judgments about the progress of selling. It applies to many aspects of complex sales situations. The discussion in the above sections was only an attempt to illustrate the conceptual and analytical breakthroughs that the X-Be framework generates in the field of exchange behavior and its sub-field of selling and sales management. As will be shown in the remainder of this chapter, other aspects and applications that illustrate the effectiveness and concreteness of the X-Be framework will demonstrate the great extent to which selling and sales management will be transformed by the proper implementation of the concepts and methods of this framework.

## CLASSIFICATION OF SALES OPPORTUNITIES

Sales opportunities characterization and management are fundamentally important for the operation of any business. The correct classification of the available sales opportunities and their statuses would not only impact the corresponding selling activities, but also provide the foundations on the basis of which other business activities (e.g., production, logistics, finance, investment, and human resources) are planned, and managed within the organization. As a subject matter, current selling and sales management knowledge has provided several instruments to help analyze sales opportunities and their statuses. Among these instruments, there are two that have become very popular: "sales pipeline" and "sales funnel." Although different in names, the fundamental logic behind these two methods is similar. Thus, we will only consider the concept of sales funnel in our discussion below.

### Problems With Sales Funnel

As a useful metaphor, the concept of sales funnel has developed into a very important sales management tool for assessing sales opportunities, planning and directing selling activities and conducting sales forecast. Such uses of the funnel concept can be found in many companies operating in the B-to-B markets. In addition, many B-to-B CRM software systems include this concept as the foundation for the analysis of the company's sales management activities and results. In general, the implementation of the sales funnel method can be either activity-based, result-based, or both (see Figure 10.1).

In general, sales managers prefer a result-based implementation of the sales funnel method. The reason for this preference is simple: salespeople

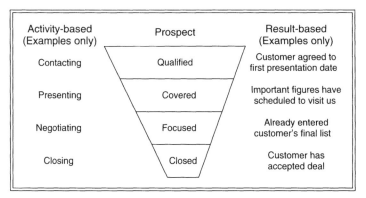

**FIGURE 10.1**   A Simple Illustration of the Sales Funnel Method.

might be good at generating all kinds of sales activities, but when it comes to results, they may deliver a few or no concrete results at all. On the other hand, an activity-based implementation would be beneficial to salespeople, as it may help in guiding them through the sales process. In any case, the sales funnel method tends to have several problems and limitations that inhibit the performance of both salespeople and managers. The following succinct list will help the reader appreciate the nature of these problems and limitations.

1. Activity-to-outcome problem: While some kinds of statistical relationships may exist between the sales activities and their outcomes, the applicability of these relationships is very limited and cannot be reliably and consistently leveraged in all of the future sales situations of the company. The success factors always differ from situation to situation. Because of this, the generalization of any relationship between sales activities and their corresponding outcomes could be the cause of a great deal of frustration and probably failure.

2. Outcome-to-activity problem: Even in the case where we are confident that the success factors (e.g., getting the key persons to visit our plant) of a given sales situation can be extrapolated to another sales situation, the knowledge of these success factors, so defined as exemplified in the above funnel, does not, unfortunately, provide us with indications and actionable information as to what next steps the salespeople and their managers should take to advance toward closing the sale.

3. Outcome-to-outcome problem: In most cases, the past successes achieved with a company's existing customers cannot be used as

a sound foundation to predict the probability of winning business with new customers. In fact, this can be a difficult task even in the case of the same customer: if the nature of the business involves an initial buy and subsequent re-buys, predicting what the repeatability of the following businesses from such a customer cannot be addressed systematically within the sales funnel methodology.

4. Overview-to-insight problem: Because sales managers tend to work at the macro level to detect patterns using the sales funnel methodology, it is often a challenging task for them to isolate the relevant details about how, why, and where their salespeople have performed well and succeeded in their selling work.

5. Cost problem: When they use the sales funnel method, salespeople tend to spend a great deal of time and effort on management and administrative tasks that are unrelated to the actual job of selling.

6. Professional problem: Salespeople and managers often appeal to the poorly defined **natural language** to communicate their insights into various opportunities in the funnel. Because of the vague nature of any natural language, it often causes not only extra communicational costs, but the very problem concerning the backbones of their professions. As a matter of fact, the extent to which one can be professional in his or her field is, first of all, dependent upon the preciseness, consistency and logic imbedded in the very core of his or her working language in the field. This is the case for all kinds of professionals such as scientists, engineers, doctors and accountants, and sales practitioners are no exception in this regard.

While the above problems and limitations provide enough incentives to look for an alternative to the sales funnel method, there is another even more serious shortcoming that this method suffers from: it does not inform salespeople about how to engineer customer value by getting them involved in the process of value formation and exchange on the part of customer. No matter how you implement the sales funnel method, whether you base it on the sales activities, the results (intermediate and final), or on both, the logic that underlies this method does not reflect the customers' buying logic and decision-making processes at all.

It has been our experience that many companies using the sales funnel method have faced all kinds of confusion in dealing with their customers. Often, salespeople manage to get many meetings with the key persons on the customer's side; they present their proposals and receive seemingly good feedbacks from the customer; then later on, they enter the customer's final list of potential suppliers and may even feel that they are enjoying a privileged relationship with this customer, only to find out at the last minute that they have lost the sale to someone else. In other cases, the business relationship may have already been established by salespeople, but not very long later, the conquered sales cease, as no more purchase orders come in; they have all gone to the competitors.

When reading about such situations, some people may react by stating the following: to avoid this type of failure, you need some special sales skills such as the ones usually used for closing, and/or you have to address problems with the after-sales service. While this is indeed true in many cases we dealt with in our professional life, there are other degenerate situations in which the failure to close the deal had nothing to do with closing skills, or after-sales service. In fact, some of the failures we reported above happened to multinational companies operating in China, and, according to feedback we received from Chinese customers, the reason why the sellers did not win the sale is simply "Peibang." "Peibang" is one of those tricky business practices in China that lead to a gentle and unexpected failure of the seller. The Chinese word "Peibang" refers to the situation where "someone is brought to execution ground but without being executed." For various reasons, some customers like to see some suppliers on the track of competition up to the last minute. These suppliers are often kept happy by the buying company during the entire purchase process, even though the latter company would have already decided not to offer the business to them. The sales funnel method will never reveal if a sales opportunity is in an unusual status such as "Peibang," but the proper implementation of the X-Be framework will.

## Power of the Classification of Sales Opportunities Within X-Be

The approach used in the X-Be framework is radically different from the sales funnel. It is designed to help overcome the difficulties listed above and to guide the salespeople and their managers focus their attention on the right sales parameters. For this purpose, sales opportunities and their corresponding statuses are characterized by analyzing customers' exchange behaviors at the fundamental level. Quantitatively, this characterization is carried out using the X-Be sales status indices, namely, the relating status, attitude, and confidence indices. You could use these indices individually or combined. In Figure 10.2, we propose a classification of sales opportunities that makes use of the relating status and confidence indices

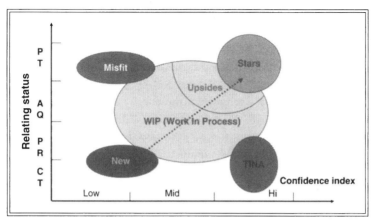

**FIGURE 10.2**  Classification of Sales Opportunities in the X-Be Framework. TINA, There Is No Alternative to Customers.

(Note the following values of Relating Status: CT, Critical Stage; PR, Public Relations Stage; AQ, Acquaintance Stage; PT, Partner Stage. For more details on these indices, refer to Chapter 8).

In our previous discussions, we showed how and why salespeople should use the relating status and confidence indices to make sound judgments and improve the effectiveness of their selling activities. But, these indices can also be integrated into an effective management tool that salespeople and their managers can use either individually or as a team to evaluate and monitor all of the company's sales opportunities. One aspect of this tool is shown in Figure 10.2 where sales opportunities are classified into six categories:

1. The "Star" – this type of sales opportunity features high values of both the confidence and relating status indices.
2. The "Upsides" – these are the sales opportunities that are characterized by a relatively high value on both dimensions. In general, effective work will upgrade them to the "Star" category.
3. The "WIP" (Works in Process) – this refers to those sales opportunities which are at the medium level on both dimensions.
4. The "New" – a sales opportunity of this type scores low on both dimensions. This is usually the case when a salesperson has just initiated the first contact with a new customer. However, no matter how long the salesperson has been working on this sales opportunity, if both scores are low, the opportunity will remain in the "New" category unless the salesperson gives it up.

The above four categories are the most common ones in sales processes. But, there are two more that are worth some discussion.

5. The "TINA (There Is No Alternative to Customers)" – this type of sales opportunity is characterized by a high score on the CI, but a rather low score on the relating status index. It often occurs in situations where (1) the sale process is that of a large corporation that dominates the market, (2) the purchasing process is that of a client who is temporarily unable to replace some products or suppliers, or (3) the clients simply have no (better) choices.

6. The "Misfit" – this refers to those sales opportunities that score very high on the relating status index, yet salespeople are unable to move toward winning the sale, as the recorded CI is in the low range. An extreme example of such a situation is when your customer needs hats, but what you can supply are socks; in this case you have no chance to succeed in closing any deal with this customer, even if you have an excellent relating status with him and he wishes you success in your sales work. In reality, though, "Misfit" is not as extreme as the "hats versus socks" situation. It usually means that some features of your sales offer (quality issues, logistic issues, financial arrangement, and so on) misfit with the customer needs. However, any identified "Misfit" could serve as valuable information for renovating and innovating on the existing sales offer (or "integrated product" using the X-Be terminology) to better fit the customer needs. Because the "Misfit" sales opportunities can be the source of valuable customer information, more discussion about them is provided below.

A sales opportunity falls in the "Misfit" category if the seller's offer misfit with the customer's buying points, selling points, and/or with customer's expected deliverability upon them. For instance, the misfit could concern the quality standard, the price, the payment terms, the logistic needs, and so on. It will be highly beneficial for the selling company to set a system through which salespeople can report accurately the specific "Misfit" factors as soon as possible. We should note, however, that these reports cannot be based on vague assumptions or hand-waving by the salespeople; otherwise, salespeople may end up using the "Misfit" category cleverly to escape the difficulties of selling, and thus mislead the company. For a sales opportunity to be labeled as a "Misfit," salespeople must prove (and the company verify) that their overall relating status indices with the influential key persons and COLs are very high.

- If no efforts can make the key persons with whom the salesperson has a favorable relating status accept the sales offer (or the integrated product), then the most probable reason for this situation is that the sales opportunity is a "Misfit."

- The earlier the salesperson can discover the "Misfit" nature of a sales opportunity, the better it is for her and her company to avoid further losses.

- The salesperson must record clearly and specifically the "Misfit" factors and report them to the relevant people and departments as valuable customer information.

- A salesperson is qualified to report a "Misfit" sales opportunity only when it is almost certain that her relating status with the customer is high.

- Managers could easily check out the relating status of a salesperson with the customer (for instance, they can call the key persons personally and verify with them the reported information). They should show gratefulness when salespeople report "Misfit" factors and provide inputs for product improvements, renovations, and innovations. Those who believe that their salespeople can "sell ice to Eskimos" should reconsider their management philosophy, as they may be pursuing the ostrich policy more than effective sales management.

**FIGURE 10.3**   Facts about the "Misfit" Sales Opportunities.

Generally speaking, when a salesperson enjoys a favorable relating status with the client, all of her work will lead to successful sales, unless the opportunity is, indeed, a "Misfit." Figure 10.3 presents a summary of the main facts about the "Misfit" opportunities.

As was previously indicated, the above categorization provides us with an effective tool for sales opportunities management. Some of the main characteristics of this tool are as follows:

1. Its development is based on the fundamental aspects of the exchange behaviors of customers. It reflects the progress of the sales process, along with the process of value formation and exchange on the part of customer. Because of this, it guides salespeople and their managers to focus and monitor the core sales parameters.

2. It is intended to help salespeople with their selling work, while at the same time reveal, as a natural by-product, the information that the management wants; there is therefore no need for extra work on administrative tasks that are unrelated to the actual job of selling.

3. It collects insights as well as live and relevant information about each sales process as it unfolds; this helps not only in the management of this individual sales process, but also contributes

to the enhancement of the existing statistics about the past sales processes, which then makes salespeople and their managers even more effective.

4. Its prediction power is increased because of its insightful structure and also because of the improved quality of the sales process statistics. As indicated above, these statistics are indeed enhanced and their extrapolations properly adjusted by the current information that is collected for the sales process at hand. In addition, the well-structured nature of the six-category classification of sales opportunities helps improve the prediction of the probability of winning a sale. This probability depends indeed on the category to which this sale belongs. For instance, one may be so lucky that she wins a sale in the "New" category (as per the Chinese saying: "even a blind cat will run into a dead mouse once in a while"), but the probability of winning sales in the "New" category is much smaller than that of winning sales in the "Star" category.

5. It can predict the repeatability of an already won business in the case where the nature of this business involves an initial buy and subsequent re-buys. For instance, if this business was won while it was in the "Star" category, its repeatability is more likely to occur than if it was won in the "WIP" category.

What is more, the above X-Be-based categorization of sales opportunities enables the selling company as well as its departments and employees to remain in sync with the current market situation, not with past statistics. It helps the company implement a business management approach that is truly client-centered. In the next sections, we will present even more applications of the X-Be-based classification of sales opportunities.

## AN X-Be-BASED SALES MANAGEMENT TOOL

If we integrate the X-Be-based classification of sales opportunities (Figure 10.2) with a bit more information about the customers, we obtain a powerful CNM System for Sales Management, such as the one shown in Table 10.2. This system builds up on the CNM System for Selling presented in Table 10.1. It aims at monitoring the sales across the whole company and developing accurate estimates for its forecasts. It also serves as a basis for the design of the appropriate actions to take in the future and helps

**TABLE 10.2  A Customer Needs Management (CNM) System for Sales Management.**

| Chief Sales Officer: | | Date Updated: | | | Serial Number: | | | |
|---|---|---|---|---|---|---|---|---|
| PPP | Client/ Product | Sale Revenue (million dollars) | | | | | Relating Status Index | Confidence Index | Explanation |
| | | Total Revenue | Q1 | Q2 | Q3 | Q4 | | | |
| FC | | | | | | | | | |
| SL | | | | | | | | | |
| SQ | | | | | | | | | |
| ND | | | | | | | | | |
| NE | | | | | | | | | |
| Stars | | | | | | | PT | H | |
| Upsides | | | | | | | AQ | M,H | |
| WIP | | | | | | | AQ,PR | M | |
| NEW | | | | | | | CT,PR | L,M | |
| Misfit | | | | | | | PT | L | |
| TINA | | | | | | | CT | H | |
| Comment | | Date | | Name | | Department | | Position | |

Note: The PPP in this chart refers to the company's PPP .

in providing appropriate feedback to the company's departments (production, finance, human resources, and so on) so that they can adjust their decisions to the level of the essential activity of the company – the sales.

The sales management concepts that are used in this CNM system are the same as those that are required by the good sales practices and that have been discussed in this book. As a result, the implementation of the proposed CNM system does not require salespeople to spend any more effort in collecting extra information for management. In fact, the information that salespeople would have gathered in the CNM System for Selling (Table 10.1) for running their selling activities will serve as input to the CNM System for Sales Management (Table 10.2). One can develop a computer software tool to automate the data processing and transfer from the first system to the second; this software tool can also be used to display the specialized management interfaces that are required to navigate the CNM System for Sales Management.

The natural logical links and high degree of compatibility between both CNM systems help create, within the selling company, one single management platform that enables salespeople, sales teams, and sales management staff to work harmoniously and effectively. This platform is built on one common language that reflects the essence of the exchange behaviors of customers, which then allows all staff members involved directly or indirectly with sales activities to communicate over the sales issues from the perspectives of both selling and sales management.

In what follows, we present just a summary of the key beneficial aspects of the CNM sales management approach that we propose in this book. As for the details about the implementation of this approach and its effective use from different perspectives, it is beyond the scope of this text.

1. The CNM System for Sales Management helps salespeople and their managers track down the complete dynamics of the sales opportunities they are working on. They can monitor the current stages at which these opportunities are in the customer's purchase process, as well as the category they belong to. Based on this information, they then carry out an analysis of the current and future sales performance of the company and design possible management actions.

2. The CNM System for Sales Management can be used to forecast the amount of sales that can be won at different time horizons with different probabilities, based on historical data and current information collected (in terms of the X-Be concepts – PPP, selling indices, category of the opportunity, and so on) by salespeople. It can also be used to estimate the probability of the repeatability of those already won sales (which would currently be at the FC stage).

3. It guides salespeople to effectively allocate their time depending on the information that has been gathered in the Table (Table 10.2) and the sales quota that they have to complete in a given period of time.

4. It empowers the sales management staff to assess the sales performance of each salesperson in a comprehensive and

systematic manner, by considering the sales already achieved, the ones that could be achieved in the future with different probabilities, and the possible re-buys from existing customers.

We should point out that what we presented above are only a few management implications of the implementation of the X-Be-based CNM Systems for Selling and Sales Management. Other positive implications are the use of result-driven time management and activity-based costing methods for sales management to objectively allocate time and cost to the selling activities. All that is required to benefit from these implications is to collect customer information in terms of the X-Be concepts – PPP, key persons, VOC, buying points, selling points, deliverability issues, relating status index, attitude index, CI, integrated product, and the development of networked resources.

## SELLING TO CONSUMERS

In the above sections, we presented the various ways the X-Be framework can be applied to help construct sound judgments about the customers, set up SMART objectives for the selling activities, and categorize sales opportunities and manage them. But the discussion focused mostly on sales situations that occur in the context of a B-to-B relationship. In this section, we look at consumer selling.

We start this discussion by pointing out that the categorization of business relationships as B-to-B or B-to-C tends to be misleading for the purpose of analyzing business interactions. The relationships that are often referred to as B-to-C can be analyzed more effectively as a B-to-B type, because the consumer never acts as a one single individual, but rather as a social being that is also part of an organization – the CISS. In addition, we argue that the notion of business "B" is too restrictive, since governments, charitable organizations, and non-governmental organizations can also get involved in exchange processes that are as important for the economy as a whole. These organizations are usually implicitly included under the umbrella of B-to-B, but, in the X-Be framework, we prefer to describe business relationships as O-to-O, that is, Organization-to-Organization, where the term "organization" refers to a *company*, a CISS, *a government, a non-governmental organization, or a charitable organization.*

For consumer selling, a good understanding of the CISS is key to effectively approaching consumers. Although the structure and behavior of the CISS tend to be different than those of a traditional organization, we argue that the X-Be concepts can still be applied to consumer selling, especially in the case of big ticket items (such as buying a car, a house, a major appliance, and so on) and products that are risky, new, or complex. There are indeed "key persons" and "COLs" that influence the consumer's decisions; these decisions will be taken through a PPP-like process that involves the notions of "VOC," "buying points," "selling points," and "deliverability issues"; the seller needs to develop and use her "networked resources," and her work will come down to designing an "integrated product" that meets the consumer's buying points and selling points and addresses the "impeding factors"; the monitoring and planning of the selling activities can be done using indices similar to the "attitude", "confidence," and "relating status" indices. But the way the X-Be should be implemented for consumer selling depends on some important aspects of the customers' behavior: their purchase involvement, product involvement, and program involvement. Depending on the nature of the product to be sold, customer's preference for interaction, and availability of communication technology, these involvements could be high, medium, or low.

If, for instance, the product is significant, risky, new, and/or complex (e.g., real-estate products, education, health-care service, and so on), the consumer's purchase involvement tends to be high. When this is the case, the X-Be framework and its management tools can be adapted relatively easily to consumer selling. The details of how this adaptation can be carried out are however beyond the scope of this book.

If, on the other hand, the product is a small-ticket item, the seller will face low or medium purchase involvement situations. The consumer will not go through all of the stages of the PPP, and the DVB will be predominant. In some of these situations, non-personal selling (telemarketing, direct mailing, internet tools, advertising, and so on) could be a cost-effective approach, and the X-Be concepts could be very useful in the design of this approach's instruments. In general, the seller may increase the effectiveness of her selling work by combining the use of other approaches such as, for instance, program involvement and product involvement. While the effectiveness of these approaches or combinations thereof is dependent on the industry and the market in which the sales company operates, a properly designed integrated selling approach (combining personal and non-personal communication and interaction with customers) will be in the benefit of both the consumers and sales company.

We should note, however, a recent trend in the area of supply and demand chains management that aims at adopting the approach of real-time and simultaneous systems management of both chains. This business management trend, to be supported by the current overwhelming development of information technology, sets the stage for a high level of mass customization and customerization of both services and products. Services and products become then indistinguishable and end up being co-produced in real-time by both the seller and the buyer (Tien et al., 2004). As a result, many purchase situations could technically move in the future from the low- and medium-involvement categories to the high-involvement category. Therefore, and as was indicated above, the X-Be framework becomes relevant to these purchase situations if consumers so choose to virtually experience with things that were not previously possible due to the high cost of communication and interaction. Even in the situations of DVB-dominated purchases, sellers could still properly characterize customer value in terms of the VOC, buying points and selling points, customer-satisfying deliverability, and so on and keep abreast of any significant change in the relevant default values (which will evolve as a result of changes in society). Sellers could also use X-Be selling status indices as a kind of survey instrument to effectively monitor the status of value integration in terms of integrated product, and so deal with competition from the perspective of customer value, as was explained in the X-Be framework.

## ON SELLING SKILLS

There are many sales skills – many "angles," "tips," "tricks," "rules," and "guidelines" to handle a sales job, probably as many as there are salespeople. But there are certainly much fewer skills which could guide salespeople consistently and successfully throughout their career. Deep down, only those sales skills which can assist in identifying potential customers, understanding their needs, engineering, and delivering the right sales offers to satisfy the identified needs may make salespeople succeed. With this in mind, in this section we will turn our attention to three categories of selling skills, which should be areas of interest for the professional development of any seller and sales organization. The skills described below will also be useful in thoroughly and successfully enacting the principles and ideas introduced in this book.

### Relating Skills

As we noted in Chapter 7, throughout the exchange relationship, a sales-person is reliant upon consistent access to important customer information. While some basic data about a customer or client company can be gleaned through public channels, invariably there will be essential information that will only emerge through communication and social networking with potential and existing customers – hence the centrality of the notion of networked resources in selling and sales management. Skills pertaining to the ability to form relationships with others – relating skills – and to develop, maintain, and update one's networked resources are of fundamental importance. Networked resources and the methods to build them were discussed in Chapter 7; here, we only emphasize this: the quality of your networked resources is measured by the amount of the relevant and important customer information that you have gained from these resources at the time you need it; it is dependent on the number of people who have the needed customer information and your relating status with them.

## Communication Skills

The communication skills presented here are distinct from the above relating skills. Whereas the latter enable the salesperson to form relationships, the former allow the salesperson to utilize those relationships to exchange critical sales information, when it is necessary. In this section, we will discuss five distinct communication skills, each of which is closely related to the X-Be principles and each of which permits the salesperson access to information essential to moving an exchange relationship forward. The five skills are the following:

1. "attitude scouting" to identify the VOC;
2. "attitude calibrating" to verify the buying points and selling points;
3. "proving" to convince the customers that you will deliver on the buying points and selling points;
4. "pace setting (i)" to ensure the effective flow of information exchange;
5. "pace setting (ii)" to sense the hidden buying points.

Let's consider each of these skills in turn.

### Attitude Scouting

In order to fully understand a key person's VOC, when engaging in the communication with him, the salesperson needs to isolate three distinct, but related streams of information:

*Background and situational information* – what is the situation in which this key person might perceive or have perceived a purchase need?

*Selecting points* – what information might be or have been perceived to be relevant to the situation where the purchase need arose?

*Selecting rationales* – what are the key person's accounts for the significance of the above-mentioned relevant information?

Attitude scouting is the ability to develop and pose specific questions that will bring these three streams of information to light, and then to evaluate the customer's response. For instance, a salesperson selling energy-efficiency equipment might ask a key person "how much electricity has our (meaning customer's) company consumed for these three years?" for the situational information, "what factors could we have better addressed when we are together to solve this costly electricity problem?" for the information of **selecting points**, and "how could we work together to best solve these concerns (**selecting points**) for the information of **selecting rationales**.

Consider the example of a salesperson attempting to sell energy-efficient solutions to a manufacturing company. First, the salesperson may obtain the situational information by enquiring into the customer's interest in energy-saving operations. So she may ask the key person how much electricity his company has consumed over the course of the last three years. If the key person replies with a larger than expected figure, the salesperson may consider it as a potential sales opportunity. To arouse his sense of purchase, she may briefly cite a couple of successful stories achieved with her company's solutions in similar situations as the key person's. In an attempt to get a clearer background about the key person's perception of the importance and urgency of solving this problem, the salesperson asks, "What specific factors in the company's operations might be contributing to this problem?" and "How do these factors concern you?" If the responses point to a clear sales opportunity, the salesperson may continue with his line of questioning in an attempt to elicit the key person's selecting points and selecting rationales, for instance, she could ask, "What are your concerns in attempting to solve this costly electricity problem" and "How might our organizations work together to address these concerns?"

**Attitude Calibrating**
Recall from Chapter 5 that what motivates a key person to buy (i.e., the buying points or selling points) has to be consistent, implicitly or explicitly, with his VOC. Thus, the salesperson needs to calibrate the buying points and selling points that the key person wants to see in a sales offer against this key person's VOC. Also, the salesperson may want to suggest new features (in the sales offer) corresponding to new buying

points and selling points, which may help detect (or induce) changes and possible evolution in the key person's VOC.

Attitude calibrating follows upon attitude scouting. With the key person's VOC (gleaned through attitude scouting) in mind, the salesperson then proceeds to consider certain questions pertaining to the nature of this key person's buying points and selling points, along the lines of the following:

Buying points: what, in a sales offer, could benefit this key person personally? (Recall that all purchases – even organizational ones – have various personal dimensions).

Selling points: what, in a sales offer, could benefit this key person socio-culturally? (Recall that all purchases – even strictly personal ones – are made with socio-cultural aspects in mind).

Thus, attitude calibrating consists in isolating and verifying a customer's buying points and selling points, by cross-referencing them with the key person's VOC (as detected during the process of attitude scouting). To achieve this goal, the salesperson can make use of various questions that she can pose to the key person.

Also, it is crucial to keep in mind that key persons assign (consciously or unconsciously) different degrees of significance to the buying points and selling points; to gauge such degrees of significance, the salesperson can make use of the selling status indices we discussed in Chapter 8.

**Proving**

"Proving" refers to the skill set of building and presenting working rationales and evidences to convince a key person that you will deliver upon the buying points and selling points you have considered integrating into the sales offer (the integrated product). Some of the important types of evidence that should be included in designing arguments are the ones that will allay the customer's sense of risk. For instance, third party's appraisals, referrals, and testimonies from satisfied customers, reputation of the sales company, and salespeople's professionalism will provide compelling evidence that the promised buying points and selling points are indeed forthcoming – in the form of the integrated product.

It is important to keep in mind that assuaging the deliverability concerns of individual key persons is often the necessary precondition for those individuals feeling confident enough about the direction the intended exchange is taking to openly voice their approval to others – thus improving the seller's CI (see Chapter 8) and increasing the likelihood of closing the sale. In this respect, managing each individual key person's sense of risk is of the utmost importance.

## Pace Setting (i)

One thing that a salesperson must always remember – indeed, even during the course of deliverability proving – is that selling is an act of interactive communication, not just demonstration. The customer's input is integral and should be the basis for any and all activity on the part of the seller. Thus, a skilled salesperson should know how much to say, and when to say it, so as to elicit the maximum useful input from the key persons. Hence our next skill, pace setting (i), or the ability to regulate the rate of information exchange with a key person, in order to ensure that communications remain productive throughout the exchange relationship. The methods for pace setting (i) are quite straightforward but many salespeople are not used to them: at timely and consistent intervals during the process of communication, the salesperson poses questions, soliciting feedback and comments from the key person. Self-discipline is the key: a sensitive sales approach generally calls for input from the customer with much more regularity than the key person might actually be inclined to volunteer it.

The success of both attitude scouting and attitude calibrating is dependent to a great extent on pace setting (i). Administered effectively, pace setting (i) serves to stimulate and maintain the attention of the key persons; to build a sense of parity and co-operation between seller and customer; to help the seller better understand the key persons' expectations; and to demonstrate the seller's interest, sensitivity, and professionalism – all of which, as we have already noted, will be advantageous throughout the exchange relationship.

## Pace Setting (ii)

*Pace setting (ii)* is related to pace setting (i), though it also draws on elements of attitude scouting. This particular skill serves to aid sellers in the detection and verification of hidden buying points. This type of buying points were discussed in Chapter 8, where we described a modified version of the "teacher's method" as a technique to detect and verify these points.

## Forward Thinking

We turn now to the third and last category of selling skills: *forward thinking*. Forward thinking is, quite simply, the ability to foresee – with some degree of clarity – the possible outcomes of a situation and to make preparations for those outcomes. A salesperson adept at forward thinking is thus able to anticipate and prepare for events in an exchange relationship before they take place, as well as to respond to events fully once they do take place. In this way, keen forward thinking serves to buttress the effectiveness of all the other selling skills described in this section.

The ability to "think forward" in a situation is determined, to a great extent, by the reliability (and comprehensiveness) of the conceptual framework through which the situation is being viewed and analyzed. In traditional selling, this "conceptual framework" is usually experience, but one of our reasons for writing this book was to afford all sellers, even novices, some of the insights that veteran salespeople might take for granted. The X-Be framework strives to uncover the logic inherent in purchasing behavior and to present it in a logical manner, so as to be as immediately and broadly applicable as possible in real-world sales settings. As psychologist Kurt Lewin puts it, "there is nothing so practical as a good theory." Throughout this book, we have attempted to advance what we believe to be one such "good theory," as well as the practical tools necessary for applying it.

## Summary

In the above discussion, we have attempted to demonstrate the relationship between specific selling skills and the attainment of necessary objectives in an exchange relationship. Our prevailing intention has been to emphasize the importance of value-adding skills for anyone involved in the business of selling – be it on the level of management, or on the front lines – the sales floor.

During the course of our discussion, we have outlined three distinct categories of selling skills. The first category consists of relating skills, which enable the salesperson to form (and maintain) relationships – relationships that will, in turn, ideally evolve into arenas for the exchange of useful information, and possibly into full-fledged exchange relationships. The second category of selling skills, communication skills, build upon relating skills by empowering the seller to take best advantage of established relationships – by exchanging, processing, and applying the information possessed by the seller's networked resources. We broke this category into four specific skills: (1) attitude scouting, for eliciting a key person's VOC; (2) attitude calibrating, for uncovering the key person's buying points and selling points; (3) deliverability proving, for addressing the customer's concerns and sense of risk with regard to the issue of deliverability upon the key person's buying points and selling points; and (4) pace setting, an effective means of regulating the rate of information exchange and uncovering hidden buying points. Finally, we turned to the last category of selling skills – forward thinking or the ability to foresee, and make preparations for, events in the exchange relationship before they take place. Although experience can endow certain salespeople with a some ability to "think forward," we argue that a better way to ensure consistent forward thinking is to understand the customer's behavior in terms of a comprehensive conceptual framework for the exchange process, such as the one set forth in this book.

## CONCLUSION

A new set of method for selling and sales management is what we presented to our readers in this chapter. All of these methods have been derived from an integrated implementation of the X-Be building blocks. A unique feature of the derived methods is their parsimonious nature; they allow salespeople and their managers to handle the highly complex and diverse phenomena of selling and sales management, while they are based on a relatively small number of elements – the X-Be building blocks and associated concepts. But what has really made all of this possible is the intrinsic logic that underlies the X-Be framework. This logic, which leverages customer's reward-oriented behaviors, has proved to be very useful and practical, as it has been demonstrated in this chapter and in the previous ones. In the next chapter, we will show that it is also theoretically sound and, as a result, it opens up the doors for more development in the areas of supply chain management, CRM, risk analysis, systems management, and engineering.

# PART TWO

# THEORETICAL FOUNDATIONS AND ADVANCED TOPICS

# 11

# THEORETICAL FOUNDATIONS

Our discussion throughout this book has focused on the topic of selling and sales management. Based on the X-Be framework, a comprehensive roadmap to effectively manage the sales activities from the low-level inter-actions between the involved people all the way to the overall and strategic planning of corporate sales was presented. But, when we were developing the ideas that underlie this framework and the corresponding roadmap, our thoughts were not limited to selling. They were much broader than that, as they were concerned with the fundamentals of reward-oriented behaviors in social interactions in general. As discussed in social exchange theory, the analysis of these behaviors can further refine our understanding of a variety of social situations in which exchange takes place. We wanted to gain some insights into the intrinsic characteristics of social interactions, and we wanted to do it by imposing the *principle of parsimony* on us.

The literature on selling and sales management is abundant, but very few authors have taken on the challenge of explaining the complexity of selling and sales management on the basis of a parsimonious framework – a framework that is made up of only a few operational elements, yet is able to account for various selling and sales management situations logically and effectively. Many contributions to the body of knowledge of sales management come down to piling-up case studies, sales stories, formal codes, and appeals to "common sense." These contributions are usually not presented in an integrated fashion from a perspective of the customer's value-pursuing behavior, which makes it difficult for the sales community to leverage them in a systematic way within the highly competitive corporate world.

In this book, we took a completely different approach. We developed an integrated, parsimonious, and logically based framework to help conduct the various selling and sales management operations in a systematic, effective, and efficient manner. As was demonstrated in the previous chapters, this framework has applications in many key activities that take place in a sales department and beyond; this includes, but not limited to, managing sales opportunities, generating sales forecast, constructing sound judgments about customers, planning sales events, managing customer objections, guiding the communication with the customers, designing adequate sales offers, developing a team-oriented environment for selling and sales management, constructively evaluating salespeople performance, effective handling of competition, activity-based costing, and practicing management by objectives. The X-Be tool that is used to carry out such activities is a *Simple Algebraic Language to Engineer Satisfaction* (SALES) of both parties involved in the exchange.

But, while the focus here is on selling and sales management, we believe that the framework can be extended to the study of other types of human interactions where some kind of value exchange needs to take place. In this respect, the X-Be framework's ideas can be used to develop insightful agent-based models to describe and simulate the behavior of emergent structures such as markets, economies, organizations, communities, and so on.

In this chapter, we leave aside the benefits and potential applications of the X-Be framework and we focus on its theoretical foundations. We do that by looking at the connections between the X-Be concepts and some selected topics that stem from various scientific disciplines. The discussion will be brief but multiple and will concern the fields of philosophy of science, decision sciences, cognitive psychology, behavioral studies, sociology, and systems engineering. The main purpose of this discussion is to highlight the contributions of these disciplines to our understanding of the issues of exchange behavior and provide indications about how we intend to advance our future research in this area.

## SALES AND PHILOSOPHY OF SCIENCE

At the heart of our framework for the exchange behavior in selling and sales management is the proposition that sales behavior, however subjective may be its particulars, and no matter how much uncertainty it may evince, can, in theory and practice, be analyzed, planned, and systematized – and thus, considered using some elements of the scientific method. If we were writing a book on another topic such as mechanics, thermodynamics, and quantum physics, we would not have to state and discuss a proposition like this one. It would have been obvious to the readers; these topics are after all part of what we call natural sciences. But in the case of selling and sales management, the reader may have legitimate reasons to be wary of claims such as these. Broad dicta about sales activity present few theoretic objects to be substantiated and discussed in scientific circles. Too, the rhetoric of science is often deployed irresponsibly, simply to add an air of legitimacy.

> Science is highly esteemed. Apparently, there is a widely held belief that there is something special about science and its methods. The naming of some claim or line of reasoning or piece of research "scientific" is done in a way that is intended to imply some kind of merit or special kind of reliability…Advertisements frequently assert that a particular product has been scientifically shown to be whiter, more potent, more sexually appealing or in some way superior to rival products…The high regard for science is not restricted to everyday life and the popular media. It is evident in the scholarly and academic world too. Many areas of study are now described as sciences by their supporters, presumably in an effort to imply that the methods used are as firmly based and as potentially fruitful as in a traditional science such as physics or biology.
> A. F. Chalmers (1982) – *What is This Thing Called Science?*

But this is not to say that the "soft" disciplines have nothing to learn from the natural sciences. The broad paradigm of observation, analysis, induction, deduction can still be of use – not merely in social disciplines (which are, it is true, striving for scientific legitimacy), but in everyday life. Our claim is that certain elements of the scientific method can be usefully applied to the study of sales for the benefit of salespeople, sales managers, and sales researchers. The approach that we propose consists in inventing a small number of operational elements on the basis of empirical studies and relevant principles and constructing a theoretical framework with these elements to account for the complex nature of selling and sales management.

At present, most sales studies are focused on piling-up business cases or sales stories. This "facts only" approach cannot reveal much, for raw facts have relevant meanings only when they are looked at within a certain conceptual framework [as per the thesis of the theory dependence of observation (Kuhn, 1962)] – they are just stimuli that would not be useful unless they are interpreted, synthesized, and converted into meaningful actions, in the same way as does data, which become useful when it is elevated to the level of information, and then knowledge. But, for a salesperson to convert raw facts into actions, she needs a theory, a conceptual framework that helps her analyze the "facts" and synthesize them. As psychologist Kurt Lewin said, indeed, "experience alone does not create knowledge" – "there is nothing so practical as a good theory". In this book, we propose such a "theory" for the field of selling and sales management – a "theory" that is embodied in the X-Be framework and its (1 + 7) elements.

We should also note that the need for such a framework to interpret "facts" and "experience" is not unique to social sciences; it is also the case in natural sciences as has been revealed in philosophy of science. Some remarks by, Francois Jacob (1995), a Nobel Prize winner for medicine, in his autobiography, *The Statue Within,* might be illuminating in this respect:

> Contrary to what I once thought, scientific progress did not consist simply in observing, in accumulating experimental facts and drawing up a theory from them. It began with the invention of a possible world, or a fragment thereof, which was then compared by experimentation to the real world. And it was this constant dialogue between imagination and experiment that allowed one to form an increasingly fine-grained conception of what is called reality.

In our research on selling and sales management, the "possible world" that we envision – and to which we aspire – is one in which selling and sales management could be analyzed using a SALES of both parties involved in the exchange. "Simple" so that all employees involved in the sales process are able to implement it with no major difficulty; "Algebraic" so that salespeople and sales managers can carry out meaningful operations on the various concepts used in the language SALES. But, to develop such a language, we need a theoretical framework on the basis of which the language alphabet and operations can be designed.

To set our inquiry for the development of such a framework on a sound track, we must first of all define what we mean by selling: Selling is the process in which a party (the seller) searches for, communicates, and interacts with another party (the buyer) for a certain exchange to take place to the satisfaction of both parties.

Selling can thus take place regardless of what form of communication and interaction is used (electronic or non-electronic, personal or non-personal) and regardless of what type of exchange will take place (items, services). Under this definition, successful selling behavior is measured by a mutually satisfactory exchange between both parties involved. With this in mind, we can initiate our inquiry for the development of a theoretical framework for selling and sales management.

The inquiry process is tripartite. Firstly, we must think about our research paradigm and decide about the beliefs and basic knowledge that we will use to account for human behavior. As we have already mentioned, these are rooted in other disciplines including decision sciences, cognitive psychology, and behavioral studies; as for the research paradigm, it is based on our belief that successful selling behavior requires an "interactivist" (as opposed to deterministic) approach. Secondly, we must make a record of our findings – those observational statements that result from the application of the beliefs and knowledge previously selected from the above disciplines, as well as those phenomena and processes that we uncover as a result of our analyses. Finally, we must organically fuse our research paradigm with our observational statements in the form of a comprehensive framework that reveals the intrinsic logic among the theoretic objects or concepts that are used to document observational statements. And this framework (i.e., the X-Be) is the font from which our account of effective selling springs.

This inquiry process went of course through several iterations before the framework presented in this book emerged.

## SALES AND DECISION MAKING

In his book, "Judgment & Choice," Robin M. Hogarth (2001) describes the process of decision making as the "most important" of all human activities. His point is fairly obvious. Decision making occurs and recurs to anyone, so it is the constant center of conscious thought in many research areas. It is not merely the single process from which most human behavior stems, but also that to which most actions and processes can be reduced. So it should come as no surprise that the process of effective selling may have to be considered in the context of *customer's decision making*, and that shall be the focus of this section.

The purchasing process does, indeed, ultimately amount to a process of decision making, though as purchases become more important and complex, the process begins to resemble more a network of decisions than a simple choice.

In any case, though the seller may try to engineer the best possible sales offer, it is ultimately the purchaser's decision to accept it into his life. So how does a person go about making a decision?

There are so many studies that have been carried out on the subject of decision making. One of most influential concepts in these studies is that of *bounded rationality*, introduced by Herbert Simon. Herbert Simon's work and that of Daniel Kahneman, on one level, exist to challenge the traditional models of economics, which suggest that persons are hyperrational, or act only to satisfy themselves and never deviate from their own preferences. Simon argues that humans are not always or not usually "rational" in that sense, and that many of their decisions are governed by "irrational" emotion. This more elastic, inclusive definition of people's relationship with reason leaves ample room for other "non-economic" factors to play a role in human decision making. For instance, an individual customer often needs, among other things, some socio-cultural justifications for the purchase he makes – hence the introduction of the notion of selling points in the X-Be framework. Decision making can be parsed by a number of criteria, so studied differently.

Nonetheless, in the context of bounded rationality, the process of decision making can be parsed by a number of criteria, and each decision can be categorized by the same means. Table 11.1 below presents a list (by no means an exhaustive one) of possible categorization standards to describe and classify decisions. The variety of these standards gives an indication of

**TABLE 11.1   Various Standards for Categorizing Decisions**

| Categorization Standard | Possible Features or Contents |
| --- | --- |
| Effective reach | Individual, Group, Organizational, National, International |
| Decision environment | Certain (enough information is available about the expected results ), risky (expected results evaluated in the probabilistic sense), completely uncertain (no information is available) |
| Types of decision | Programmed (determined by past experience), non-programmed (learning and adapting), associative choice |
| Nature of criteria used for decision making | Intuitive (feeling only), judgmental (rules of thumb), defined (a set of clearly defined rules) |
| Nature of problems in decision making | Clearly defined, fuzzy, undefined |
| Time dimension | Short-term, mid-term, long-term |
| Nature of decision | Routine, non-routine |
| Importance to decision maker | Low, moderate, high |
| Involvement of decision maker | Low, limited, extensive |
| Decision-making model | Classical, behavioral, garbage can model |
| Classical model | Decision makers act in a world of complete certainty |
| Behavioral model | Beliefs and perceptions need to be taken into account |
| Garbage can model | The main components of the decision-making process – problems, solutions, participants, and choice opportunities – as all mixed up in the garbage can of organization |

the wide range of possible customer decisions and behaviors, which tend to challenge sales researchers. And, like any decision making, purchasing behavior is ultimately a forward-looking enterprise, one that attempts to bring predictions to fruition, but which is shaped (and necessarily limited) by one's own perception and imagination. People make decisions in the hopes of precipitating the value they have envisioned or hypothesized, and that value is not guaranteed. In other words, the future as imagined or hypothesized gives rise to purchasing behavior, if not necessarily to the actual planned outcome.

For our purposes, we developed the PPP model to capture the major possible customer buying behaviors. We did so with the following considerations in mind:

1. The PPP reflects the main principles that have been researched in the field of decision analysis.
2. It allows sufficient flexibility for other factors influencing human decisions to be integrated into it (conversion of the PPP model into buying map after studying the VOC, buying points, selling points, and deliverability) in a logic manner.

## SALES AND COGNITIVE PSYCHOLOGY

In his famous book "Cognitive Psychology," Neisser (1967) summed up the term "cognition" best: "...The term 'cognition' refers to all processes by which the sensory input is transformed, reduced, elaborated, stored, recovered, and used, ...it is apparent that cognition is involved in everything a human being might possibly do; that every psychological phenomena is a cognitive phenomena."

Thus, studies of value exchange behavior at the interpersonal level should obviously look at the cognition of both parties involved. In particular, the analysis of the perceptions of the key persons on the customer side is essential for effective selling. The following selected topics on cognition are of particular interest to us, although many other topics and issues researched in cognitive psychology remain so attractive to us.

### Attention and Perception

If effective selling can be whittled down to a process of customer's decision making, we should ultimately be able to reduce it further to the fundamental cognitive processes of the customer who makes purchase decisions – hence the extension of our inquiry into the realm of psychology.

Particularly pertinent to the sales process is the nature of attention. It colors consumer interest, shapes a purchaser's attitude toward the sales offer in question, and directs the purchaser's relationship to the seller. In their 1978 article, "Mechanisms of attention", S.W. Keele and W.T. Neill argued that attention was at the very heart of cognitive psychology and that an understanding and appreciation of it was essential to any student of human behavior. The modern world bustles urgently and constantly with information; it is the sort of world about which the French philosopher Jacques Derrida could pronounce, *il n'ya pas de hors-texte* – "there is nothing outside of text," or, more accurately, "there is nothing that is not text." But, at the individual level, choosing amongst the "noise" is essential for functioning, communicating, and understanding, and humans "choose" information by affording it selective attention.

As William James puts it, "the essence of genius is to know what to overlook." Conversely, the reader may infer that the selectivity of attention can also give rise to errors – errors stemming from preconception, the "halo effect," projection and prejudice. But to James, experience itself was ultimately the sum of one's attentive "choices," and he warned that chaos of inundation would be the necessary result if subjectivity and selectivity were to be lost. Selectivity is, in short, all we have.

In the end, the factors that influence and determine the selection of one's attentive focus are largely three-fold. They stem from the following:

- Object or person to be perceived (i.e., external factors).
  (the shape or size of an object; color, sound, scent, or thermal contrast or intensity; motion, dynamic or static; novelty or familiarity; appearance frequency, etc.)
- Internal (subjective) factors.
  (desire and need; experience and knowledge; cultural/developmental background and context; the emotion of the moment, etc.)
- Background environment in which the person who holds the internal factors perceives the (external) object or person.
  (physical setting such as noise and tranquility; social setting such as the various relationships involved, etc.)

In light of this, it should be evident that any study of exchange behavior and buying decision making should keep in mind the centrality and individual particularity of customer's attention. An earlier but famous sales formula called AIDA (A: attention, I: interest, D: desire, A: action) is a simple yet reasonable reflection of purchase behaviors. As we expand our discussion into more complex realms of psychology, these basic tenets should be retained – because they are at the obvious heart of any effective selling.

## Gestalt Psychology

Because humans are selectively attentive creatures, and because of the profusion of informational "noise" which assails the senses constantly, the sensations and perceptions which govern our immediate reactions must be received and formed very quickly. We attempt to form an impression of the "whole form" of something on first glance, or first sensation. Human perception tends not to be atomistic when formed at first place – assembling a whole picture from clearly identified constituent fragments – but rather emerges, thanks to the marvelous capacity of the human brain for interpolation and extrapolation, and also its discomfort with openness and ambiguity. Consider the visual sense, we may arrange a series of widely spaced dots in a circle and see a circle; we may place two isosceles triangles atop a small circle and see a rabbit. It applies to other senses as well; milk chocolate has a characteristic flavor quite distinct from the respective flavors of cocoa, cocoa butter, and milk. Our immediate sensations of things tend to be integrated ones – "whole forms," rather than some coherent assemblage of logical elements. This is the general theoretical thrust of the psychological principal known as *Gestalt* theory. That immediate impression of an object's whole form, afforded by the senses as a result of limited stimuli and parsed by the brain as more or less explicable, is thus termed a *Gestalt guess*. These "guesses" are at the root of our most primordial interactions with the world around us.

## From a Guess to Thinking (a Process of Conceptualization)

Once a guess has been formulated, attention becomes more focused; more stimuli could be gathered and evaluated with the biasing power of this guess. Those stimuli that accord with those reasons that are relevant and important in the eyes of the Gestalt guess are selected; the brain allows them to shade and pare the image of the guess. Thus does the "whole form" acquire detail, to the point at last that it emerges, not as some nebulous wisp, but rather as a substantial object, and the process by which this object takes shape is the process of conceptualization that follows upon Gestalt guesses. It is in this way that the disparate elements of an object are grouped together to give rise to a more clear, meaningful and/or confident understanding about the perceived object. Again, the process abides necessarily by reason – much in the same way that customer behavior abides generally by default values (to use the X-Be terminology), which represent the long-term memory, and which is activated by a Gestalt guess. To illustrate this process, let us imagine an example.

Suppose an unschooled individual, walking by the ocean one day, encounters a whale poking its head above the waters. Its size and rapidity attract the observer's attention. Intermittently, the massive creature appears and reappears, enough for the observer to come to an early supposition about what it might be. He sees its eyes; he sees its fins; he appreciates the animal's size and shape. For, indeed, he has already realized that it is an animal, not some peculiar chimera, that he has encountered. Calling upon these limited stimuli, and his limited zoographic knowledge (his default value: a movable creature found in water must be fish), his initial Gestalt guess is that it is a type of enormous fish. But this "fish" is like nothing he has ever seen, and though he remains under the impression that it is one, certain stimuli – he having noticed the fact that the whale keeps surfacing, apparently for air – lead him to doubt his Gestalt guess. Fish, after all, gather air through gills and do not often surface; they do not have blowholes as this creature does. He decides to investigate further; for, by now, he has already entered the process of conceptualization.

So he proceeds to the nearest library and, with the help of the librarian, finds the most handsomely illustrated book that was available on sea life. He happens upon a photograph that resembles the creature whose frolicking he has witnessed. Still under the impression that the animal is a fish, if possibly an exceptional one, he notes, perhaps in disbelief, that the text underneath the picture, courteously read to him by the same librarian who accepts to provide help to the individual, refers to the animal as a "whale," the earth's largest *mammal*. Quickly he consults the lexicon in the back of the book and confirms that fish do not breathe air and that mammals do, and yet, he has never seen – or even heard of – a mammal living in the sea. It seems to him that either his own definition of what a mammal is needs renovation or the book is in error. So he is faced with a choice.

- Abide by his first impression. Conclude that the text in the book – which appears a little outdated – is wrong; finalize his conceptualization of the "whale" as a sort of enormous, *exceptional* fish, but nothing more than a fish, or
- Forsake his first impression – his Gestalt guess – and abide by the text of the book. What needs renovation in this case is his own definition of "mammal."

To us, reason suggests that the latter be the correct path to take, but that is only because we tend to consider books authoritative; we take for granted the remarkable capacity of language to prevaricate and mislead. It may be equally likely for our unschooled individual thus to take the first option, redefining his own sense of the word "fish" to allow for breathing. In any event, his conceptualization of the animal evolved organically and selectively on the basis of new information.

Of course, this whole above process can also be applied to the way a person's need might emerge, before the earliest PPP. In this case, the peculiar chimera – the whale, in our above example – is the human sense of want. It is first glimpsed dimly, apprehended roughly; then it becomes shaded, complicated by new stimuli and knowledge as they come. Indeed, the process ultimately yields two maxims for elucidating sales cognition.

1. A purchase need cannot emerge without certain default values or VOC already being in place in the potential purchaser.

   Just as our naïve observer's initial assumption about the whale being a sort of fish was predicated on his knowing what a fish is, a customer's impression that he needs something is predicated upon him knowing that there perhaps exists a corresponding area of purchase needs in his life. Hence the old aphorism about a great salesperson being able to sell an air conditioner to an Inuit: the latter will certainly not want for cold, and will be not merely unresponsive to this particular sales pitch, but will probably not even be able to conceive of a situation in which he might have use for it.

2. The more detailed and specific are the potential purchaser's VOC, the more specific will become her purchase needs.

   The potential purchaser's initial Gestalt guess was an early, rough estimation of a sense of purchase need. The more information influences him, the more knowledge with which he has to consider this need, the more detailed and specific will be his impression of the sales offer that ultimately satisfies him. This "focusing" of his impressions has been a process of conceptualization for his emergence of a purchase need.

   In this sense, the initial Gestalt guess, a selective initial judgment of what one's purchase needs are and how they may be satisfied, is the "conceptual embryo" for the rest of the purchasing process (see Figure 11.1).

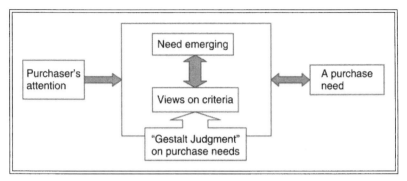

**FIGURE 11.1**   A Gestalt Account for an Emerging Need.

## Default Values Versus Learning Processes

But the process of need cognition does not always necessarily "begin at the beginning." Experience affords us all certain cognitive "shortcuts" that absolve us of the laborious exercise outlined above, of starting with very little information and coming to an eventual, more informed conclusion. On the basis of our discussion so far, we know these shortcuts as default values – the result of direct or indirect experiences of similar events or similar environments assimilated into one's system of values. In the field of psychology, they would be termed heuristics and biases. Armed with them, we are able to come to conclusions regarding complex problems, or on the basis of incomplete information, without resorting to much analysis. The result is the sort of spontaneous judgment that leads consumers to tend to believe, for example

- that expensive products are superior;
- that well-known brand can be expected to provide more consistently good products, than lesser known brands;
- that a product recommended by experts must have merit.

Related to the concept of default values are the concepts of "default rule" regarding the overregularization behavior (e.g., Marcus, 1996), and "heuristic judgment" which has been explored by numerous experts in various fields in a number of publications (e.g., Chaiken & Trope, 1999; Kahneman & Tversky, 2000). The general tenor of the discussion is that such cognitive "shortcuts" are a learned behavior, certainly, but once an actionable value – or judgment – is instilled, it can be hard to dislodge. Robert B. Cialdini, having spent three years studying the various ways in which this line of thinking manifests itself in social life, noted with some frustration that these shortcuts are ineluctable (Cialdini, 2006). (This has troubling implications for, among other things, interpersonal prejudice.)

These "instant" judgments, biases, and prejudices are the result of the brain having "learnt" or otherwise acquired a direct, apparent, or causal relationship between two objects. (In the case of consumer behavior, an example might be the perceived relationship between price and quality.) These relationships may be acquired by any number of different learning processes.

1. Conditioning
   a. classical ("Pavlovian") conditioning – automatic stimulus response,
   b. operant conditioning: certain behavior leads to a constant consequence.
2. Cognition
   a. iconic rote learning – concepts are associated "by heart" without conditioning or reasoning,
   b. vicarious learning – behaviors learnt by watching the consequences of others' actions,
   c. reasoning – using thinking to parse information.

And it is intellectually labor saving to seize upon these learnt behaviors and apply them in as many situations as they seem to be effective – even if a given situation is not positively analogous to the one that gave rise to the bias in the first place. In other words, heuristic judgments and biases are often consulted even when they are not completely appropriate. This has implications, of course, to the realm of sales. For our purposes, default values can be a hindrance or a boon to sales success, depending on the seller's ability to identify them and use them appropriately. Even to an established seller or "brand," they can pose a problem, if, for example, default values represent a consumer stereotype – one that must be subverted if, for example, a new product is to be introduced.

On the other hand, we human beings seem to be getting programmed on a continuous basis as a result of our learning. The VOC on the basis of which customer value is judged in the sales offer at hand could remain fairly constant, or be highly changeable depending on the situation in which the purchase need occurs and the "intensity" of the relevant default values in the purchaser who is experiencing the purchase need. But, in any case, the purchaser's VOC seem to constantly advise him as to what information could be relevant (selecting points) and if and how this information is important (selecting rationales) to the purchase at hand.

Before proceeding to the next section about the discipline of behavioral studies, we have three more points to make about the concept of VOC and the related subject issues.

1. A customer's perception of value could settle either directly on some obvious characteristics of the sales offer that are clearly part of the customer's selecting points or on some other unobvious secondary (or inferential) features that should be accounted for in the selecting rationales, or on both.
2. A customer may continue his learning process when interacting with his environment in which sellers' activities take place. The extent to which the customer is inclined to learn through his interactions with these sellers in a particular purchasing process is at least affected by the relevant default values, sense of significance of the purchase at hand, and his personality. The PPP model has explicitly incorporated the first two factors.
3. While certain concepts such as customer traits and personality may be useful in some aspects of selling, we do not believe that they are reliable enough in identifying the customer's perception of the value he is pursuing. They do not guarantee the consistency of the purchasing behaviors of the customer across different situations and, thus, could cause unnecessary confusions for sellers. Instead, we emphasize the use of the customer's VOC in the situation where the purchase has arisen. But this is not to say that the personality issue has been ruled out within X-Be. In fact, customers' different tendency to rely on default values and emphasis on buying points or selling points across different

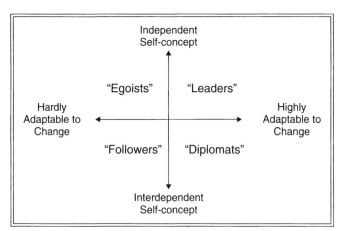

**FIGURE 11.2** Different Customer's Personalities Associated with X-Be Elements: (1) The above concept of "adaptability to change" refers to one's behavioral tendency to rely on his or her default values; (2) Independent or Interdependent Self-Concept (e.g., Abe et al, 1996) is indicated here by personal emphasis on buying points or selling points, respectively.

purchasing situations may manifest their different personalities on these two important dimensions: (1) adaptability to change (strong default value behavior leads to low adaptability) and (2) independent or interdependent self-concept (people with strong independent self-concept emphasize more on buying points than selling points, while those with strong interdependent self-concept more on selling points than buying points). Figure 11.2 might be interesting to those who want to handle customer's personality issues when considering their selling activities.

## SALES AND BEHAVIORAL STUDIES

In our previous discussions, we have repeatedly raised the issue of the rationality of the buying behavior of customers. To many people, the concept of rational behavior means being logical, agreeable to reason. Here, we would like to refer it to in a more inclusive way: a rational behavior is a behavior that is agreeable to some set of reasons, no matter what these reasons are or how they have been defined by the individual under observation.

Rational behavior, to a large extent, may be predicated upon selective attention. Once a mind is attentive to something (event, object, situation, etc.), its behavior toward it is governed by many factors, but mostly falling under the following three categories:

- thoughts and sensations regarding the current event/situation that is being experienced;
- memories of thoughts and sensations toward similar events/situations from the past, if there are any;
- default values as discussed in the previous section.

But while these factors may govern positive responses (i.e., what to do), and generate behaviors, a further three types of factors tend to restrict behaviors.

- The individual's personality (e.g., introverted or extroverted).
- Thoughts of "reward" or "punishment" for a given behavior – consideration (based upon current stimuli or memory) of whether a given behavior will yield pleasure or pain.
- Thoughts of whether this is the right occasion for a given behavior.

The above statements, which reflect various principles from psychology and behavioral studies, summarize our own understanding of what generate behavior and what restricts it, in the context of value-exchange behavior.

## Reward-Oriented Behavior

The research of behavioral psychologists has uncovered the fact that reward-oriented behaviors exist not only in children and adults, but also in animals, both tamed and wild. Some of the most famous experiments in this vein were undertaken by Ivan Pavlov, who demonstrated that reward-oriented behavior can be conditioned even when no reward is present: a dog can be made to salivate at the sound of a dinner bell, even if food is never proffered.

In the development of the X-Be framework, and based on the research of many behavioral psychologists, we have made the assumption that purchasing behavior is a kind of reward-oriented behavior, no matter how complex it may seem to be. And a purchaser, involved in a purchasing process, communication, or interaction with sellers, is viewed as a value-chasing agent.

## Types of Reward for Purchasing Behavior

As was indicated earlier in this book, the concept of customer value is commonly understood in the economic/accounting sense, that is, the difference between the total benefits and the total costs of a sales offer to the customer; an equivalent understanding has also been adopted in social exchange theory, which studies human relationships and interdependence.

For our purposes, to effectively assist people in selling (i.e., in all of those behaviors, including any types of communication and interaction, that aim at winning customers), the concept of customer value is decomposed into identifiable buying motivators falling within two different categories: buying points (specific personal benefits) and selling points (specific socio-cultural factors that help justify the purchasing behavior). Our definition of customer value is thus "customer value is the set of VOC-endorsed buying points and selling points in a sales offer." According to this definition, cost reductions could be perceived by the purchaser either in the buying points or in the selling points or both. This definition is more relevant to the work of salespeople who are, after all, always engaged in a game of psychology and behavior when they communicate and interact with customers. In addition, it helps develop selling status indices – attitude index and CI – which are very useful and add a great deal of value to the field of selling and sales management, as was explained in Chapter 10.

When we talk about buying points, the emphasis is on the customer as an individual. But, as explained earlier in the book, effective selling has to take into consideration the socio-cultural factors that face a key person, especially in organizational selling and in situations where the conditions of the garbage can model prevail. So, when we discuss the concept of selling points, another kind of reward for purchasing behavior, our principal focus is on group psychology and organizational behavior.

## Purchasing Risks and Deliverability

To deal with the customer's sense of purchasing risks which are usually reflected in those genuine objections from the customer (not the objections that customers tend to use as buying 'tricks' to obtain more features and lower prices), the concept of customer-oriented *deliverability* upon buying points and selling points is introduced in the X-Be framework. The way this concept is defined makes it very closely associated with the risk aversion behavior, which is often present in decision making and is well documented in many research publications. As such, the concept of deliverability provides salespeople and sales managers with an effective instrument to heed, (debate,) ponder, discuss, analyze, and address customer's perceived purchasing risks in the entire purchase process.

When the concept of deliverability is added to the other X-Be building blocks (namely ,VOC, buying points, and selling points), we obtain a small set of working concepts that defines the very essence of all kinds of selling (personal, non-personal, consumer selling, and organizational selling) in a simple behavioral formula:

Selling $= f($VOC, buying points and selling points, deliverability$)$

This insightful result is nothing but an implementation and illustration of the well-known scientific principle of parsimony. Thanks to this principle and to the X-Be framework, we are now able to define, characterize, and think about so many issues, concepts, and phenomena in selling and sales management on the basis of the elements of this framework. Here are a few examples:

1. What is a purchase need? *It is a set of VOC-endorsed* buying points *and* selling points.
2. What is a product? *It is a set of VOC-endorsed* buying points *and* selling points *with certain deliverability.*

3. What is competition? *It is a set of impeding factors which can always be linked to a set of VOC-endorsed buying points and selling points that, in the perception of one or more key persons, the seller has difficulties delivering to the satisfaction of the latter key persons.*
4. How do we assess the seller's impressions and feelings? *By using the selling status indices that are based on the concepts of buying points and selling points* (see below).
5. What is selling, the seller's job? *As was indicated above, it is a behavioral function f of the VOC, buying points, and* selling point*s and deliverability of these points.*

## Assessment of Selling Status

Attitude is usually defined as a disposition toward something or someone. It is generally agreed that attitude consists of three components (so called the ABC of attitude), namely, the following:

- A: Affective component (feeling, mood and emotion),
- B: Behavioral component (overt behaviors), and
- C: Cognitive component (thoughts and considerations).

In Chapter 8, we deployed the concept of attitude to formulate two of our indices of the selling status: attitude index and CI. The concept of attitude is the one employed quite widely by behavioral scientists as a measure of behavioral dispositions, but our usage of attitude is unique to our work, especially in regard to the CI. The attitude index is defined as the extent to which the buying points motivate the key person to act and buy. It helps characterize the degree of importance that this key person assigns to each buying point. As such, it measures the customer's impression and feeling on how effective the offer will be in bringing him closer to happiness. The CI, on the other hand, is defined as the extent to which a key person has publicly acknowledged the selling points of the sales offer, the seller herself or her company; "extent," here, is understood to refer both to (1) the amount and prominence of acknowledgment and to (2) the type of forum in which acknowledgment was made.

A great deal of research in behavioral psychology indicates that there are variations in the extent to which attitude and behavior are consistent, though effective social communication seems to be predicated on this consistency. In our selling status indices, we implemented the notion of attitude in such a way that these variations are mitigated. The reader is referred to the discussion of attitude index and CI in Chapter 8 – both indices are anchored at specified observables (customer's overt behaviors).

## SALES AND OTHER SUBJECT AREAS

In the previous sections, we discussed the topic of sales and the elements of the X-Be framework, as well as their connections to the subject areas of philosophy of science, decision sciences, cognitive psychology, and behavioral studies. In this section, we discuss the remainder of the X-Be elements. The foundational knowledge that is used to support these elements is scattered in various disciplines and sub-disciplines, such as sociology, psychology, and philosophy. But, some rationales are also the result of our own understanding and experience in the area of selling and sales management.

One of the concepts we did not discuss in the previous sections is that of key persons. We introduced this concept to deal with the emergent behavior of both organizations and consumers. The term "emergent" is understood in the sense that "the whole represents something over and above the sum of its parts." It was first coined by the psychologist George H. Lewes in his publication "Problems of Life and Mind" (1874–1879). For our purposes, we handle this emergent nature of organizations by adopting a pragmatic approach; we focus on the key persons and their influential powers. Several authors in the field of sales management have discussed similar concepts such as the notion of buying center and its members (Bonoma, 2006). In the X-Be framework, the concept of key persons refers to the behavioral roles that are directly related to the process of value formation and exchange; these roles are analyzed from three different perspectives – money, product and purchasing process, which are used to decide about who qualifies to be a key person, (1) money side – budget approver, budget user, and budge advisor; (2) product side – product approver, product user, and product adviser; and (3) process side – purchaser. A key person could assume one or more of these roles in a purchase process. Conversely, anyone who could significantly influence the buying decision making process may have to assume one or more roles on either the money side, product side, or process side, or any combination thereof.

The concept of influential power of a person over others is defined in a social exchange sense by the following three factors:

1. this person possesses "something";
2. this "something" is valued by others;
3. the influential power of this person is measured by the degree of importance that is assigned to this "something" by the others.

Based on this definition of influential power, we describe a COL is a key person whose opinions are significantly influential among other key persons in a purchase process. Thus, this definition might not reflect exactly the same concept as that of opinion leader in marketing textbooks.

The concepts of appropriate communicator and networked resources may have some connections with the concept of interpersonal relationships and that of influential power. However, the concept of networked resources has been explored in the X-Be framework mainly from the perspective of customer information collection and management.

The relating status index is defined as a measure of the amount of useful information [i.e, information beneficial to the selling process at hand) received (by the seller] from a key person during or after interaction with him.

The important and unique concept of relating status index (as one of the selling status indices) is introduced to measure the quality of a sales relationship in terms of the exchange of useful information. The basis for defining the relating status index is the communicational phenomenon, referred to as "communication filter," which tends to develop during the communication and interaction between the key person and the seller. It seems that the notion of "communication filter" is also a reflection of a person's social and professional maturity in the sense of whether he knows the extent to which and the occasions on which he could or should communicate with someone else.

Throughout this book, we have considered the seller to be the one who is more active in the exchange relationship. This is because we have made the assumption that selling is taking place in a relationship in which the seller is relatively more interested than the buyer in having this relationship consummated, which is the case most, but not all, of the time in free market economies. As a consequence of the principle of least interest (Waller, 1938) – the least interested partner in a relationship has the greater power – the seller will be more actively involved in the exchange relationships than her customers. Thus, our study starts with the analysis of the purchasing process for the benefit of sellers.

Finally, we would like to point out that the thinking that underlies all of the ideas in this book is based on a new paradigm for systems analysis and modeling; we like to refer to this paradigm as "interactivism." The customer behavior cannot be predicted deterministically – not even stochastically. It is the result of so many interactions that are constantly taking place between the customer and his surrounding (which includes the seller herself); if only the impact of these interactions were negligible or small enough, the customer behavior could be considered deterministic or stochastic (respectively). But this impact tends to be very high in most cases. A simple example that illustrates this fact is the theory of psychological reactance (Brehm, 1966); if a certain action on a person is perceived (by this person) to unfairly restrict his freedom, this action will produce completely the opposite of the expected result (this is why the $(1+7)$ building blocks of the X-Be framework, together with their derived working concepts and tools, are all rooted in the buying logic of a customer to ensure the effectiveness of the selling and sales management operations). The outcomes of the behavior of one person depend at least in part on the behavior of the other person interacting with the first one, and vice versa. This also means that the concept of value in the context of exchange behavior may be better understood as a result of the communications and interactions among the parties involved in the exchange. Considering that exchangeable and exchanged value is directly related to the customer's perception which is itself subject to the impact of social interactions, it is legitimate to claim that selling, as a kind of social interaction, contributes significantly to the formation of customer value, rather than just communicates the value of a marketing offer normally designed for a large enough segment. In this regard, it is our view that the fundamentals of exchange behavior in selling could be, at least to a certain extent, accounted for by social interdependence theories in social psychology.

## CONCLUSION

In this chapter, we discussed the connections of our research on exchange behavior in selling and sales management with selected topics in various disciplines, including philosophy of science, decision sciences, cognitive psychology, behavioral studies, and sociology. Our main goal through the analysis of these connections is to demonstrate that, despite the complexity and highly soft nature of selling and sales management, it may still be possible to systemize this field and study it from a scientific perspective. In the next chapter, "Advanced Topics for Researchers," we show how selling and sales management can be handled as a systems engineering problem and how X-Be can contribute significantly to this endeavor.

# 12

# ADVANCED TOPICS FOR RESEARCHERS

The authors had a long debate about what should be the length of this chapter and what topics should be covered in it. It is our belief indeed that, although X-Be has been presented in this book specifically for the context of selling and sales management, the fundamentals of this framework can be expanded and adapted to cover several other types of social interactions from different perspectives. In the end, we decided to limit this chapter to only two sections:

1. An example to illustrate how the ideas presented in this book can be implemented in real-world cases.
2. The new direction (that is systems engineering) to which we intend to take our research in the field of selling and sales management.

## ILLUSTRATIVE EXAMPLE OF HOW X-Be CAN BE IMPLEMENTED

In this section, we present an example[1] that provides the reader with a concrete idea about how the X-Be framework can be implemented in a sales organization. To help focus on the X-Be process, we deliberately kept the scenarios of the example very simple. The reader should also keep in mind that this example presents only a few facets of the X-Be framework.

Assume that the company named "CNMER" uses the X-Be framework to manage their customers' needs and sales activities. "ANYPROD" is the

---

[1] The authors would like to acknowledge the contribution of Mr. Yingbo Li to the development of this example.

company's product, whose price ranges between $1 million and $5 million depending on the product's configuration. Salesperson "S" is working for "CNMER" and sales manager "SM" is the supervisor of "S." For a clear illustration of the usage of X-Be, it is assumed that the following X-Be configuration example is given.

## X-Be Configuration Example

1. The current level of X-Be maturity is 0.8 for CNMER and 0.6 for "S" (maximum is 1).
2. The relationship $f$CI that expresses the confidence index CI as a function of the attitude index AI is known to us. Given an AI value, the computer could calculate the CI value according to $f$CI. If there is more than one key person involved in the current stage of the purchase process, the integrated formula to be used for estimating the CI is ($\sum$ CI of each key person $>$ × $<$ influence percentage of the key person$>$), where, $\sum$ represents sum. For example, if there are two key persons involved whose CI and influence percentage are 0.2, 40% and 0.3, 60%, respectively, the integrated CI value is $0.2 \times 40\% + 0.3 \times 60\% = 0.26$.
3. The "sales success rate" (SSR) is computed as a function of CI and the stage (NE, ND, SQ) of the organizational PPP. Three relationships $f_{NE}$CI, $f_{ND}$CI, and $f_{SQ}$ CI are used to estimate SSR. If the current stage of PPP and the current value of CI are available, the computer can easily figure out the value of SSR from the relationships $f_{NE}$CI, $f_{ND}$CI, and $f_{SQ}$CI. The "Conservative Sale" formula is b × ($f_{NE}$CI, $f_{ND}$CI, or $f_{SQ}$ CI) × RI × m$/$M, and the "Confident Sale" formula is $b \times (f_{NE}$CI, $f_{ND}$CI, or $f_{SQ}$CI$) \times$ m$/$M. In these formulas, "m" represents X-Be Maturity of salesperson "S," "M" represents the X-Be Maturity of company "CNMER," "RI" is the Relating Status Index, and "b" represents the budget of the customer. For an integrated sales forecast in a time period, the integrated formula is $\sum$[b × ($f_{NE}$CI, $f_{ND}$ CI, or $f_{SQ}$CI) × m$/$M] or $\sum$[b × ($f_{NE}$CI, $f_{ND}$CI, or $f_{SQ}$CI) × RI × m$/$M]. For example, assume "S" has two sales processes at her disposal, and the PPP will reach the SL stage in a month. The customer's budget, PPP stage, CI, RI in the two sales processes are "100, NE, 0.7, 0.6" and "200, ND, 0.9, 0.8," respectively. Given this information (on CI and stage of PPP), assume that, using $f_{NE}$CI and $f_{ND}$CI, the SSR for the two sales processes were found to be 6% and 35% respectively. Thus, a sales forecast for "S" in the next month is

"Conservative Sale" $100 \times 6\% \times 0.6 \times 0.6/0.8 + 200 \times 35\% \times 0.8 \times 0.6/0.8 = 44.7$ and "Confident Sale" $100 \times 6\% \times 0.6/0.8 + 200 \times 35\% \times 0.6/0.8 = 57$.

4. Formula to evaluate the performance of the sales operator "S." Assume that CNMER opted for the following formula to evaluate its salespeople:

$$\text{Evaluation formula: } B + (C \times m/M) + E + F,$$

where B, C, E and F are as follows:

| Item | Symbol | Score Range |
|------|--------|-------------|
| Real sale | B | 0–50 (previous quarter) |
| Sales forecast | C | 0–30 (next quarter) |
| Networked resources | E | 0–20 |
| Submit a pattern (see below for pattern examples) | F | 0.1–5 |

To evaluate the sales forecast C, the following formula is used:

$$(\text{Conservative sale} + \text{Confident sale})/\text{quota} \times 2,$$

where "quota" is the sales quota that is assigned to "S" by "SM."

5. Rules regarding the assessment of sales events by "SM." "SM" gets to assess the design of a sales event if (1) its time cost is over 1 day or (2) its money cost is more than \$100.

6. A few examples of the patterns that can appear in the X-Be Pattern Library.

An example for the table of the PPP characteristics pattern.

| PPP | PPP Characteristics |
|-----|---------------------|
| SQ | The targeted company has built a purchase team |

An example for the table of the key person's characteristics pattern

| Purchase Role (PR) | KP Characteristics |
|--------------------|--------------------|
| Product approver | Vice President |
| Product user | IT manager |
| Money approver | CFO |

An example for the table of the PR/VOC [Selecting points (SeP)] characteristics pattern

| PR | VOC-SeP Characteristics |
|---|---|
| Product approver | Top-quality, Professional |
| Money approver | Cost-effective |
| Product user | Manageable |

An example for the table of the VOC (SeP)/VOC [Selecting rationales (SR)] characteristics pattern

| VOC-SeP | VOC-SR Characteristics |
|---|---|
| Professional | Veteran in the industry |
| Top-quality | CMM/ISO compliant |
| Cost-effective | Low-cost, as there are other priorities in the company. In any case, it has to be within budget |
| Manageable | As automated as possible, must be highly stable |

An example for the table of the VOC (SR)/buying points-selling points characteristics pattern.

| VOC-SR | BPs-SPs |
|---|---|
| Veteran | Over 10 years experience in ANYPROD business |
| CMM/ISO | At least CMM level 3 |
| Low-cost,within budget | Maximum 10% of the total budget allocated for such expenditures |

An example for the table of the selling points/CI characteristics pattern.

| SPs | CI Characteristics | CI Estimate |
|---|---|---|
| At least CMM level 3 | A key person gave a few positive words, privately to "S," on the company CNMER | 0.4 |

An example for the table of the buying point-selling point/Appropriate Communicator (AC) characteristics pattern.

| BPs-SPs | AC Characteristics |
|---|---|
| At least CMM level 3<br>Maximum 10% of the total<br>budget allocated for such expenditures | CMM Manager in the company CNMER<br>Salesperson "S" or Sales Manager "SM" |

The above tables represent just a few examples of the X-Be patterns that have to be developed within the company CNMER from the records of salesperson's experience, the experience of other salespeople in the company and/or the work of consultants.

## ACTIONS

Let us now describe a possible scenario of how X-Be can be implemented in CNMER.

In the beginning of a new quarter, "SM" starts up, on her terminal the X-Be software system, assigns a $3.5 million quota to "S," and submits that information to the business logic server. The "SM" receives a "successful submission" message on her terminal. The business logic server pushes the "quota" information to "S." "S" receives the quota information through her own terminal. Based on the knowledge of this "quota," "S" should plan her work for the new quarter. She may need to check her current X-Be-based sales processes first; for this purpose, "S" sends a "Get current X-Be status for the new quarter" request to the business logic server; the Statistical Data Analysis Module handles the request and responds with the following form to "S":

| X-Be-Based Processes | Sales Process 1 | Sales Process 2 | Sales Process 3 | Sum |
|---|---|---|---|---|
| Budget | 2 million | 5 million | 4 million | – |
| Current stage of PPP | NE | ND | SQ | – |
| CI | 0.7 | 0.9 | 0.9 | – |
| Sales success rate | 6% | 35% | 70% | – |
| RI | 0.5 | 0.8 | 0.8 | – |
| Conservative Sale | $0.045 million | $1.05 million | $1.68 million | $2.775 million |
| Confident Sale | $0.09 million | $1.313 million | $2.1 million | $3.503 million |

The above form shows three sales processes, the PPP of which will reach SL stage within the new quarter. The total Confident Sale for this quarter is $2.775 million, and the total Conservative Sale is $3.503 million. The above values are calculated with the foregoing formulas, $\sum[b \times (f_{NE}CI, f_{ND}CI, \text{or } f_{SQ}CI) \times m/M]$ and $\sum[b \times (f_{NE}CI, f_{ND}CI, \text{or } f_{SQ}CI) \times RI \times m/M]$. Thus, the integrated sales forecast is $(2.775 + 3.503)/2 = $3.139$ million. Compared to the "quota" of $3.5 million, the integrated sales forecast is lower. On the salesperson's terminal, "S" could read a message about it: "In order to complete the 'quota' of $3.5 million, "S" needs to get at least $0.361 more of integrated sales forecast."

In order to get more integrated sales forecast, "S" may want to set up a new X-Be-based sales process. "S" searches the Sales Opportunities from her Networked Resources database and finds that there is a budget from the company ANYONE to make a purchase within the next few months. After having confirmed the budget information and the time information from her Networked Resources, "S" set up a new X-Be-based process named "ANYONE case" in the X-Be software system.

After having gone through several sales events design and implementation processes, the "ANYONE case" in the X-Be software system has now accumulated several X-Be elements and patterns (which have been input by "S") from those events and structured them into a series X-Be visualized snapshots (VS). Figure 12.1 shows version 9 of these snapshots for the "ANYONE case."

This figure depicts the following items:

1. The name of the account being managed in this snapshot and the sales team responsible for it.
2. A control slider and control button that allows the user to move (back and forward) to other snapshot versions (for instance, if the slider is moved a bit to the left, version 8 of the snapshots will be displayed).
3. The budget allocated by the customer for this purchase ($4 million).
4. The date and time at which the SL stage of PPP will be attained (SL Deadline), which means that, by that date and time, ANYONE would have already paid its money.
5. The current stage (SQ) of the PPP.
6. The current cost of managing the ANYONE account, that is, how much money has been spent so far in the previous PPP stages ($35,000 on this snapshot).
7. The amount of money that has been received from ANYONE.

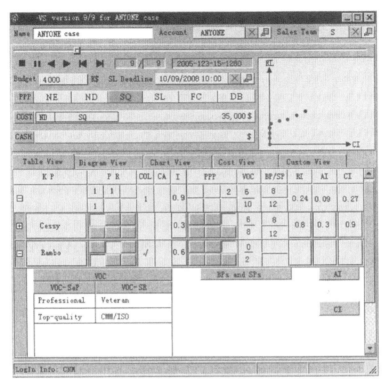

**FIGURE 12.1**   Version 9 of the X-Be visualized snapshots (VS) for the "ANYONE case."

8. A chart that plots information about the selling indices SI, which reflect the performance of the whole ExBe process – the X-coordinate of the chart displayed in this snapshot is the CI, and the Y-coordinate is the relating status index (RI). At this point of the ExBe process (version 9 of the snapshots), there are nine points in the chart (note that other indices can be plotted as well).

9. A "table view" of the current snapshot version. This view shows the following:

a. The key person information related to the ANYONE account. As illustrated, there are two key persons in the displayed version of the snapshots: "Cessy" and "Rambo."

b. The PR information of the key person – the six blocks, followed left-to-right and top-down, indicate the following:

   i. PR-MA (Money Approval) [1 key person: "Cessy"],

   ii. PR-MS (Money-related Suggestion) [1 key person: "Rambo"],

   iii. PR-MU (Money Use or Management),

   iv. PR-PA (Product Approval) [1 key person: "Rambo"],

v. PR-PS (Product-related Suggestion), and

vi. PR-PU (Product Use or Management).

c. The COL information. The key person "Rambo" is the only COL in the current snapshot.

d. The key person Rambo's influence is 0.6, and key person Cessy's influence is 0.3.

e. The individual (as opposed to organizational) PPP information for the key person – the six blocks, followed left-to-right and top-down, are NE, ND, SQ, SL, FC, and DB. Both Cessy's and Rambo's individual PPP are in the SQ stage.

f. The VOC information of the key person, which shows that "S" has picked up 8 VOC for "Cessy," 6 of those VOC have been given buying points/selling points; "S" has also picked up two VOC for "Rambo," none of them has been given buying point/selling point yet.

g. The buying points/selling points information of the key person, which shows that "S" has given "Cessy" 8 buying points/selling points; no buying point/selling point has been given to "Rambo."

h. The selling status indices RI, AI, and CI. The values for Cessy's RI, AI, and CI are 0.8, 0.3, and 0.9, respectively. The integrated RI, AI, and CI are 0.24, 0.09, and 0.27, respectively. "S" cannot yet get any SI from key person "Rambo."

10. The VOC-SeP, VOC-SR, buying points/selling points, AI, and CI for key person "Rambo" (sign "–," not "+" is displayed at the left of the name "Rambo" on the figure), which shows that there are only two VOC for "Rambo."

Based on the above X-Be snapshot, "S" may want to design a sales event in order to provide buying points/selling points to the two VOC of key person "Rambo." "S" goes to the sales event design process module of the X-Be software system and begins to design a specific sales event. For this purpose, "S" enters into the "Identify organizational PPP" module and, based on available information from the previous sales events, decides that the PPP is still in the SQ stage. "S" moves then to the next step for "Identification of key person" and selects key person "Rambo" as the targeted key person in the sales event to be designed. Then, in the next step, "S" selects the following VOC as the targeted VOC in the sales event to be designed.

| VOC-SeP | VOC-SR |
|---|---|
| 1 Professional | Veteran |
| 2 Top-quality | CMM/ISO |

The first line shows that the key person "Rambo" is concerned with the "Professional" aspect of the company, and he thinks that "A company with a long history" means "Professional"; the second line shows that key person "Rambo" is concerned with the "quality" aspect, and he finds that "A company with CMM/ISO certification" means "Top-quality."

"S" moves to the next step and selects (from the X-Be pattern library) the following buying points/selling points, for instance, to satisfy the above VOC of the key person "Rambo":

1 "10 year experience in ANYPROD" for the "Veteran" VOC-SR
2 "CMM level 3" for the "CMM/ISO" VOC-SR

The first line means that "S" assumes that having a "10 year experience in ANYPROD" represents a good evidence that her company meets the key person's criterion "A company with a long history," that is a "Veteran" (key person Rambo's first VOC-SR). Similarly, the second line means that "S" assumes that the fact that CNMER has a "CMM level 3" certification is a proof that the second VOC-SR "Top-quality" is satisfied. The above decisions regarding the buying points/selling points are in the "design state" (as opposed to "conclusion state").

In the next step, "S" checks the selling points/SI pattern in the X-Be pattern library and finds the following suggestion appropriate to her case: "Organize a visit to CNMER and prompt key person to make public comments." Thus, "S" decides to design a sales event that consists in taking the following two actions: (1) arranging a visit by the key person "Rambo" and other key persons to CNMER so that they can be introduced to the company's CMM-3 quality certification system and (2) after the two VOC "Professional" and "Top-quality" are satisfied, prompting the COL "Rambo" to make public comments about the selling point "CMM level 3."

In the next step, "S" selects the following appropriate communicators (AC) from the buying points-selling points/AC pattern:

| BPs-SPs | AC |
|---|---|
| 1 "10 year experience in ANYPROD" | Senior staff |
| 2 "CMM level 3" | CMM Manager |

These two lines mean that "S" thinks that a "Senior Staff" and the "CMM Manager" are the appropriate candidates to communicate the information about having a "10 year experience in ANYPROD" and the information about the "CMM level 3" certification, respectively.

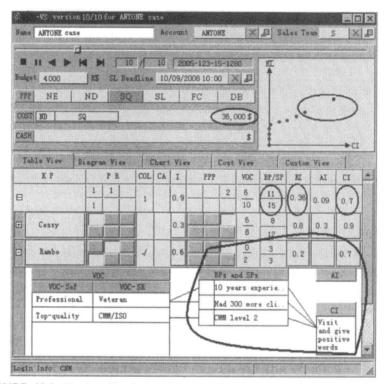

**FIGURE 12.2** Version 10 of the X-Be visualized snapshots (VS) for the "ANY-ONE case."

In the next step, "S" provides an action plan for the above sales event and specifies a budget of $1,000. After "SM" and "S" discuss and assess the action plan, "SM" approves or disapproves the design; to keep the example simple, we will assume that "SM" finds this design reasonable and approves it.

After the approval, "S" implements the sales event according to the design, picks up further X-Be elements and patterns from the sales event, and updates the data in the X-Be software system. After that, the X-Be visualized snapshot (VS) is updated to version 10. Figure 12.2, which depicts this version of the snapshots, provides the following information:

- The PPP is still in the SQ stage;
- The cost has increased to $36,000 (in contrast to $35,000 in the previous snapshot);
- The plot shows one extra SI point;

- Compared to version 9, three more buying points-selling points that have been added to the X-Be snapshot;
- The integrated RI increased by 0.12, and the CI increased by 0.43 (in contrast to the previous snapshot).

"S" picked up three buying points/selling points that pertain to the key person "Rambo." In the sales event, "S" assigned a value of 0.2 to RI (based on the usefulness of the information that she obtained from the key person) and a value of 0.7 to CI for the key person "Rambo" (based on the extent to which the key person has acknowledged the selling points). In addition, "S" has found, during the sales event, another buying point/selling point for key person Rambo: "CNMER has more than 300 clients." "S" submits the new buying point/selling point to the X-Be pattern library and gets an extra score of 0.1 (symbol F in the salesperson's evaluation formula).

The "Confident Sale" for the ANYONE sales process is 4 million $\times$ $f_{SQ}$ 0.7 $\times$ 0.6/0.8 = 4 million $\times$ 35% $\times$ 0.6/0.8 = 1.5 million. The conservative sale is \$1.05 million $\times$ 0.36 = \$0.378 million. Thus, the integrated sales forecast is (1.05 million + 0.378 million)/(1.05 million + 0.378 million) 2 = \$ 0.714 million 2 = \$ 0.714 million. At version 10 of the X-Be snapshots, the sales forecast for the new quarter is then \$3.139 million + \$0.714 million = \$3.853 million. Referring back to the formula for the evaluation of salespeople, we can use the following values for the items B, C, E, F:

| | | |
|---|---|---|
| Real Sale | B | 50 (previous quarter) |
| Sales forecast | C | (3.853/3.5)×30 = 33 (next quarter) |
| Network resources | E | 15 (estimate) |
| Submit a pattern | F | 0.1 |

According to the evaluation formula $B \times C \times m/M + E + F$, the score for "S" is $50 + 33 \times 0.6/0.8 + 15 + 0.1 = 89.85$.

## SELLING AND SALES MANAGEMENT: A SYSTEMS ENGINEERING PERSPECTIVE

In this last section, we provide a discussion of the field of selling and sales management from a systems engineering perspective. The purpose of this discussion is to explain to the reader a new direction to which we intend to take this field by implementing the X-Be framework and its concepts.

Because of the mathematical nature of the ideas presented in this section, we decided to make the discussion as brief as possible.

Traditionally management has been defined in terms of planning, organizing, coordinating, and controlling of resources to achieve a certain set of objectives. The nature of the work that takes place in each of these phases depends on the system – let us call it S – that needs to be managed. However, there are a few aspects that are common to the management of all systems. We discuss these aspects below, and we use the sales management field as an example to illustrate the ideas.

1. The system S is not static. It is subject to various types of changes in time and space. For instance, in the case of sales management, the hiring and laying-off of salespeople, expansion of distribution networks, the emergence of a new competitor in the market, the various types of promotions, the changes in customer perceptions of value are all changes that affect the management of sales. Let us assume that these changes can be represented by a vector $\vec{u}$ that takes values in a certain vector space $U$.

2. The changes that occur in the system are the result of either of the following:
   - the manager's actions,
   - or actions from the external world.

   Thus, let us subdivide $\vec{u}$ into two sub-vectors, $\vec{u}_m$ and $\vec{u}_e$, with:

$$\vec{u}_m \in U_m \subset U$$

$$\vec{u}_e \in U_e \subset U$$

$$U = U_m \oplus U_e$$

   where, $\vec{u}_m$ represents the manager's actions and $\vec{u}_e$ represents the external actions. Using the systems engineering terminology, $\vec{u}_m$ will be referred to as the input and $\vec{u}_e$ as the perturbation.

3. The manager takes the actions $\vec{u}_m$ to achieve a certain objective. In the case of sales management, let us assume that this objective consists in maximizing the total sales $J_T$ (which is dependent on both $\vec{u}_m$ and $\vec{u}_e$) over a certain period of time $T$, say, the next quarter for example. The manager has to carry out this maximization, while respecting various constraints on $\vec{u}_m$. For instance, she cannot have an infinite budget to hire any number of salespeople, and so on. Also, since the external perturbations cannot be determined ahead of time, they have to be hypothesized.

We can now use the above concepts to state the sales management problem as a systems engineering problem:

$$\text{Find } \vec{u}_{\mathrm{m}} \text{ that maximizes } J_T(\vec{u}_{\mathrm{m}}, \vec{u}_{\mathrm{e}})$$

$$\begin{cases} \text{within the constraints on } \vec{u}_{\mathrm{m}} \\ \text{and} \\ \text{a reasonable hypothesis on } \vec{u}_{\mathrm{e}} \end{cases}$$

This is an optimal control problem that can be approached using the tools of control theory (for information about this topic, the reader can be referred to any textbook on optimal control), and it is in this direction that we would like to take the field of selling and sales management. But there are a few challenges that need to be addressed before we can successfully apply control theory to this field. Here we discuss briefly three of these challenges, which are all on our research agenda. We also highlight the connections between each one of these challenges and the X-Be framework.

The first challenge concerns the issue of information representation. In the above discussion, we represented the changes that affect the system S using the vector space structure (space $U$ and its elements $\vec{u}$), which then assumes that it will relatively be easy to define what the vector coordinates should be. In real-world cases, however, vectors may not provide an adequate technique to describe the various objects we need to handle in the area of sales management; for instance, how can we make use of the vector space structure to characterize a sales (or value-exchange) relationship, customer value, customer satisfaction, impacts of competition, salesperson's felling, and impressions about her customers? These are complex concepts that may or may not lend themselves to a vectorized description. But, thanks to the X-Be framework, we now have a language that helps characterize many of these concepts in a specific manner:

- The purchasing process is described as a collection of five phases (NE, ND, SQ, SL, FC);
- Purchasing decision making is the result of the actions of the key persons (from money side, product side, or process side) in the organization;
- The voice of customer can be parsed using the VOC, the buying points and selling points (more on this later in this section);
- Customer value is described in terms of the customer buying points and selling points;

- A product is a set of VOC-endorsed buying points and selling points with certain deliverability;
- Competition is described as a set of impeding factors which can always be linked to a set of VOC-endorsed buying points and selling points that the seller has difficulties delivering.
- A value-exchange relationship is defined as depicted in Figure 6.1.

Such characterizations help in reducing the complexity of the domain of selling and sales management into a set of working elements that are relatively easily measurable. This is an important step toward implementing the vector space structure as a tool for information representation in this domain, but there are other tools that can also be used for this purpose. One of them consists in making use of kernel learning methods (Schölkopf and Smola, 2002) which does not impose a vector space structure on the description of real-world objects; all that is required is that the input space can be somehow mapped onto a Hilbert space (which is itself a vector space). Another approach may come down to a simple implementation of knowledge management principles (defining a domain schema and a KB) to capture salespeople inputs and judgments about their interactions with the customers (Guergachi et al., 2004).

The second challenge concerns the adequacy of classical control theory. At the beginning of this section, we introduced the entity "system S," but we did not define specifically what it is. In classical control theory, which is based on Newtonian physics, among the first steps that one needs to go through is the definition of the system S under study: what are its boundaries and what are its components? Once we have defined this physical system, we can describe the relationships that govern the interactions among its components as well as the impact of the changes $\vec{u}$ on these components. In the case of management of sales, the definition of what S should be is not always a trivial task. Is it going to be the sales department? Or, a certain specific sales process? Or, all of the sales processes? Or the whole company? Or, should it be the set {saleperson and her customers} composed of a specific salesperson and her (current and potential) customers? All these are possible candidates to be the system S. But, the difficulty with classical control theory does not end here; it has another shortcoming with regard to the nature of the control actions $\vec{u}_m$ that it tries to determine: it assumes that all the coordinates of $\vec{u}_m$ are operational actions. In other words, the structure of the system S under study (say, for instance, a chemical plant, or an engine) is fixed, and the optimization of the behavior of S comes down to manipulating operational control variables only. But, in the case of sales management, the management actions can be structural as well: replacement of a company's sales force, merger of two companies, replacement of the sales manager are all management actions that lead to structural changes. In fact, the separation line between operational and structural management actions becomes increasingly blurred in the case of management of sales and in many other business cases as well. For instance, while a reduction in the price could be considered an operational action, we cannot be so sure about the classification (operational versus structural) of a change in the packaging of the product; also, the replacement of a salesperson in the company's sales department could be considered as a structural change, but how about the intensive training of an existing salesperson, or a major overhaul of the sales practices in the sales department? It is not easy to classify them as operational or structural. This blurred separation between these two types of actions is another reason why defining the boundaries of the system S to be studied is not an easy task; the structure of the system changes over time and some of these changes can themselves be used as control/management actions. We should also note that the above-described phenomena are not unique to business systems; they are also very common in biological systems as well. To deal with such limitations of classical control theory, various new paradigms have been proposed (Beck, 2005; Casti, 2002). In the context of the X-Be framework, we approach the question of control/management of sales using the selling status indices. As was explained in Chapter 10, these indices can indeed be implemented to design CNM systems for selling, sales management, and sales opportunities classification.

The third challenge is where our X-Be framework has made significant contributions. It concerns the observablility of the system under study. Observability is one of the main issues that needs to be addressed before deciding about the best control (or management) strategy to be applied. Most systems that we deal with nowadays are "black boxes," in the sense that we cannot measure their internal states directly; all we can do is estimate, if we can, these states thorough output measurements. Take for instance the system:

$$S = \{\text{the customer and his environment}\} \qquad (1)$$

Selling comes down to understanding what the customer wants, that is, what he has in mind and how he perceives his needs (in the environment where he lives), so that the sales organization can devise the right product that helps address them. Because of the complexity of our modern economies, customer needs are not straightforward anymore, as we are indeed very far from the era where people looked at satisfying just their basic physiological needs. Yet, unless we have a good understanding or, using the systems engineering vocabulary, a good estimation of what the customer has in mind, we have very little chance to succeed in selling.

In many of the existing frameworks for selling and sales management, practitioners used what has been traditionally called the 'Voice of Customer' ($VOC_{cust}$) to describe the needs of this customer. In the X-Be framework, we do not agree on this approach. In other words, using the systems engineering terminology, we do not believe that the capture of the output $y = VOC_{cust}$ will make the system S observable. We believe that $VOC_{cust}$ is fluffy, noisy, and vague to the extent that it cannot provide a reliable description of the complex nature of customer needs.

One of the goals of the X-Be framework is to improve the observability of the system S. When a customer buys and pays for something, he does so because of a certain reason $R$. This statement can be expressed logically as:

$$[buy = True] \Rightarrow R \qquad (2)$$

This reason $R$ comes down to the fact that the buy will, in the perception of the customer, add a certain value, in the marketing/economic sense of the term, to this customer's personal and social life, directly or indirectly. Let us refer to this value as $x$. The challenge to represent the object $x$ in a meaningful and mathematical way is still on. Many authors have adopted the view that value is a kind of "perceived benefits minus perceived sacrifice." We believe that this view provides only one facet of what value really is. While it helps compute value after it was created, it provides no practical method for creating it; thus, it is of no use to a salesperson. This is why many salespeople and sales departments have adopted $VOC_{cust}$ as a base to do their job and create value; the assumption behind this adoption is that:

$$VOC_{cust} \approx x \qquad (3)$$

But, as we said earlier, this assumption is not a reasonable one, especially in complex sales (including but not limited to organizational sales) where the process of value creation is far from straightforward; in many cases, indeed, even the customer does not have a clear idea of what $x$ is.

If we consider $x$ as a hidden (state) variable of the system S defined in Equation (1), we re-write Equation (3) as follows:

$$VOC_{cust} = h(x)$$

or, if we refer to $VOC_{cust}$ as $y$:

$$y = h(x), \tag{4}$$

where $h$ is a function. In Equation (4), only one output $y$ is observed; but, if we can find a way to help salespeople observe more outputs, say $y_1, y_2, \ldots, y_n$, that are directly related to $x$, then the observability of the system S should normally improve. In the X-Be framework, we devised three outputs that are relatively easily observable by salespeople (by using the sales skills described at the end of Chapter 10) and that are directly related to $x$:

1. the VOC – this refers to the views of the customer on the criteria that he uses to judge $x$;
2. the buying points – these refer to the personal benefits that the key person (in the customer's organization), as an individual, gains from the product $P$ that claims to fulfill $x$;
3. the selling point – these refer to those aspects of the product $P$ that help the key person, as a social being, justify his purchase to those to whom he is beholden.

If we refer to VOC, buying point, and selling point as $y_1, y_2$, and $y_3$ respectively, then Equation (4) would be replaced by:

$$\begin{cases} y_1 = h_1(x) \\ y_2 = h_2(x), \\ y_3 = h_3(x) \end{cases} \tag{5}$$

where $h_1, h_2, h_3$ are functions that relate $y_i$ to $x$. The X-Be framework does not have a technique to mathematically express $x$ in terms of $y_1, y_2$, and $y_3$ [i.e., inverse Equations (5)], as this depends on the trading environment characterized by many factors such as industry, business, market, and competition, as well as the particular buyer–seller interactions. Thus, while Equations (5) improve the observability of the system S, the task to find what $x$ is after having captured $y_1, y_2$, and $y_3$ is still left to the salesperson. However, as explained in Chapter 8, the selling status indices provide effective tools for the seller to make sensible judgments about x. The salesperson who use these indices properly should be able to reasonably inverse Equations (5) by appealing to the customer's buying logic which has been captured in the X-Be framework.

## CONCLUSION

A synthesis, in the form of an example, of the current results of our research (Section 1), along with a description of the future direction of this research (Section 2), is what we presented in this chapter. We also would like to draw the readers' attention to the fact that X-Be, as it was introduced in this book, describes the interaction and exchange (at the interpersonal level) between two individuals who assume the following roles – buyer and seller. By changing the nature of these roles, we should be able to adapt X-Be to describe other types of social and business interactions and exchanges in a systematic fashion. In our future research, we intend to investigate these possible adaptations as well.

# REFERENCES

Abe, S., Bagozzi, R.P., Sadarangani, P. (1996) "An investigation of construct validity and generalizability of the self-concept: self-consciousness in Japan and the United States", Journal of International Consumer Marketing, 8, 97–123.

Beck, M.B. (2005). "Environmental foresight and structural change", Environmental Modelling & Software, 20, pp 651–670.

Blau, M.P. (1964). "Exchange and Power in Social Life", New York: John Wiley & Sons, Inc.

Bonoma, V.T. (2006). Major sales: who really does the buying? Harvard Business Review, 84(7/8), p 172.

Brehm, J.W. (1966). "Theory of Psychological Reactance", New York: Academic Press.

Casti, J.L. (2002). "Biologizing control theory: how to make a control system come alive", Complexity, 7(4), pp 10–12.

Chaiken, S., Trope, Y. (1999). "Dual-Process Theories in Social Psychology", New York: Guilford Press.

Chalmers, A.F. (1982). "What is This Thing Called Science?" (2nd edition), WA: The open University Press.

Cialdini, R.B. (2006). "Influence: The Psychology of Persuasion", New York: Collins.

Cohen, M.D., March, J.G., Olsen, J.P. (1972). "A garbage can model of organizational choice", Administrative Science Quarterly, 17(1), pp 1–25.

Fishbein, M., Ajzen, I. (1975). "Belief, Attitude, Intention, and Behavior: An Introduction to Theory and Research", MA: Addison-Wesley.

Guergachi, A., Shah, B., Pille, P. (2004). "Sales Forecasting: Initial Steps Toward the Development of a Computerized Information System for the Integration of Judgmental Forecasts and Computationally-Based Approaches", 8th World Multi-Conference on Systemics, Cybernetics and Informatics, Florida, US.

Hawkins, D.I., Best, R., Coney, A.K. (2003). "Consumer Behavior: Building Marketing Strategy", New York: McGraw-Hill.

Hogarth, R.M. (2001). "Judgment and Choice", New York: John Wiley.

Jacob, F. (1995). "The Statue Within: An Autobiography", New York: Cold Spring Harbor Laboratory Press.

Katz, D. (1960). "The Functional approach to the study of attitudes", Public Opinion Quarterly, 24, pp 163–204.

Kahneman, D., Tversky, A. (2000). "Choices, Values and Frames", New York: Cambridge University Press.

Keele, S.W., Neill, W.T. (1978). "Mechanisms of attention". Carterette, E.C., Friedman, P. (Eds.), Handbook of Perception, Vol. 9, pp 3–47. New York: Academic Press.

Kogut, B., Zander, U. (1992). "Knowledge of the firm, combinative capabilities, and the replication of technology", Organization Science, 3, pp 383–397.

Kotler, P. (1996). "Marketing Management: Analysis, Planning, Implementation, and Control", New Jersey: Prentice Hall.

Kotler, P., Keller, L.K. (2005). "Marketing Management" (12th edition), New Jersey: Prentice Hall.

Kuhn, T.S. (1962). "The Structure of Scientific Revolutions", Chicago: University of Chicago Press.

LaPiere, R.T. (1934). "Attitudes vs. Actions", Social Forces, 3, pp 230–237.

Lewes, G.H. (1874–1879). "Problems of Life and Mind", London: Truebner & Co., 5 vols.

Marcus, G.F. (1996). "Why do children say 'breaked'?", Current Directions in Psychological Science, 5, pp 81–85, The American Psychological Society.

Mead, G.H. (1934). "Mind, Self, and Society", Chicago: The University of Chicago Press.

Meyer, M.H., Utterback, J.M. (1993). "The Product Family and the Dynamics of Core Capability", Sloan Management Review, 34(3) pp 29–47.

Neisser, U. (1967). "Cognitive Psychology", New Jersey: Prentice-Hall.

Porter, M.E. (2004). "Competitive Strategy", New York: Free Press.

Pralahad, C.K., Hamel, G. (1990), "The Core Competence of the Corporation", Harvard Business Review, May–June, pp 79–91.

Schölkopf, B., Smola, A. (2002). "Learning with Kernels", Cambridge, MA: MIT Press.

Sheng, P. (2002). "What is This Thing Called Selling?" Beijing, China: China Social Sciences Press.

Sheng, P., et al. (2005), "Selling Behavior", Beijing, China: China Social Sciences Press.

Simon, H.A. (1984). "Models of Bounded Rationality", Vol. 1, Cambridge, MA: MIT Press.

Staw, M.B. (1981). "The escalation of Commitment to a Course of Action", Academy of Management Review, 6, pp 577–587.

Tien, J.M., Krishnamurthy, A., Yasar, A. (2004). "Towards real-time customized management of supply and demand chains", Journal of Systems Science and Systems Engineering, 13(3), pp 257–278.

Waller, W. (1938). "The Family: A dynamic Interpretation", New York: Gordon.

Warner, M. (2001). "Blind Optimism, Thick Skin, and A Cell Phone Sudha Shah is Selling Software in a Crummy Economy", Fortune Magazine.

Webster, E.F., Wind, Y. (1972a), "Organizational Buying Behavior", New Jersey: Prentice-Hall.

Webster, E.F., Wind, Y. (1972b), "A General Model for Understanding Organizational Buying Behavior", Journal of Marketing, 36(2), pp 12–19.

Wernerfelt, B. (1984). "Resource-Based View of the Firm", Strategic Management Journal, 5, pp 171–180.

# INDEX

For Product Safety Concerns and Information please contact our EU representative GPSR@taylorandfrancis.com Taylor & Francis Verlag GmbH, Kaufingerstraße 24, 80331 München, Germany